Covered Bridges and the Birth of American Engineering

Executive Editors

Justine Christianson
Christopher H. Marston

Authors

James Barker
Lola Bennett
Joseph Conwill
Sheila Rimal Duwadi
Dario Gasparini
Richard O'Connor
Matthew Reckard
Rachel Herring Sangree

Associate Editors

Michael R. Harrison
David A. Simmons

Hsitoric American Engineering Record
National Park Service
Washington, D.C.
2015

U.S. Department
of Transportation

**Federal Highway
Administration**

This study is part of the Research, Technology and Education portion of the **National Historic Covered Bridge Preservation** (NHCBP) Program administered by the Federal Highway Administration. The NHCBP program includes preservation, rehabilitation and restoration of covered bridges that are listed or are eligible for listing on the National Register of Historic Places; research for better means of restoring, and protecting these bridges; development of educational aids; and technology transfer to disseminate information on covered bridges in order to preserve the Nation's cultural heritage.

This study is conducted under a joint agreement between the Federal Highway Administration– Turner Fairbank Highway Research Center, and the National Park Service–Historic American Engineering Record (HAER).

Federal Highway Administration Program Manager–Sheila Rimal Duwadi, P.E.

HAER National Covered Bridges Recording Project Leader–Christopher H. Marston

Published in 2015 by the Historic American Engineering Record, National Park Service, Washington, D.C.

Library of Congress Control Number: 2015955439

ISBN: 978-0-578-17106-7

Book design by Michael Bechetti, Creative Communication Services, Department of the Interior, Washington, D.C.

Book printed by Westminster Printing, Santa Ana, Calif.

Distributed by the Historic American Engineering Record

Cover The Kidd's Mill Bridge (1868) in Mercer County, Pennsylvania, is a early example of a truss patented by Ohioan Robert W. Smith, whose prefabricated wooden bridges successfully competed with iron ones during the late 1860s-early 1870s. HAER PA-662-7, Jet Lowe, photographer, 2006.

Title Page Cutaway perspective view of a 3-D model of J.J. Daniels' West Union Bridge (1876) in Parke County, Indiana, using data collected through Leica laser scanning. HAER IN-105, sheet 1, Jeremy Mauro, Benjamin Shakelton, Christopher H. Marston, delineators, 2014.

Dedicated to Eric N. DeLony

Eric DeLony's love of historic bridges, such as the Thomas Viaduct (1835) seen here, led to many initiatives to document historic bridges around the country during his thirty-year career at HAER from 1971-2003. Christopher H. Marston, photographer, 2012.

Contents

Introduction and Acknowledgments

by Justine Christianson and Christopher H. Marston

A covered bridge in a bucolic setting has become a quintessentially American image, one meant to evoke a pastoral vision of nineteenth-century America. Underneath the housing of a covered bridge, however, is a more complex story. By manipulating a basic form—the triangle—civil engineers and builders developed truss types suitable for different topographies, spans, and modes of transportation. These wood trusses were later adapted for use with metal, which generally usurped wood bridge construction in the first part of the twentieth century. This book examines the development of wood trusses and covered bridge construction, explores the function of trusses in covered bridges, and looks at the preservation and future of these distinctly American bridges.

The Historic American Engineering Record's multi-year, multi-faceted National Covered Bridges Recording Project extended from 2002 to 2015 thanks to funding from the Federal Highway Administration's National Historic Covered Bridge Preservation (NHCBP) Program. Eric DeLony, former chief of the Historic American Engineering Record (HAER), developed this comprehensive documentation project. Sheila Rimal Duwadi and her predecessor, Steve Ernst, of the Federal Highway Administration (FHWA), ably administered the funding. At the core of the project has been the documentation of covered bridges across the United States. A total of eighty covered bridges have been documented with large-format photographs and written historical reports. Measured drawings have been completed on thirty-one bridges, and engineering analyses of several truss types were performed on sixteen structures. From this comprehensive examination of covered bridges, it has been possible to develop both historical narratives and analyses of wood-truss design and development in the United States.

Such an ambitious project would not have been possible without the aid of the numerous scholars, students, professionals, and community members who contributed in myriad ways. First, thanks are due to the advisory group of covered bridge experts, engineers, and Federal Highway Administration and National Park Service personnel who met in Washington, D.C., in February 2002 to develop the project. Led by Eric DeLony, the participants included Jim Barker, John Bowie, Steve Buonopane, Ben Brungraber, Joseph Conwill, Neal Daniels, Steve Ernst, David Fischetti, Dario Gasparini, Judy Hayward, Nick Jones, Emory Kemp, Chris Leedham, Jan Lewandoski, Christopher H. Marston, Tom McGrath, Richard O'Connor, Phil Pierce, John Sprinkle, Laurie Trippett, Tom Visser, Tom Vitanza, and David Wright. Their discussions helped set the course for the documentation that informs this book.

Scores of students and preservation professionals have participated in the documentation of covered bridges. Field teams spent days climbing in and around the trusses in all kinds of weather and under various conditions, obtaining measurements for use in the numerous drawings produced for HAER and as part of the preparation of descriptions and analyses for the written historical reports and engineering reports. Special thanks go to all who provided access to bridges and research facilities across the country to facilitate the documentation.

HAER summer field team members (2002–2014) included: Lola Bennett, Mark M. Brown, Kimberly Clauer, Vuong Dang, Sarah Dangelas, Alicia Decatur, William Dickinson, Pavel Gorokhov, Dave Groff, Amy James, Dylan Lamar, Douglas Parker, Megan Reese, Bradley Rowley, Hummam Salih, and Benjamin Shakelton. Several field team members were interns from the International Council on Monuments and Sites (ICOMOS) U.S. summer exchange program, which provided a remarkable cross-cultural experience: Csaba Bartha, Silvia Nadine Bauer, Dr. Philip S. C. Caston, Charu Chaudhry, Francesca da Porto, Magdalena Karakova, Arnold Kriesel, Francesco Lanza, Dorottya Makay, Michiko Tanaka, and Shweta Vardia.

Dr. Dario Gasparini, Dr. Stephen Buonopane, Professor John Ochsendorf, Dr. Rachel Sangree, Dr. Benjamin Schafer, and Justin Spivey served as engineering consultants to the field teams and produced several engineering reports. In addition, the following academic and professional partners also produced documentation: David Ames, University of Delaware; Richard K. Anderson, Jr., Cultural Resource Documentation Services; Jim Barker, Dave Millen, Matthew Reckard, Ken Sutton, Paula Sutton, and Jingyuan Zhou, J.A. Barker Engineering, Inc.; Jim Berilla, Neal Harnar, and Kamil Nizamiev, Case Western Reserve University; Hannah Blum, Johns Hopkins University; Randy Bosnel, Smith Neubecker & Associates; Brad Dameron, Ball State University; and Sarah Ebright and Alex Smith, Bucknell University.

Many current and former HAER staff members worked on this project, including Thomas Behrens, Naomi Hernandez, J. Lawrence Lee, Dana Lockett, Anne E. Kidd, Jet Lowe, Anne Mason, Kristen O'Connell, Richard O'Connor, James Rosenthal, and Jeremy Mauro. The late Jack Boucher photographed several covered bridges for HABS and HAER over his sixty-year career. The National Park Service's Cultural Resources Geographic Information Systems facility staff (John Knoerl, Deidre McCarthy, James Stein, and Matt Stutts) provided invaluable assistance in mapping extant covered bridges. NPS's Historic Preservation Training Center (HPTC) has been a NHCBP program partner since 2002. Tom McGrath, former superintendent of HPTC, served as chair of the First National Covered Bridge Conference in 2003. Tom Vitanza served as lead editor of the forthcoming *Guidelines for Rehabilitating Historic Covered Bridges*, a collaborative effort of the NPS and FHWA, which will provide guidance for rehabilitating covered bridges to the Secretary of the Interior's Standards for Rehabilitating Historic Properties.

USDA Forest Service's Forest Products Laboratory partners Mike Ritter and Karen Martinson set a high bar with their related research projects for the NHCBP program. Brent Phares at Iowa State University oversees the National Center for Wood Transportation Structures Web site (http://www.woodcenter.org), which is the repository for the online version of the World Guide to Covered Bridges and the proceedings of the Second National Covered Bridge Conference. The 2013 Dayton conference served as a celebration of the NHCBP program as well as a ten-year update on the state of covered bridge preservation, both nationally and internationally. The following helped make the event a great success: Christopher H. Marston (conference chair), David A. Simmons (paper chair), Sheila Duwadi, Dario Gasparini, Dave Kirwin, Jane Lightner, Doug Miller, Terry Miller, Dorothy Printup, Steve Simmons, and Bill Vermes.

A significant debt of gratitude is also owed to several key people. Lola Bennett and Joseph Conwill have been involved in the HAER National Covered Bridges Recording Project since its inception and have graciously answered a multitude of questions about covered bridges throughout the years with incomparable patience. In addition to writing fifty-eight HAER historical reports, Lola also wrote five nominations and the comprehensive covered bridges context study for the National Historic Landmarks Program and served as the initial curator of the traveling exhibit *Covered Bridges: Spanning the American Landscape*. The National Society for the Preservation of Covered Bridges and its late president, David Wright, provided a wealth of information for chapter 7, and Bill Caswell assisted with providing images from the society's extensive archives. Bridgewright Timothy Andrews provided valuable information on historic construction methods. Michael R. Harrison and David A. Simmons brought their considerable knowledge and editing skills to improving the manuscript.

The majority of images come from the Historic American Buildings Survey and the Historic American Engineering Record collections at the Library of Congress. We owe a debt to Anne Mason, collections manager, HABS/HAER/HALS, and to Ford Peatross and his staff at the Library of Congress for maintaining this remarkable collection.

The other images used in this book come from many collections, both institutional and personal. We would like to thank the following for their assistance: Ron Anthony, Anthony & Associates, Inc.; Pamalla Anderson, Southern Methodist University; Brian K. Brashaw, University of Minnesota–Duluth; Aimee Brooks, Columbus Museum; Bill Caswell and Joseph Conwill, National Society for the Preservation of Covered Bridges; Bill Cockrell, Oregon Covered Bridge Society; Johanna Descher, École Nationale des Ponts et Chaussées; Paul Espinosa, George Peabody Library, The Sheridan Libraries, Johns Hopkins University; James Garvin; Hopkinton (New Hampshire) Historical Society; Dario Gasparini and Gerhard Welsch, Case Western Reserve University; Pavel Gorokhov; Jean-Pierre Jerome, Parks Canada; Hillary S. Kativa, Historical Society of Pennsylvania; Matthew Kierstead; Tevis Kimball, Jones Library, Inc.; Katherine Krile, Smithsonian Institution Traveling Exhibition Service; Francesco Lanza; Athena LaTocha, National Academy Museum; Jane Lightner, Preble County Historical Society; Bill Patterson; Jack Peters; Lizanne Reger, Smithsonian Institution's National Portrait Gallery; David A. Simmons, Ohio History Connection; Jim Smedley, Maryland Covered Bridges Web site and Theodore Burr Covered Bridge Society; Will Truax; Tom Vitanza; Robert M. Vogel; Thomas E. Walczak, Theodore Burr Covered Bridge Society; and the Miriam Wood Collection.

Finally, we greatly appreciate all the covered bridge enthusiasts, historical societies, preservationists, engineers, builders, craftsman, and other professionals who work every day to preserve and save covered bridges for future generations.

Portfolio of Covered Bridge Trusses Recorded by the Historic American Engineering Record

Edited by Christopher H. Marston

This section previews the variety of wooden truss types typically found in covered bridges from the HAER Collection. Many other HABS and HAER images are used throughout the book to illustrate the many aspects of covered bridge engineering.

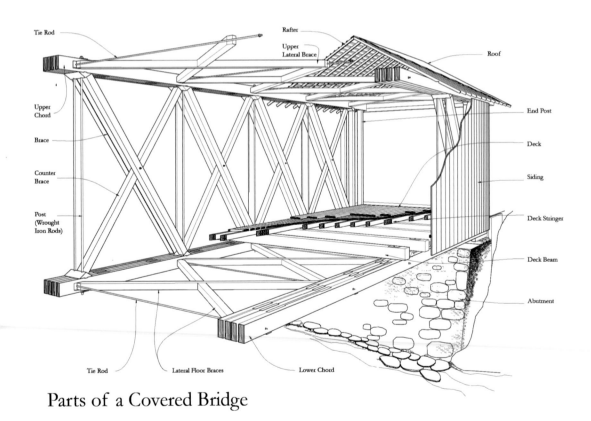

Parts of a Covered Bridge

Figure 0.1 Diagram created by Lola Bennett, Thomas Behrens, Charu Chaudhry, and Christopher H. Marston, 2006.

Truss Types found in Covered Bridges

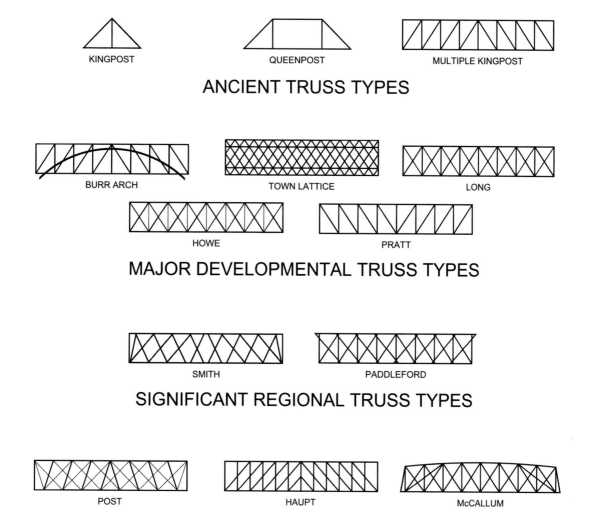

ANCIENT TRUSS TYPES
KINGPOST — QUEENPOST — MULTIPLE KINGPOST

MAJOR DEVELOPMENTAL TRUSS TYPES
BURR ARCH — TOWN LATTICE — LONG — HOWE — PRATT

SIGNIFICANT REGIONAL TRUSS TYPES
SMITH — PADDLEFORD

MINOR TRUSS TYPES
POST — HAUPT — McCALLUM — CHILDS — PARTRIDGE — BROWN — INVERTED BOWSTRING — WHEELER

Figure 0.2 Diagram by Thomas Behrens, Lola Bennett, Pavel Gorokhov, and Christopher H. Marston, 2006, 2014.

Ancient Truss Types

Kingpost Truss

Figure 0.3 Pine Brook Bridge (1872) in Washington County, Vermont, is a 48-foot-long kingpost-truss bridge, rehabilitated by Milton Graton in 1977. The kingpost truss, a simple truss design commonly used for roof framing for centuries, was a common truss type sufficient for modest spans. There are only about twenty historic examples of kingpost-truss covered bridges remaining in the United States. HAER VT-37-8, Jet Lowe, photographer, 2006.

Figure 0.4 Located in Douglas County, Oregon, Neal Lane Bridge (1939), a 42-foot-long kingpost-truss bridge, features paired 1 3/4-inch-diameter iron rods as its center posts. It is the only kingpost design surviving of the many wood trusses built from standard plans by the Oregon State Highway Commission. HAER OR-126-5, Jet Lowe, photographer, 2004.

Queenpost Truss

Figure 0.5 The Flint Bridge (1874) in scenic Orange County, Vermont, is a queenpost-truss bridge restored by Milton Graton in 1969. HAER VT-29-5, Jet Lowe, photographer, 2003.

Multiple-Kingpost Truss

Figure 0.6 A variant of the multiple kingpost with later modifications, Taftsville Bridge (1836) displays aspects of an early craftsman tradition such as the multiple braces at the end of the trusses as seen in the foreground. HAER documented the Windsor County, Vermont, bridge prior to its rehabilitation after Hurricane Irene. HAER VT-30-8, Jet Lowe, photographer, 2003.

Figure 0.7 The multiple-kingpost Humpback Bridge (1857) in Alleghany County, Virginia, displays marked camber. This National Historic Landmark is the last surviving original structure on the James River and Kanawha Turnpike, a major thoroughfare across the Appalachian Mountains. HAER VA-1-15, Jack Boucher, photographer, 1971.

Figure 0.8 Kenyon (Blacksmith Shop) Bridge, a 96-foot-long multiple-kingpost truss in Sullivan County, New Hampshire, was constructed by James Tasker in 1882. HAER NH-40-4, Jet Lowe, photographer, 2003.

Major Developmental Truss Types

Burr-Arch Truss

Figure 0.9 The Village Bridge (1833) in Washington County, Vermont, is a Burr-arch truss bridge noted for its hand-tooled knee braces added by Milton Graton during repairs in the early 1970s. The hand-tooled knee braces replaced steel sway braces added during the mid-twentieth century. HAER VT-34-4, Jet Lowe, photographer, 2004.

Figure 0.10 The Burr-arch truss on the Duck Creek Aqueduct (1846) in Franklin County, Indiana, features flared posts and is the sole remaining covered wood aqueduct in the country. It was designated a National Historic Landmark in 2014. HAER IN-108-2, James Rosenthal, photographer, 2004.

Figure 0.11 Barrackville Bridge (1853) in Marion County, West Virginia, is a 131-foot span Burr-arch truss bridge. HAER documented the bridge following rehabilitation by Emory Kemp in 1999. It is one of three extant bridges completed by West Virginia bridge builder Lemuel Chenoweth. HAER WV-8-23, Jet Lowe, photographer, 2002.

Figure 0.12 Built by Indiana master builder J. J. Daniels, Jackson Bridge (1861) in Parke County, Indiana, is a Burr-arch truss with paired diagonals, posts, and arches. With a span of 207 feet, the Jackson Bridge is the nation's longest single-span wood truss that still carries vehicular traffic. HAER IN-48-7, James Rosenthal, photographer, 2004.

Figure 0.13 Pine Grove Bridge (1884) between Chester and Lancaster Counties, Pennsylvania, is one of eleven bridges by Elias McMellen that still stand. Although it has been rehabilitated, it still exhibits some of the finest examples of Burr-arch truss framing. HAER PA-586-7, Jet Lowe, photographer, 2002.

Town Lattices

Figure 0.14 Built in 1829, the Bath-Haverhill Bridge in Grafton County, New Hampshire, is the oldest existing Town lattice bridge in the country. The laminated arches were added in 1922 to increase load capacity. HAER NH-33-14, Jet Lowe, photographer, 2003.

Figure 0.15 The Beaverkill Bridge (1865) is distinctive for its fan-like radiating planks at the ends of the lattice trusses. Carpenter John Davidson built this regional variation of the Town lattice in Sullivan County, New York, where two other examples survive from the 1860s. HAER NY-329-5, Jet Lowe, photographer, 2003.

Figure 0.16 The Town lattice on the 110-foot span Holliwell Bridge (1880) is braced by a pair of queenpost trusses. It was constructed by Harvey P. Jones and George K. Foster, who together built at least five covered bridges in Madison County, Iowa. HAER IA-64-22, Jet Lowe, photographer, 2004.

Figure 0.17 One of the bridges of Madison County, the Roseman Bridge (1883) is a Town lattice truss bridge with auxiliary queenpost trusses. HAER IA-95-6, Jet Lowe, photographer, 2004.

Figure 0.18 The Cornish-Windsor Bridge (1866) across the Connecticut River between Sullivan County, New Hampshire, and Windsor County, Vermont, is a notched Town lattice truss built by James Tasker and Bela Fletcher. With two spans of over 200 feet each, it is one of the longest historic covered bridges in the country. HAER NH-8-10, Jet Lowe, photographer, 1984.

Figure 0.19 Watson Mill Bridge (1885) in Madison County, Georgia, is one of the extant covered bridges by Washington W. King, eldest son of Horace King, a freed slave who became a prolific bridge builder in the South. HAER GA-140-13, Jet Lowe, photographer, 2004.

Figure 0.20 The two-span, double-web Town lattice Contoocook Railroad Bridge (1889), which spans the Contoocook River in Merrimack County, New Hampshire, was built under the supervision of J. P. Snow of the Boston and Maine Railroad. HAER NH-38-9, Jet Lowe, photographer, 2003.

Figure 0.21 The 320-foot-long, three-span Swann Bridge (1933) features upper lateral bracing in a lattice web above its Town lattice trusses. One of three surviving wood bridges built in Blount County, Alabama, during the 1930s, it represents one of the last regions of covered bridge construction in the country. HAER AL-201-10, Jet Lowe, photographer, 2002.

Figure 0.22 The interior view of Milton and Arnold Graton's Hall Bridge (1982) in Windham County, Vermont, showcases the twentieth-century craftsmen's knowledge of traditional timber framing and detailing in constructing a modern authentic covered bridge. HAER VT-40-11, Jet Lowe, photographer, 2009.

Long Truss

Figure 0.23 To span the Schoharie River, Nichols Powers used a double-barrel Long truss with arch for the Blenheim Bridge (1855) in Schoharie County, New York. In 1964, it was the first covered bridge to be designated as a National Historic Landmark. The bridge was destroyed by flooding in 2011. HAER NY-331-9, Jet Lowe, photographer, 2004.

Figure 0.24 The Eldean Bridge (1860) in Miami County, Ohio, is one of the few remaining Long trusses that still retain their adjustable wooden wedges at the counterbrace panel points for prestressing. The designer of the truss, Col. Stephen Long, is credited with introducing mathematical theory to American bridge design. HAER OH-122-10, Jet Lowe, photographer, 2002.

Howe Truss

Figure 0.25 A Howe truss with arch carries the 233-foot span of the Bridgeport Bridge (1862) in Nevada County, California, built during the Comstock Lode Gold Rush by the Virginia City Turnpike Company. Massachusetts millwright William Howe introduced iron tension members into American bridge trusses. HAER CA-41-9 (CT), Jet Lowe, photographer, 1984.

Figure 0.26 Knight's Ferry Bridge (1863) in Stanislaus County, California, is a 379-foot-long, four-span Howe truss built as a major crossing on the Stockton to Sonora Road. Its high integrity as one of the best remaining examples of a wood and iron Howe truss contributed to its designation as a National Historic Landmark in 2012. HAER CA-314-8, Jet Lowe, photographer, 2004.

Figure 0.27 The 154-foot-long Howe truss Doe River Bridge (1884) in Carter County, Tennessee, is covered by a hip roof, a feature common in Europe but rarely found on American covered bridges. HAER TN-41-14 (CT), Jet Lowe, photographer, 2002.

Figure 0.28 Joseph Britton's Pine Bluff Bridge (1886) is one of several Howe trusses built by Britton and his sons in Putnam County, Indiana. HAER IN-103-4, James Rosenthal, photographer, 2004.

Figure 0.29 Built by the Rutland Railroad in 1897, the 94-foot Howe truss Shoreham Railroad Bridge is now a feature on a picturesque recreational trail in Addison County, Vermont. HAER VT-32-9 (CT), Jet Lowe, photographer, 2003.

Figure 0.30 Clark's Railroad Bridge (1904) in Grafton County, New Hampshire, which was originally located upstate in Coos County on an important link on the granite-hauling Barre Branch Railroad, features substantial Howe trusses. Today it remains active on the steam excursion line at Clark's Trading Post. HAER NH-39-8, Jet Lowe, photographer, 2003.

Figure 0.31 The 36-foot-long Snyder Brook Bridge (1918) in Coos County, New Hampshire, is a rare surviving Howe boxed pony truss (with supplemental outriggers), a once common bridge type built for short spans by the Boston and Maine Railroad. HAER NH-49-4, Jet Lowe, photographer, 2009.

Figure 0.32 Larwood Bridge (1941) was one of several covered bridges built by the Linn County, Oregon, Engineering Department from 1920 through the 1940s from a standard Howe plan. The open-sided housing used throughout Linn County provided increased visibility and reduced wind resistance. HAER OR-124-25, Jet Lowe, photographer, 2004.

Figure 0.33 The Office Bridge (1944) in Lane County, Oregon, features a 180-foot-long Howe truss with paired braces and single counters measuring 14 inches x 16 inches. The massive bridge carried logging truck traffic for the Westfir lumber mill until the plant closed in 1977. HAER OR-125-6, Jet Lowe, photographer, 2004.

Pratt Truss

Figure 0.34 Although burned by arsonists in 1980, the Sulphite Railroad Bridge (1896) in Merrimack County, New Hampshire, survives as an example of a wood and iron Pratt deck truss. Patented by Thomas and Caleb Pratt in 1844, the Pratt truss reversed the configuration of the Howe truss, placing the short web members in compression and the long web members in tension, which reduced the danger of structural failure through buckling. Few timber Pratt-truss bridges were built, but the type was successfully adapted to iron and steel. By the late nineteenth century, the all-metal Pratt truss was the standard American truss for moderate railroad and highway spans. HAER NH-36-7, Jet Lowe, photographer, 2003.

Regional Truss Types

Figure 0.35 This end panel of Kidd's Mill Bridge (1868) in Mercer County, Pennsylvania, shows the extra, steeply inclined compression brace common to trusses patented by Robert W. Smith, who successfully introduced industrial processes into covered bridge construction through his two Ohio companies. HAER PA-622-5, Jet Lowe, photographer, 2006.

Figure 0.36 The Powder Works Bridge (1872) in Santa Cruz County, California, is a triple-web Smith truss built by William Gorrill's Pacific Bridge Company, which introduced the Smith patent to the northwestern part of the country and built several wooden bridges in California and Oregon in the 1870s. HAER CA-313-9, Jet Lowe, photographer, 2004.

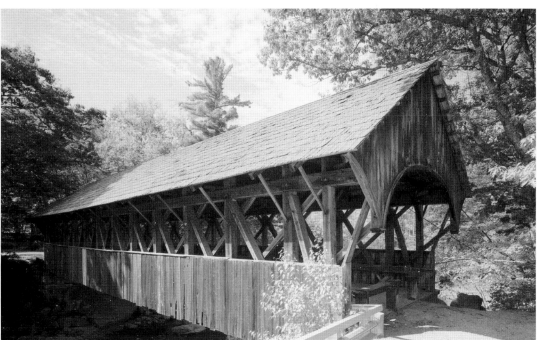

Figure 0.37 Sunday River Bridge (1872) in Oxford County, Maine, is a fine example of a Paddleford truss. Invented by bridge builder Peter Paddleford in the 1830s, the Paddleford truss dominated covered bridge construction throughout much of northern New England for more than half a century. Jet Lowe, HAER ME-69-1, photographer, 2003.

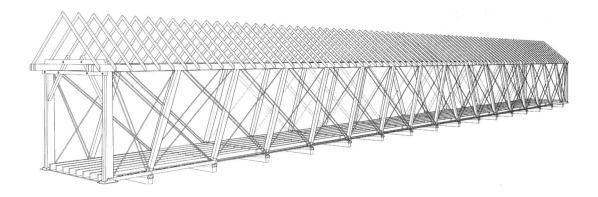

Figure 0.38 Erie Railroad engineer Simeon Post's patented truss featured parallel inclined compression and tension members. It was popular on railroads throughout the 1860s and 1870s. The combination wood and iron Post truss was used on the Bell's Ford Bridge (1868), a road crossing over White's River in Jackson County, Indiana. The structure's western span collapsed in 1999; the eastern span collapsed in 2006. HAER IN-46, sheet 1, Matthew Reckard, Ken Sutton, and Randy Bosnel, J. A. Barker Engineering, delineators, 2004.

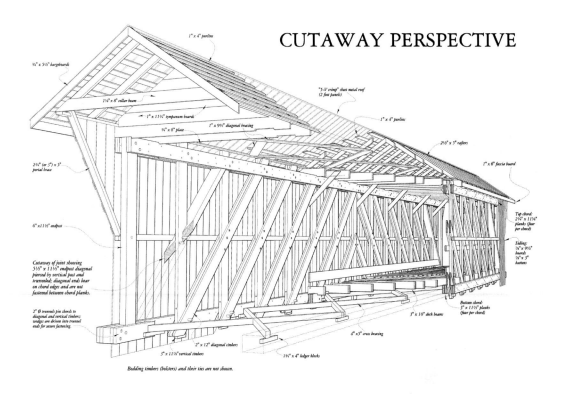

Figure 0.39 Using Gen. Herman Haupt's 1851 patent drawing in his influential book, *General Theory of Bridge Construction*, Andrew Ramsour built the Bunker Hill Bridge in Catawba County, North Carolina, in 1894; it is the last surviving example of the Haupt truss. HAER NC-46, sheet 5, Richard K. Anderson, delineator, 2004.

Figure 0.40 Patented by Daniel McCallum in 1851, the McCallum truss featured an arched upper chord and prestressed counterbraces and was used on North American railroads during the 1860s. The Powerscourt Bridge (1861), crossing the Chateauguay River in Huntingdon County, Quebec, is the only surviving example of this truss type. HAER NY-332-8, Jet Lowe, photographer, 2003.

Figure 0.41 Harshman Bridge (1894) is one of seven surviving Childs trusses built by Everett Sherman in Preble County, Ohio, in the 1880s and 1890s. Horace Childs, a nephew and agent of Stephen Long, patented the design in 1846. HAER OH-126-10, Jet Lowe, photographer, 2004.

Figure 0.42 Pottersburg Bridge (1872) is one of five surviving Partridge trusses. A prolific builder based in Union County, Ohio, Reuben Partridge patented a truss design similar to the Smith truss. HAER OH-125-9, Jet Lowe, photographer, 2003.

Figure 0.43 White's Bridge (1869) in Kent County, Michigan, was the best surviving example of this truss patented in 1857 by Josiah Brown before it was lost in a fire in 2013. The regional Brown truss featured paired braces and single counters notched and bolted at the chords. HAER MI-331-8, Jet Lowe, photographer, 2004.

Figure 0.44 The inverted Bowstring truss on the Germantown Bridge (1865) in Montgomery County, Ohio, is a combination wood and iron rigid suspension truss, in which all compression members are wood and the inverted, arched iron suspension chain is in tension. A rare surviving example of the transitional bridge building period from wood to iron, it is an example of the early work of David H. Morrison, founder of the Columbia Bridge Works of Dayton, Ohio. HAER OH-87-2, Joseph Elliott, photographer, 1992.

Figure 0.45 The Bennett's Mill Bridge (1875) in Greenup County, Kentucky, was the sole surviving historic Wheeler truss until it was rebuilt in 2004. Isaac Wheeler's truss design, featuring paired tension members, double-offset compression members, and an intermediate chord, was briefly popular in the Sciotoville, Ohio, area from 1870 to 1875. HAER KY-49-9, Jet Lowe, photographer, 2004.

Figure 0.46 The original Hancock-Greenfield Bridge in Hillsborough County, New Hampshire, was destroyed by a flood in 1936. New Hampshire Highway Department engineer Henry B. Pratt Jr. designed a replacement covered bridge that met modern regulations with the use of steel timber connectors manufactured by the Timber Engineering Company (TECO), which allowed the bridge to handle heavier loads. Constructed in 1937 by Hagan Thibodeau Construction using federal funds, this modern TECO truss has the distinction of being the first permanent highway span in the United States to use timber connectors. HAER NH-42-7, Jet Lowe, photographer, 2003.

Chapter 1

HAER and the Documentation of Covered Bridges

by Richard O'Connor

T he Historic American Buildings Survey (HABS), established in 1933 as one of the federal government's first historic preservation programs, began recording covered bridges in the 1930s, along with numerous other buildings and structure types. In HABS Bulletin No. 3, prepared under the Civil Works Program, Charles Peterson wrote,

> *It is intended that the survey shall cover structures of all types, from the smallest utilitarian structures to the largest and most monumental. Barns, bridges, mills, toll houses, jails, and in short buildings of every description are to be included so that a complete picture of the culture of the time as reflected in the buildings of the period may be put on record.*[1]

Documentation of American bridges by HABS with large-format photographs, written historical reports, and hand-measured drawings was more than a token effort. Over the next four decades, HABS recorded sixty-two covered bridges, constituting just over a third of those now part of the Historic American Buildings Survey /

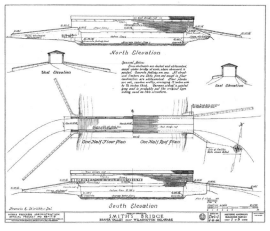

Figure 1.1. In 1936, HABS documented Smith's Bridge, a Burr-arch truss that spanned Brandywine Creek in New Castle County, Delaware. HABS documentation provides a lasting record of the bridge, which was destroyed by arson in 1961. **Top:** 1.1a) HABS DE-1-1, W. Gould White, photographer. **Above:** 1.1b) HABS DE-1, sheet 2, Frances E. Stirlith, delineator.

Historic American Engineering Record / Historic American Landscapes Survey (HABS/HAER/HALS) Collection at the Library of Congress's Prints and Photographs Division, a small but important part of the collection's current 41,000-plus sites and structures.

The Historic American Engineering Record picked up where HABS left off. The American Society of Civil Engineers, along with the National Park Service and the Library of Congress, established the HAER program in 1969, with subsequent endorsements from four other engineering societies. Bridges are unquestionably the most ubiquitous historic engineering structures on the landscape, existing wherever roads cross streams and rivers and span valleys. From its inception, HAER made bridges—wood, stone, iron, steel, and concrete—a focal point for documentation. As a subset, covered bridges are the oldest of these, with some extant structures dating to the first half of the nineteenth century.

Bridges fit well with HAER's core mission to document endangered historic engineering and industrial structures. Because bridges are continually exposed to the harshest natural elements, rot and rust tax even the most vigilant preventive maintenance programs, but it has been the unrelenting quest for structures that can withstand heavier loads and greater speeds that has doomed many of our historic bridges. Like their counterpart industrial buildings, historic bridges rarely have alternative uses that would convey a new lease on life. As Robert Vogel, curator emeritus of mechanical and

Figure 1. 2 HAER documented its first covered bridge, Humpback Covered Bridge in Alleghany County, Virginia, in 1970. So named because of its marked camber, the bridge was designated a National Historic Landmark in 2012 as the best surviving example of a timber multiple-kingpost truss, making it an outstanding example of nineteenth-century bridge construction. HAER VA-1-6, Jack Boucher, photographer, 1971.

civil engineering at the Smithsonian Institution and an early contributor to the HAER program, wrote, "A historic bridge . . . can never be anything but that, and once it is no longer needed at a certain place; or cannot cope with modern traffic loadings; or has deteriorated beyond repair only rarely will its original owner or any organization be willing to carry the continuing maintenance costs for its preservation merely as a monument."[2] The result, he notes, is that we "resort to a poor second course" preparing documentation that will outlive the structure, which is actually a primary purpose of the HABS, HAER, and HALS programs. In a striking statistic, of the sixty-two covered bridges documented by HABS between 1933 and 1969, thirty-six have been "lost"— destroyed or demolished by the forces of nature and man.

HAER, like its counterpart HABS decades earlier, developed systematic, methodological approaches to understanding the universe of historic engineering structures and determining which among those warranted more in-depth documentation. First and foremost was the inventory that located and identified engineering sites and structures in a given geographic area, evaluated their integrity and historical value, and established a need for further recording or a context for the nomination of similar resources to the National Register of Historic Places. The programs produced dozens of state and regional inventories in the 1970s and 1980s, starting with the HABS-sponsored *New England Textile Mill Survey* in 1968 and the first HAER study the following year, *A Report of the Mohawk-Hudson Area Survey.* The most recent of the inventories covered nine central and western Pennsylvania counties in the late 1980s and early 1990s.[3] HAER also worked with officials from state departments of transportation over three decades to develop extensive state bridge surveys, starting with Virginia in 1970.[4] A multi-year partnership between the Federal Highway Administration (FHWA) and the National Park Service (NPS) resulted in the documentation of hundreds of bridges in nearly fifty national parks in HAER's National Park Service Park Roads and Bridges Project from 1988 to 2002.[5]

Inventory and survey underpinned HAER's participation in the FHWA's National Historic Covered Bridge Preservation (NHCBP) Program. Fortunately, the National Society for the Preservation of Covered Bridges, a group of covered bridge experts and advocates, has published and updated its *World Guide to Covered Bridges* since 1956. The *World Guide* provides basic location, age, and dimensional data on the 800 or so known covered bridges in the United States, from which HAER developed a targeted, comprehensive documentation and study plan for its National Covered Bridges Recording Project. In February 2002, HAER convened a planning meeting of twenty-three preservation engineers and architects, timber framers, historians, transportation and preservation officials, and other experts in the field to develop a list of the most historically significant covered bridges in the United States. Several of these specialists consulted with HAER for the duration of the project. From the list they developed, HAER has selected and documented in greater detail eighty covered bridges considered by meeting participants to be the most significant.

In addition to the planning meeting and HAER documentation, other components of HAER's work, done in conjunction with the NHCBP program, have built upon and expanded HAER's traditional documentation, contributing in a variety of ways to the NHCBP program's preservation goals. Typical, comprehensive HAER documentation consists of measured and interpretive drawings, large-format photographs, and historical reports that are generally a combination of description and narrative. For the NHCBP program, HAER has worked with professional engineers, engineering students, and several universities (Case Western Reserve, Johns Hopkins, Bucknell, and Massachusetts Institute of Technology) to develop engineering analyses of a variety of covered bridge truss systems, including the Burr, Town, Long, Howe, multiple-kingpost, queenpost, Pratt, Childs, and Smith. These studies (on sixteen bridges) have subjected historical structures to modern engineering testing techniques to reveal the ways they behave under load and to answer other, more specific, questions.

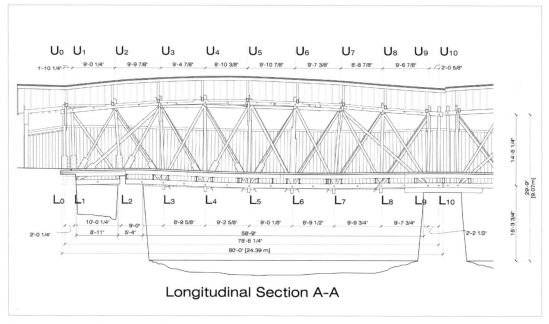

Longitudinal Section A-A

Figure 1. 3 An essential component of the NHCBP program has been HAER documentation undertaken by teams of HAER staff members, students and professionals, as in this field team on site at Powerscourt Bridge (1861) in Huntingdon County, Quebec, in 2003. **Top:** 1.3a) From left to right: Jean-Pierre Jerome and Christian Ouimet of Heritage Conservation Services, Parks Canada; Naomi Hernandez, Thomas Behrens, Lola Bennett, Dana Lockett, and Christopher Marston, HAER staff members. Courtesy of Jean-Pierre Jerome, 2003. **Above:** 1.3b) HAER NY-332, sheet 4, Thomas Behrens, delineator, 2003.

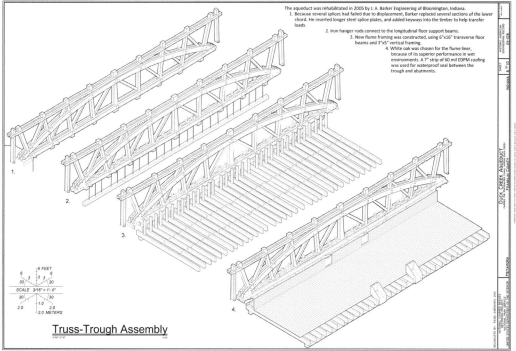

The aqueduct was rehabilitated in 2005 by J. A. Barker Engineering of Bloomington, Indiana.
1. Because several splices had failed due to displacement, Barker replaced several sections of the lower chord. He inserted longer steel splice plates, and added keyways into the timber to help transfer loads.

2. Iron hanger rods connect to the longitudinal floor support beams.

3. New flume framing was constructed, using 6"x16" transverse floor beams and 3"x5" vertical framing.

4. White oak was chosen for the flume liner, because of its superior performance in wet environments. A 7" strip of 60 mil EDPM roofing was used for waterproof seal between the trough and abutments.

Truss-Trough Assembly

Figure 1.4 The Duck Creek Aqueduct (1846) in Franklin County, Indiana, with its Burr-arch truss exemplifies how covered bridge technology was adapted to a variety of transportation systems in the nineteenth century. The Secretary of the Interior designated the aqueduct as a National Historic Landmark in 2014. **Top:** 1.4a) HAER IN-108-4, James Rosenthal, photographer, 2004. **Above:** 1.4b) HAER IN-108, sheet 6, Pavel Gorokhov, delineator, 2012.

As part of the NHCBP program work plan, HAER coordinated and undertook the preparation of a National Historic Landmark (NHL) theme study and subsequent nominations for covered bridges. Theme studies assess the national significance of groups of resources and are the first step in the development of NHL nominations, the highest official recognition of historic properties designated by the Secretary of the Interior. In particular, theme studies provide the broadest possible context for assessing the significance of individual resources against the backdrop of all other similar resources. The *World Guide*, the experts' workshop, and detailed HAER documentation provided the information necessary to develop the theme study and individual nominations. Five bridge nominations have successfully completed the formal process, resulting in all five bridges being named National Historic Landmarks: Knight's Ferry Bridge, an 1863 Howe truss in Stanislaus County, California; the 1857 Humpback Bridge in Alleghany County, Virginia, the best surviving example of a timber, multiple-kingpost truss; Brown Bridge, an 1880 Town lattice truss in Rutland County, Vermont, and the best surviving example of the work of Nichols Powers; the 1846 Duck Creek Aqueduct in Metamora, Indiana, the only surviving covered wood aqueduct in the United States; and the California Powder Works Bridge, an 1872 Smith truss in Santa Cruz County, California.

Several partnerships have extended the programs' reach. The NPS's Historic Preservation Training Center (HPTC) took the lead in convening the First National Covered Bridge Conference, a "best practices" workshop in Burlington, Vermont, in June 2003. This event brought together over two hundred engineers, contractors, craftspeople, highway administrators, and covered bridge preservation organizations to make formal presentations and exchange knowledge of "state of the art" covered bridge preservation, repair, and maintenance techniques. In addition to accomplishing these goals, the Burlington conference also resulted in the ratification of the "Burlington Charter for the Preservation of Historic Covered Bridges," a set of goals "for insuring the long term safeguarding of historic covered bridges."[6] HPTC is also developing the *Guidelines for Rehabilitating Historic Covered Bridges* to disseminate information concerning the preservation and maintenance of covered bridges according to the *Secretary of the Interior's Standards for the Treatment of Historic Properties*. In partnership with the Smithsonian Institution Traveling Exhibition Service (SITES), HAER mounted *Covered Bridges: Spanning the American Landscape*, designed to heighten the public's awareness of covered bridges and to educate people about their history, their engineering features, and the threats to their existence. The exhibition travelled continuously for more than three years to numerous locations across the country.[7]

One vital component of the project from its onset has been an update of the *World Guide*. Building on over a half century of dedicated compiling, updating, and publishing by the

Figure 1. 5 *Covered Bridges: Spanning the American Landscape* traveled around the country from 2006 to 2009. The opening panel is shown here at the Altoona Heritage Discovery Center in Pennsylvania. Courtesy of Smithsonian Institution Traveling Exhibition Service, 2009.

National Society for the Preservation of Covered Bridges and a number of individuals, the National Park Service's Cultural Resources Geographic Information Systems (CRGIS) facility created a database and Web application that translates the paper-based *World Guide* into a searchable and illustrated digital inventory of covered bridges. Users can search for bridges by name, location, year built, *World Guide* number, and even the type of truss used. In addition to the attribute data one would find within the *World Guide* for a selected bridge, the application also displays interactive Google maps for locations of existing bridges, geo-tagged photographs of the bridge and/or its surroundings via the Panoramio photo-sharing service, interactive Google Street Views (when available), and a selection of statistical charts generated on the fly based upon user inputs. Additionally, users can find connections between existing bridges and lost bridges based upon a shared location. A select set of known and approved bridge experts can log on to the site and update the database dynamically, and edits can then be quickly viewed by the general public. The Web site is hosted by Iowa State University's National Center for Wood Transportation Structures and can be viewed at http://woodcenter.org/CoveredBridges/.

As of this writing, HAER and its partners are in the process of completing several other initiatives. HAER convened the Second National Covered Bridge Conference in Dayton, Ohio, in June 2013, ten years after the one held in Burlington.[8] Ongoing research projects include the reconstruction and intensive load and environmental testing of a Howe pony truss, analyzing the performance of existing covered bridge floor systems, and load testing a full-size, half-span model of a Burr-arch truss.

Figure 1.6 Participants of the Second National Covered Bridge Conference in Dayton in June 2013 toured the covered bridges of Preble County, Ohio. Courtesy of Jane Lightner, Preble County Historical Society.

A decade has passed since Eric DeLony, former chief of the HAER program and HAER's first permanent staff member, convened the first covered bridge planning meeting in Washington, D.C. After organizing and leading extensive bridge documentation projects ranging from Washington State's concrete structures to Chicago's bascules to Pennsylvania's cast- and wrought-iron bridges, DeLony ended his federal career working with Steve Ernst and Sheila Duwadi to formalize HAER's participation in FHWA's National Historic Covered Bridge Preservation Program. With a long track record of engineering documentation, a wealth of wide-ranging expertise on which to draw, and multi-year funding, DeLony established the HAER covered bridge agenda as a model project, cascading from a comprehensive inventory to thorough documentation to detailed engineering studies, all geared toward preservation of fragile historic engineering resources. In this business, it doesn't get any better than that.

Endnotes

1 U.S. Department of the Interior, Office of National Parks, Buildings and Reservations, Historic American Buildings Survey, HABS Bulletin No. 3, December 20, 1933, 1.

2 Robert Vogel, ed., *A Report of the Mohawk-Hudson Area Survey* (Washington, D.C.: Smithsonian Institution Press, 1973), 1.

3 Robert Vogel, *New England Textile Mill Survey: Report of the First Summer's Work, June–September 1967* (Washington, D.C.: Smithsonian Institution Press, 1968). As part of America's Industrial Heritage Project (AIHP), HAER published surveys of historic industrial and engineering sites in nine counties in southwest Pennsylvania, including Bedford, Blair, Cambria, Fayette, Fulton, Huntington, Indiana, Somerset, and Westmoreland.

4 The first covered bridge recorded by HAER was the Humpback Covered Bridge (HAER No. VA-1) in 1970. Notable HAER bridge surveys undertaken between 1986 and 2000 include examples in Ohio, Wisconsin, Massachusetts, Arkansas, Oregon, Washington, Iowa, Texas, Pennsylvania, Missouri, Illinois, and California.

5 A portfolio of selected drawings is found in Timothy Davis, Todd A. Croteau, and Christopher H. Marston, *America's National Park Roads and Parkways* (Baltimore: The Johns Hopkins University Press, 2004).

6 The Burlington Charter and information on the 2003 "Covered Bridge Preservation: National Best Practices Conference" are available at http://www.uvm.edu/coveredbridges/charter.html.

7 More information on the traveling exhibition is on SITES's Web site, http://www.sites.si.edu/exhibitions/exhibits/archived_exhibitions/bridges/main.htm. See also Christopher Marston, " 'Covered Bridges: Spanning the American Landscape' Traveling Exhibit Debuts in Harrisburg," *Society for Industrial Archeology Newsletter* 35, no. 2, (Spring 2006): 1–3.

8 The program and presentations from the Dayton conference are available at http://www.woodcenter.org/2013-national-covered-bridge-conference/papers.cfm.

Overview of the National Historic Covered Bridge Preservation Program

by Sheila Rimal Duwadi

The Federal Highway Administration (FHWA) has been administering the National Historic Covered Bridge Preservation (NHCBP) Program since 1998, as legislated in highway bills starting with the Transportation Equity Act for the 21st Century (TEA-21) and continuing through the Safe, Accountable, Flexible, Efficient Transportation Equity Act—A Legacy for Users, or SAFETEA-LU for short. Between 2000 and 2012, the program provided funding in two key areas: grants to preserve, rehabilitate, and restore historic covered bridges; and for research, education, and technology transfer. During this period, over 200 historic covered bridges in twenty-four states that are listed or have been determined eligible for listing in the National Register of Historic Places have been saved.[1]

Figure 2.1 Figure 2.1 Gilpin's Falls Covered Bridge (1860) in Cecil County, Maryland, was in danger of collapse due to decaying members. An award of $1,040,000 from the NHCBP program funded a sensitive rehabilitation project in 2009–2010. Left: 2.1a) The deteriorating bridge awaiting repair. Carol M. Highsmith Archive, Library of Congress, Prints and Photographs Division, Washington, D.C., between 1980-2006. Right: 2.1b) Stabilizing the truss during Tim Andrews' rehabilitation. HAER MD-174-4, David Ames, photographer, 2009.

Research, education, and technology transfer focused on finding means and methods for repairing, strengthening, and preserving covered bridges; producing documentation, including educational videos and manuals; and offering workshops and seminars. The FHWA achieved much in this effort through close collaboration and shared resources with the National Park Service's Historic American Engineering Record (HAER) and the U. S. Department of Agriculture (USDA), Forest Service's Forest Products Laboratory (FPL). Countless numbers of engineers, historians, researchers, scientists, and others have been involved in this effort. As studies are completed, they are made available at the National Center for Wood Transportation Structures' Web site at www.woodcenter.org.

What follows is a discussion of some of the highlights of the research, education, and technology transfer projects.

The *Covered Bridge Manual*, one of the first projects completed, serves as a guide for inspection, repair, rehabilitation, and restoration of historic covered bridges and provides techniques that reflect the latest developments in the preservation field, including both theoretical and practical aspects of inspection, as well as historic and traditional construction. Since the goal of most owners is to have their covered bridges carry modern traffic, developing a manual that illustrated the right blend of the new and the traditional, with guidance on how to preserve the historic integrity exhibited in the original architectural, structural, and material characteristics of the bridge, was necessary. Published in 2005, it has been a valuable resource in preserving these structures.[2]

If unprotected, wood can be damaged from biological activity, and many covered bridges have had to be repaired as a result of structural deterioration. During the period historic covered bridges were built, there were few chemical treatments available to prevent fungi and insects from attacking and colonizing the wood. While covering wood trusses with roofs and sides kept the wood dry and slowed the deterioration of the wood members, moisture could still migrate over time, resulting in suitable conditions for colonization by wood-destroying organisms. Therefore, a priority has been the identification of chemical preservative treatments that prevent wood deterioration while still being safe and acceptable to the historic preservation community.

Fire is another concern as arsonists have targeted wood covered bridges. While large dimension timbers have inherent fire-resistive characteristics that can eliminate the need for fire retardant treatments (FRTs), this is not always true of small-sized members. FRTs can add an extra layer of protection, allowing more response time for the authorities. However, there has been a reluctance to use FRTs, as older treatments were known to affect the structural properties of wood and accelerate the corrosion of fasteners. A new generation of products is now available that reduces these problems.

Researchers at Oregon State University and at Mississippi State University, respectively, conducted studies to identify and evaluate chemical preservative treatments and fire retardant treatments for use in covered bridges that would be effective and yet still acceptable for historic preservation purposes. The *Guide for In-Place Treatment of Wood in Historic Covered and Modern Bridges*, published in 2012, compiles the results of these studies into a practical document.[3] In addition, the *Covered Bridge Security Manual* provides cost-effective, tested systems that can be used to protect against vandalism.[4]

Corrosion of Fasteners in Wood Treated with Newer Wood Preservatives and *Guide for Materials Selection and Design for Metals Used in Contact with Copper-Treated Wood* report on the corrosion effects of newer preservatives on metals and provide references for engineers to aid in selecting treated wood for building projects. The publications also provide design strategies to minimize corrosion of metals in contact with treated wood.[5] *Evaluating Naturally Durable Wood Species for Repair and Rehabilitation of Above-Ground Components of Covered Bridges* examines seven wood species for their durability without the use of chemical wood preservatives and provides a guide for the use of naturally durable wood species in the rehabilitation of covered bridges.[6]

A condition assessment of a bridge is essential to determining the structure's safety. In accordance with the National Bridge Inspection Standards, all bridges greater than 20 feet in length and on public roads are required by law to be inspected every two years. While visual inspection to determine condition is by far the most prevalent form of inspection for all bridge types, more advanced technologies continue to be developed, although these have mostly been for use in evaluating steel and concrete structures. The project "Advanced Field Evaluation Tools for Condition Assessment of Wood Members in Covered Bridges" will identify, adapt, and evaluate innovative, low-cost technologies bridge inspectors can use to examine wood members and more accurately determine the condition of a covered bridge.

In addition to damage to covered bridges caused by age, environment, arson, and increasingly heavy loads, natural hazards such as floods have had devastating impacts on these historic structures. As Hurricane Irene moved up the northeastern United States in 2011, for example, the major rainfall and subsequent flooding associated with the storm damaged a significant number of roadways and bridges in Pennsylvania, New York, Massachusetts, Vermont, and New Hampshire. Several covered bridges were washed away during this event. Physical and analytical tests are being conducted at the FHWA's Turner-Fairbank Highway Research Center to simulate the hydraulic flows anticipated in similar weather events in order to develop design equations and coefficients for drag, lift, and overturning forces, and to develop design details to strengthen bridge members and improve the hydraulic safety of covered bridges.

Educational materials have been developed thanks to funding from the NHCBP program. The comprehensive *Educational Guide on the History of Covered Bridges in the United States*, developed by the Institute for the History of Technology and Industrial Archaeology at West Virginia University, was designed for use by K–12 educators teaching math, science, and American history. It is available both in print and online formats. The guide is divided into sections for grades K–5, 6–9, and 9–12 and includes printable lesson plans for educators, a list of covered bridges erected in the United States, individual bridge histories, and a companion disk with interactive and animated elements for students. Graphic elements consist of images and descriptive drawings that convey bridge type, year built, design loads, traffic, wood species, information on the designer/builder, and much more.[7] In another educational outreach effort, funding was provided to Indiana University for a documentary entitled *Spanning Time: America's Covered Bridges*, which has been broadcast nationwide on public television.[8]

The program has also funded efforts by the National Park Service's Historic American Engineering Record (HAER) to accurately document historic covered bridges, as described in chapter 1. Such documentation is essential because it creates a lasting record of structures that can be quickly destroyed, as in the case of the Blenheim Covered Bridge in New York, which was swept away by raging waters during Hurricane Irene. In addition to covered bridge documentation, HAER and the National Park Service's Cultural Resources Geographic Information Systems facility have created an interactive Web site using data from the *World Guide to Covered Bridges*. This site is available at http://www.woodcenter.org/CoveredBridges/.

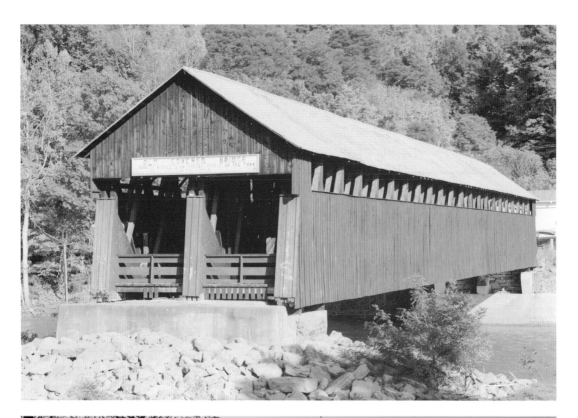

Figure 2.2 Hurricane Irene washed away Blenheim Bridge (1855), a National Historic Landmark, in September 2011. At 210 feet, the bridge had one of the longest clear spans of any surviving covered bridge and was a rare surviving double-barrel Long truss. **Top:** 2.2a) Before, HAER NY-331-3, Jet Lowe, photographer, 2004. **Above:** 2.2b) After, Matthew Kierstead, photographer, 2012.

Accurately documenting a covered bridge, as done according to HAER standards, requires taking detailed field measurements of the bridge and its various components. The use of laser scanner technology to produce as-built drawings, which is less labor intensive than traditional measuring techniques but can produce the same level of detail, is also being investigated as part of the NHCBP program. Two different scanning technologies have been studied. The HAER program used a Leica scanner to record ten historic covered bridges as part of its surveys.[9] The University of Minnesota–Duluth tested a FARO scanner on six Midwestern bridges and produced its findings in the report *Use of Laser Scanning Technology to Obtain As-Built Records*. When feasible, laser scanning technology can shorten the recording process.[10]

Figure 2.3 New technologies for documentation include HAER's Leica C10 scanner and the FARO scanner used by the University of Minnesota–Duluth. **Top Left:** 2.3a) A Leica C10 scanner was used to document the West Union Bridge (HAER IN-105). Jeremy Mauro, photographer, 2013. **Top Right:** 2.3b) Resulting point cloud of West Union Bridge. Scan data by Jeremy Mauro, 2013. **Left:** 2.3c) A FARO scanner was used to document the Cedarburg Covered Bridge in Wisconsin. Brian K. Brashaw, photographer, 2010.

Figure 2.4 The rehabilitation of the Long truss on the Blair Bridge (1869) in Grafton, New Hampshire, required the use of staging, a technique discussed in the forthcoming "Guidebook for Restoring Structural Integrity of Covered Bridge Members." Ron Anthony of Anthony & Associates, Inc., photographer, 2012.

To educate engineering and architecture students about the structural behavior and evolution of wooden truss designs, Johns Hopkins University is developing educational models for four significant trusses—the Burr, Town, Long, and Howe. Scale plans for 100-foot trusses will allow users at a consortium of engineering schools to construct their own models and learn the aspects of each design.

Because historic covered bridges carried much lighter loads in the past than they do today, several studies have been funded to better understand the load-carrying capacities of covered bridges, to develop methods to strengthen members and establish more accurate rating procedures, and to identify ways to decrease dead load. In *Strengthening Historic Covered Bridges to Carry Modern Traffic*, West Virginia University assessed the use of fiber-reinforced polymers as a means of strengthening components.[11] Studies still in process through the Forest Products Laboratory include "Improved Ratings for Covered Bridges through Load Testing," which will develop rating procedures for reliably determining safe load-carrying capacity. "Improved Analytical Techniques for Historic Covered Bridges" will recommend improved analytical methods that have been validated using field load-test data. "Lightweight Floor Replacement Systems" will assess the use in covered bridges of floor systems that have been proven for bridge applications, and "Guidebook for Restoring Structural Integrity of Covered Bridge Members" will discuss the steps necessary for decision makers to identify effective rehabilitation techniques for restoring the structural integrity of covered bridge members.[12]

Unlike the properties of steel and concrete, engineering properties of wood can vary both within and between species. Additionally, wood is orthotropic, which means its material properties vary depending on grain direction. Therefore, the design values for wood given in specifications and standards are based on statistical samples with a conservative safety factor to account for the variability. Often the species, sources, and grades of existing woods in historic covered bridges are difficult to identify, and the current practice is to assume a species and select wood values from existing specifications. As part of "Species Identification and Field-Grading of Woods in Covered Bridges," a field manual is being developed to help determine the timber species and identify the grade so that engineering properties can be more reliably predicted.

Figure 2.5 FHWA funded a joint project between HAER, Case Western Reserve University, and the National Society for the Preservation of Covered Bridges to study the Moose Brook Bridge (1918) in Gorham, New Hampshire, a Howe truss that was a victim of arson in 2004. The original castings were restored, and bridgewright Tim Andrews reconstructed the salvaged trusses for testing in Case Western's lab. **Top** 2.5a) The burned trusses sat idle for five years. HAER NH-48-3, Jet Lowe, photographer, 2009. **Above** 2.5b) The first truss assembled in the tab. Photograph courtesy Dario Gasparini, 2011.

The timber trusses used in historic covered bridges set the stage for modern-day trusses. The bridge builders and engineers of the past ingeniously designed the truss and arch systems that make up these bridges to carry and transfer loads safely. The NHBCP program supports several projects studying these designs. William Howe's patented truss permitted tightening of the tension rods to induce compression in the wood diagonals. The "Howe Truss Design and Performance" study will provide a better understanding of William Howe's design by studying the Moose Brook Bridge, a Howe boxed pony truss, through both analytical and full-scale experimental tests. Similarly, Burr-arch truss systems will be examined to develop a better understanding of the design and connection details of Theodore Burr's designs. Portions of the recovered Bartonsville Covered Bridge will be used to study the performance of Town lattice trusses and the interaction of the lattice system in carrying and distributing loads in order to develop more precisely calibrated models.

Covered bridges represent the technological heritage of the United States. Developing techniques and methodologies that utilize the right blend of the new and the traditional and that result in preserving the historic integrity of the bridge, including its original architectural, structural, and material characteristics, has been the thrust of the National Historic Covered Bridge Preservation Program. In addition, disseminating knowledge about various aspects of covered bridges to all sectors of the American public remains a primary goal.

Endnotes

[1] Detailed lists of year by year project funding can be found on the Federal Highway Administration Web site, http://www.fhwa.dot.gov/bridge/covered.cfm.

[2] Philip C. Pierce, Robert L. Brungraber, Abba Lichtenstein, Scott Sabol, J. J. Morrell, and S. T. Lebow, *Covered Bridge Manual* (U.S. Department of Transportation, Federal Highway Administration, Publication No. FHWA-HRT-04-098, April 2005). The report is available online at http://www.fhwa. dot.gov/publications/research/infrastructure/structures/04098/04098.pdf.

[3] Stan Lebow, Grant Kirker, Robert White, Terry Amburgey, H. Michael Barnes, Michael Sanders, and Jeff Morrell, *Guide for In-Place Treatment of Wood in Historic Covered and Modern Bridges* (U.S. Department of Agriculture, Forest Service, Forest Products Laboratory, in cooperation with the U.S. Department of Transportation, Federal Highway Administration, General Technical Report FPL-GTR-205, 2012). The report is available online at http://www.fpl.fs.fed.us/documnts/fplgtr/fpl_gtr205.pdf.

[4] Brent Phares, Terry Wipf, Ryan Sievers, and Travis Hosteng, *Covered Bridge Security Manual* (U.S. Department of Agriculture, Forest Service, Forest Products Laboratory, in cooperation with the U.S. Department of Transportation, Federal Highway Administration, General Technical Report FPL-GTR-223, 2012). The report is available online at http://www.fpl.fs.fed.us/documnts/fplgtr/fpl_gtr223.pdf.

[5] Samuel L. Zelinka, *Corrosion of Fasteners in Wood Treated with Newer Wood Preservatives* (U. S. Department of Agriculture, Forest Service, Forest Products Laboratory, in cooperation with the U. S. Department of Transportation, Federal Highway Administration, General Technical Report FPL-GTR-220, 2013); Samuel L. Zelinka, *Guide for Material Selection and Design for Metals Used in Contact with Copper-Treated Wood* (U. S. Department of Agriculture, Forest Service, Forest Products Laboratory, in cooperation with the U. S. Department of Transportation, Federal Highway Administration, General Technical Report FPL-GTR-227, 2013). The reports are available online at http://www.fpl.fs.fed.us/documnts/fplgtr/fpl_gtr220.pdf and http://www.fpl.fs.fed.us/documnts/fplgtr/fpl_gtr227.pdf, respectively.

[6] Grant T. Kirker, Carol A. Clausen, A. B. Blodgett, Stan T. Lebow, *Evaluating Naturally Durable Wood Species for Repair and Rehabilitation of Above-Ground Components of Covered Bridges* (U. S. Department of Agriculture, Forest Service, Forest Products Laboratory, in cooperation with the U. S. Department of Transportation, Federal Highway Administration, General Technical Report FPL-GTR-224, 2013). The report is available online at http://www.fpl.fs.fed.us/documnts/fplgtr/fpl_gtr224.pdf.

[7] Institute for the History of Technology and Industrial Archeology, West Virginia University, *Educational Guide on the History of Covered Bridges in the United States*, available at http://www.woodcenter.org/covered_bridges_education.

[8] *Spanning Time: America's Covered Bridges*, DVD (Bloomington, Ind.: WTIU, 2004). More information is available at http://www.indiana.edu/~radiotv/wtiu/bridges/#.

[9] Jeremy Mauro, "Strategies for Documenting Covered Bridges Using 3D Laser Scanning and 3D Modeling," Second National Covered Bridges Conference, Dayton, Ohio, 2013, available at http://www.woodcenter.org/2013-national-covered-bridge-conference/papers.cfm.

[10] Robert J. Ross, Brian K. Brashaw, and Samuel J. Anderson, "Use of Laser Scanning Technology to Obtain As-Built Records of Historic Covered Bridges" (U. S. Department of Agriculture, Forest Service, Forest Products Laboratory, in cooperation with the U. S. Department of Transportation, Federal Highway Administration, General Technical Report FPL-RP-669, 2012). The report is available online at http://www.fpl.fs.fed.us/documnts/fplrp/fpl_rp669.pdf.

Endnotes

11 "Strengthening Historic Covered Bridges to Carry Modern Traffic," FHWA TechBrief, FHWA-HR-07-041. The brief is available online at https://www.fhwa.dot.gov/publications/research/infrastructure/bridge/07041/07041.pdf.

12 All of these reports are still in development as of this writing. Upon completion, they should be available at Iowa State University's National Center for Wood Transportation Structures' Web site, http://woodcenter.org.

Chapter 3

History of Covered Bridges in the United States

by Lola Bennett

Figure 3.1 Charles Whitney wrote in the introduction to Rosalie Wells's 1931 *Covered Bridges in America*, "The present generation does not. . . realize the important role which the timber bridge played in the early development of the American continent. But for the abundance of timber and the ingenuity of the American bridge builder, the construction of bridges across the many rivers would have been impossible when bridges were so much needed to carry the highways and railways into undeveloped country." Fort River Bridge (1840) in Hampshire County, Massachusetts, carried vehicular traffic until it was lost to arson in 1962. The structure was captured around the turn of the twentieth century by renowned local author and photographer Clifton Johnson. Courtesy of Jones Library, Inc., Amherst, Massachusetts.

Americans did not invent covered bridges, but they built them in unprecedented numbers as the nation expanded across the continent in the nineteenth century.[1] In the process, they refined timber-truss design to a degree never seen before. While the practice of building framed timber bridges first occurred in Western Europe, American bridge builders quickly set the standard for timber-bridge construction, producing a succession of innovative designs that made possible the construction of sturdy and cost-effective bridges capable of spanning long distances and safely carrying heavy, moving loads. Concomitantly, these builders recognized the value of covering a timber bridge's framework to ensure the structure's longevity. By the end of the first quarter of the nineteenth century, the covered bridge was a ubiquitous part of the American landscape. At the height of covered bridge building, around 1870, there were well over 10,000 covered bridges in the United States.[2]

The historic era of covered bridge building—the period when timber bridges were built because wood was abundant and cheap, and when practical knowledge of timber-framing techniques was passed down through successive generations of builders—began in the early 1800s and ended in the 1950s in the United States. The dates defining this era vary from region to region, but the practice of building covered bridges lasted about a century in most parts of the country. In the Mid-Atlantic region, covered bridges were built from 1805 until about 1920; in New England, from about 1810 until about 1910; in the Midwest, from the 1810s until the 1920s; in the South, from about 1820 until the 1930s; and in the Pacific Northwest, from the 1850s until the 1950s. By the 1950s, the economic competitiveness of timber bridges had disappeared, and the historic era of covered bridge building ended. While some covered bridges were built after this time—and they are still occasionally built today in a few scattered parts of the country—these revival-era covered bridges differ from their predecessors in that they are not part of the continuous building tradition that characterized the historic era of covered bridge construction, and the impetus behind them is nostalgia, rather than economy.[3]

Origins of the Covered Bridge

Timber bridges have been built in forested regions of the world for centuries.[4] Wood is an excellent material for building; it is strong, relatively lightweight, and can be worked with common hand tools. Since most species of wood suitable for structural applications deteriorate rapidly when exposed to the weather, early bridge builders quickly learned the value of covering wood bridges with roofs and siding to protect the underlying framework. A wood bridge left uncovered may last fifteen years, but when properly covered and cared for, it can last indefinitely. A few covered bridges in Europe have survived for well over four centuries. Schlossbrücke (1514) in Zwingen, Switzerland, and Spreuerbrücke (1568) in Luzern, Switzerland, are two fine examples.

Carpenters in the forested regions of Europe began to refine the technology of framed timber bridges during the eighteenth century. Swiss brothers Johannes and Hans Ulrich Grubenmann built some noteworthy spans during that time, including the Schaffhausen and Wettingen bridges in Switzerland. European architects, scholars, and aristocrats studied these bridges, and descriptions and illustrations of the spans appeared in contemporary travel publications and technical literature. The Schaffhausen Bridge (1758) across the Rhine River was a two-span bridge of about 360 feet whose length was achieved by an intricate strut-braced beam design. The Wettingen Bridge (1766) across the Limmat River was a 200-foot single-span structure and is believed to have been the first use of a true arch in a timber bridge. While the builders relied on empirical methods and their bridges

Figure 3.2 A testament to the value of covering timber bridges, Hyde Hall Bridge (1825) in Otsego County, New York, is believed to be the oldest extant covered bridge in the nation. It is one of several covered bridges in the United States that are nearing the two-century mark. HABS NY-263-2, unknown photographer, ca. 1958.

were heavily built and complex structures, the Grubenmann brothers did boldly demonstrate the potential for long-span wood bridges, earning them international renown and lucrative contracts. Napoleon's forces destroyed the Schaffhausen and Wettingen bridges in 1799, but several other Grubenmann covered bridges still survive in Switzerland, including Hundwilertobel (1778) at Hundwil and Kubelbrücke (1780) at Kubel.[5]

American builders were undoubtedly aware of—and perhaps inspired by—European covered bridges, but there is scant evidence to document a direct transfer of knowledge from Europe to North America; rather, it is likely that Americans independently developed the practice of covering wood bridges as the need for durable spans arose. Shortly after construction of long-span timber bridges began, the practice of covering them was rapidly adopted here.

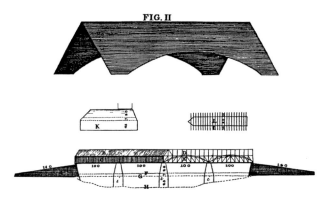

Figure 3.3 This drawing, entitled "Plan of a Bridge to be Built over Schuylkill," was published anonymously in *The Columbian Magazine* in January 1787. While this is the first published plan of a covered bridge, there is no record of one being built in the United States until the Schuylkill Permanent Bridge in 1805.

Early American Bridges

Bridges were rare in colonial America. Logs, stone slabs, and, occasionally, stone arches spanned small streams, but larger waterways had to be crossed by ford or ferry. Overland travel was hazardous, slow, and uncertain, with delays and accidents common.[6] A few ambitious river crossings were constructed as timber pile-and-beam structures, but, with few exceptions, long-span bridges were not built in the United States until after the Revolutionary War, when the growing volume of transportation and improving economic conditions justified the expenditure of material and labor.[7] This environment, coupled with a spirit of ingenuity and access to an abundant and cheap supply of timber, spurred the development of timber-bridge design in the United States.

Col. Enoch Hale took a bold first step in advancing American timber-bridge building in 1785 when he erected the nation's first long-span framed timber bridge across the Connecticut River between Walpole, New Hampshire, and Bellows Falls, Vermont. This bridge was part of the overland route from Boston to Montreal and was heralded as a great achievement in its day. Hale's braced beam bridge (as distinct from a truss bridge) was supported on rubble stone abutments and a timber pier rising from a small island in the middle of the river. The *Massachusetts Spy* stated, "Col. Enoch Hale hath erected a Bridge across Connecticut River, on the Great-Falls, at his own expense. This bridge is thought to exceed any ever built in America, in strength, elegance and publick utility."[8] Although Colonel Hale's bridge successfully carried traffic for a decade, its design was uniquely suited to its site and could not be easily replicated elsewhere. Within just a few years, more sophisticated techniques would be used to span America's waterways.

Creating structures of lengths much greater than a single log or beam was one of the initial challenges facing timber-bridge builders and required construction of a frame structure known as a truss. The truss, which utilizes the stable geometry of linked triangles to carry a load over a void, has been used for centuries for centering masonry arches and for constructing roofs. Introduced into European bridge building in the Middle Ages, the truss is the most efficient way to build long spans using wood. Italian architect Andrea Palladio popularized the concept of truss bridges in his influential treatise *The Four Books of Architecture*, which was first published in 1570.[9]

Figure 3.4 A portrait of Timothy Palmer was prepared and engraved by Louis Lement about 1804. Courtesy of George B. Pease Collection, National Society for the Preservation of Covered Bridges.

Born in Rowley, Massachusetts, in 1751, housewright Timothy Palmer is credited with making a quantum leap forward in bridge building by introducing long-span truss bridges to North America.[10] As a young man, he apprenticed with architect Moody Spofford, best known for his New England churches. In 1792, Palmer took up bridge building, erecting America's first long-span truss bridge across the Merrimack River at Newburyport, Massachusetts.[11] Containing over 6,000 tons of timber, the 1,030-foot-long structure had pile-and-beam approaches, a draw span over the main channel, and two trussed arch spans, the larger of which measured 160 feet in length. One contemporary writer described it as follows: "The two large arches (one of which is superior to any thing of the kind on the continent) . . . appear to unite elegance, strength and firmness beyond the most sanguine expectation."[12] Palmer's trusses closely resemble one of the plans published in Andrea Palladio's book, which was available in the United States at the time, revealing, perhaps, the inspiration for the design.[13] Palmer patented his truss design in 1797 and was much in demand as a bridge builder, erecting major timber spans across the Merrimack, Kennebec, Connecticut, Piscataqua, Schuylkill, Potomac, and Delaware rivers.[14]

America's First Covered Bridge

In the late eighteenth century, Philadelphia was the largest and wealthiest city in the United States, but it had few bridges spanning its major waterways. A stone-arch bridge had carried the King's Highway across Pennypack Creek for a century, but the deep and fast-flowing Schuylkill River posed a much greater challenge. As one nineteenth-century writer noted, "the character of this river is wild, and, in times of floods, rapid and formidable; and, to any structures of slight materials, ruinous and irresistible."[15] Ferry service had been established in 1723, but it was often slowed or stopped entirely by floods or ice.

In 1798, a group of forward-thinking citizens led by Judge Richard Peters incorporated the Schuylkill Permanent Bridge Company for the purpose of erecting a toll bridge over the Schuylkill River along the line of Market Street. The board of directors originally hired British engineer William Weston to build a stone bridge, but construction of the foundations proved so costly that, within a few months, the company was forced to consider alternative plans. Weston then designed an iron bridge for the Schuylkill crossing, but the directors were reluctant to attempt such a large span with the relatively untested material. After consulting with Timothy Palmer, at that time the nation's preeminent bridge builder, the directors opted to build a timber superstructure on the foundations of the aborted stone-arch span.

Figure 3.5 *Schuylkill Bridge, High Street, Philadelphia*, engraving by William Russell Birch, ca. 1804. Completed in 1805, the Schuylkill Permanent Bridge is the first documented covered bridge in the United States. It stood for forty-five years until replaced in 1850. This image depicts the bridge prior to being covered, with the completed structure shown in the inset. Courtesy of Library of Congress, Prints and Photographs Division, Washington, D.C.

In the spring of 1804, Timothy Palmer and his assistant Samuel Carr traveled to Philadelphia to erect the bridge superstructure. Over the next few months, a 195-foot trussed arch center span flanked by two 150-foot trussed arch spans rose from the foundations. Opened to traffic on January 1, 1805, the Schuylkill Permanent Bridge was heralded as an engineering masterpiece and "an honour to its inventor for its originality of architecture, and its excellence of mechanism."[16] Due to the extraordinarily high cost of construction—$300,000—the board of directors corresponded with Palmer about the possibility of covering the bridge to protect their investment from the weather. In his reply, Palmer affirmed the board's decision with this statement:

> *I am an advocate for weather boarding and roofing, although there are some that say I argue much against my own interest. . . . It is sincerely my opinion that the Schuylkill bridge will last thirty and perhaps forty years, if well covered. . . . I think it would be sporting with property to suffer this beautiful piece of architecture . . . which has been built at so great expense and danger, to fall into ruins in 10 or 12 years!* [17]

The company directors hired Philadelphia architect Adam Traquair to design the covering of the bridge and carpenter Owen Biddle to execute it, stating that the housing "compelled ornament, and some elegance of design, lest it should disgrace the environs of a great City."[18] In addition to its numerous architectural embellishments, including statues by sculptor William Rush, the structure was given two coats of ornamental stone plaster and sprinkled with stone dust to resemble a stone bridge. The Schuylkill Permanent Bridge had become the first documented covered bridge in North America. Speaking for the board of directors, Judge Peters expressed the hope that the Schuylkill Permanent Bridge would serve as an example "in all pontifical wooden structures of magnitude, hereafter."[19]

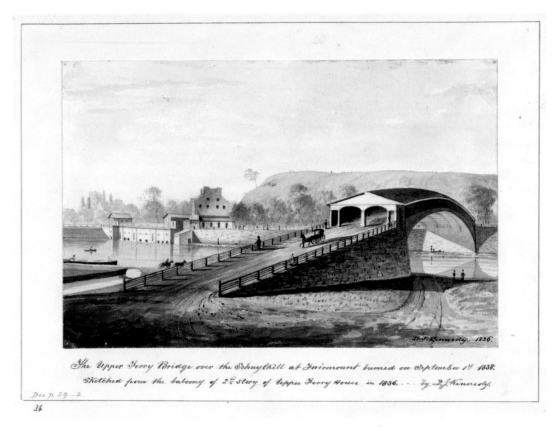

Figure 3.6 *Upper Ferry Bridge over the Schuylkill*, watercolor by David J. Kennedy, 1836. Erected in 1812 by German-born mechanic Lewis Wernwag, the Upper Ferry Bridge, also known as the Colossus, was an early masterpiece of American civil engineering. Spanning the Schuylkill River at Philadelphia, the 340-foot structure was the longest clear-span bridge in the world at the time of its construction, and the second-longest timber bridge built during the historic era of covered bridge construction. The Colossus carried traffic for a quarter of a century before it was destroyed by fire in 1838. Courtesy of Historical Society of Pennsylvania, Philadelphia, Pennsylvania, David J. Kennedy watercolors.

Diffusion and Proliferation of Covered Bridges

Internal improvements were one of the first priorities of the young nation, with transportation networks desperately needed to improve communication, expand commerce, and unite the country. The Louisiana Purchase of 1803 doubled the land area of the United States, and, over the next half-century, American settlers headed west in increasing numbers. Timber bridges were an ideal solution to some of the many transportation hurdles facing settlers. Constructing a timber bridge only required readily available materials and common hand tools, and skilled carpenters could erect the superstructure of an average-sized bridge within a few weeks. Consequently, hundreds of covered bridges were constructed, first in major urban centers and then in increasingly rural areas as people moved westward.

By 1810, adding roofs and siding to timber bridges was common practice in the United States, and there were covered bridges at most major crossings in southern and western New England, southeastern New York, eastern Pennsylvania, and New Jersey. From this core area, covered bridges spread to the northeast, south, and west at a rapid pace. By 1820, covered bridge building had reached northern New England, Maryland, southwestern Pennsylvania, and southeastern Ohio; by 1830, western Ohio and the Carolinas; by 1840, southern Indiana and the deep South; and, by 1850, there were covered bridges in most regions with European settlements in the United States and Canada.[20] The number of covered bridges continued to increase until about 1870, by which time there were well over ten thousand of them in the United States. Covered bridges would eventually be found in forty-one states. The few areas where covered bridges were not found include the heart of the Rocky Mountain region, and the northern and southern plains. The reasons for this vary from region to region but include the absence of major river crossings and readily available timber, topography more suited to other types of bridges, late-period settlement, and low population density.

Figure 3.7 This ca. 1880 photograph, taken in Contoocook Village, Hopkinton, New Hampshire, shows the 1849 Concord and Claremont Railroad Bridge on the left; another covered bridge, which still survives, replaced that bridge in 1889. The town of Hopkinton built the roadway bridge on the right in 1853; it was replaced in 1936 with a stone-faced concrete bridge. Courtesy of Hopkinton Historical Society, Hopkinton, New Hampshire.

Covered bridges helped achieve the safe, efficient, and economical overland transportation that was a key aspect of the nation's growth and economic development. They were adapted to the needs of many types of transportation corridors, including turnpikes, canals, and railroads. The rapid growth of the railroads in the mid-1800s placed new demands on bridges. In particular, the increasing weight of locomotives and rolling stock and the need for rigidity encouraged technical advancements in the design of timber-truss bridges.

Developments in Timber-Truss Design

The social and economic climate of the nineteenth century favored the flowering of timber-bridge building in America. The demand for bridges was great, wood was plentiful, and ambition was high. As a result, American builders produced, in rapid succession, a series of remarkable advancements in the design and construction of timber bridges. Between 1790 and 1840, timber bridge forms progressed from rudimentary pile-and-beam spans to scientifically designed, long-span trusses capable of carrying railroad loadings. These advancements addressed the overall challenge confronting bridge builders: to create economical and efficient structures that could span long distances, that were easy to erect and maintain, and that were strong enough to carry heavy, moving loads. Over time, this led to increased standardization in bridge design.

The earliest significant covered bridges depended on arch construction, as builders sought to capitalize on the inherent strength of that structural form.[21] Within a decade, however, truss construction came to dominate the field of American bridge building. Since the truss is the most efficient way to build long spans of wood, the majority of surviving covered bridges in the United States (more than 98 percent) are truss bridges.[22] America's early bridge builders relied on simple truss designs that had been used for roof framing since at least the Middle Ages, specifically the kingpost, queenpost, and multiple-kingpost trusses, which were sufficient for modest spans. These truss types continued to be used into the twentieth century. Approximately 24 percent of the extant covered bridges in the United States use one of these simple truss types.[23] Later, these simple truss types became the basis for more sophisticated timber bridge designs, like the Burr, Town, and Howe trusses, that could span even greater distances. Dozens of patents were granted for timber bridges before 1850, but only a small percentage of these designs were ever successfully built. Fewer still gained widespread acceptance. More than 60 percent of the surviving covered bridges in the United States use trusses developed by a small group of American bridge builders in the first half of the nineteenth century. The major truss types and their creators are discussed below.

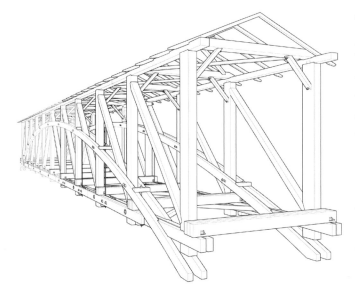

Figure 3.8 None of Theodore Burr's Pennsylvania bridges remain, but many of the nation's best examples of Burr-arch trusses are found in this state. Pine Grove Bridge (1884) completed over Octoraro Creek between Chester County and Lancaster County, is an example and one of at least twenty-five covered bridges erected by Capt. Elias McMellen, a prolific Pennsylvania bridge builder. HAER PA-586, sheet 2, Vuong Dang and Dave Groff, delineators, 2002.

Theodore Burr is a major figure in the history of covered bridge building. He is credited with the invention of the Burr-arch truss and with building a number of significant covered bridges throughout his twenty-year career. Born in Torrington, Connecticut, in 1771, Burr learned construction at an early age from his father, who was a miller and millwright. In 1800, Burr built his first bridge, a simple timber-stringer span, across the Chenango River on the Catskill Turnpike at Oxford, New York. He subsequently experimented with a wide variety of timber arch designs for bridges that spanned the Hudson, Mohawk, Delaware, and Susquehanna rivers. In 1806 and again in 1817, Burr received patents for the bridge design that bears his name.[24] Burr's masterpiece was the short-lived McCall's Ferry Bridge (1815), which, with a clear span of 360 feet, 4 inches, was the longest timber arch span erected during the historic era of covered bridge building. In 1822, Burr died under mysterious circumstances while supervising construction of a bridge at Middletown, Pennsylvania. The Union Bridge (1804), which spanned the Hudson River at Waterford, New York, was the last survivor of the bridges Burr designed; it was destroyed by fire in 1909.

Burr's patented arch-truss configuration was not entirely new, as a similar plan had been published in *Columbian Magazine* in 1787, yet he was apparently the first bridge builder to make practical use of this design. The Burr-arch truss was an innovative design in which a separate segmental arch was superimposed on a multiple-kingpost truss. Its structural action was such that the arch bolstered the truss, while at the same time being stabilized by it, resulting in a complex interaction. A major advantage of this design, and a contributing factor to its popularity, was that it allowed for a level deck (in contrast to the arched decks of earlier spans built by Timothy Palmer and Lewis Wernwag), an important feature for multiple-span bridges, and, later, for railroad bridges. The Burr-arch truss was the first patented bridge truss to gain widespread acceptance among bridge builders, although Burr reportedly collected few royalties from it. It was also one of the most popular timber-truss types of the nineteenth century and beyond, as it was still used in some areas until about 1920.[25]

Of the thousands of Burr-arch truss covered bridges that were built during the historic era of covered bridge building, about 185 examples survive in the United States, with some of the finest examples located in Pennsylvania and Indiana.[26]

By 1820, the potential span length of timber bridges had been extended to over 350 feet, and the practicality of the truss principle had been tested, even though its theory was still not fully understood. Combination arch-truss bridges were commonly built at major crossings, but the use of hewn timbers, traditional mortise and tenon joints, and the massive piers and abutments required to resist the thrust of the arch made construction of such bridges expensive and labor intensive. In response, builders began looking for ways to simplify construction so that substantial bridges could be built quickly and affordably in more locations. The fact that local governments (rather than private corporations) were beginning to finance public roads and bridges by this time further encouraged the development of simpler and more economical bridge designs.

Ithiel Town was an influential American architect and the inventor of the Town lattice truss, which was notable as one of the first attempts to eliminate traditional joinery in timber-bridge design. Born in Thompson, Connecticut, in 1784, Town studied architecture as a young man under renowned architect Asher Benjamin. From 1829 to 1835, Town was a partner of Alexander Jackson Davis, who was a major proponent of the Greek Revival style of architecture. The firm of Town and Davis designed churches, state capitols, and other institutional and academic buildings along the East Coast. Town also made a significant contribution to the field of engineering when he began designing bridges. In 1818, he erected North Carolina's first covered bridge across the Yadkin River near Salisbury.[27] In 1820 and again in 1835, Town patented his bridge truss and aggressively promoted the design, receiving patent royalties of one dollar per running foot of bridge.[28] Ithiel Town supervised only a few bridges himself, none of which survive.

Figure 3.9 *Ithiel Town*, Nathaniel Jocelyn, oil on canvas, 36-1/8 x 29 inches. Courtesy of National Academy Museum, New York, Gift of George Dudley Seymour, 1941, 662-P.

The Town lattice truss design consisted of a lattice web of overlapping planks fastened together with treenails (wood pins). In 1821, Town published a pamphlet describing this design as "the most simple, permanent, and economical, both in erecting and repairing" and advocating this less expensive method of bridge construction as a solution to "the great and increasing demand for wooden bridges

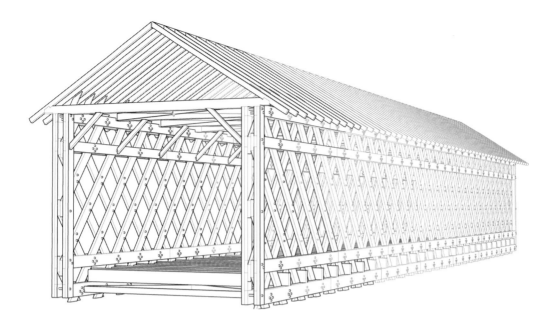

Figure 3.10 Brown Bridge (1880) in Rutland County, Vermont, is an outstanding example of a Town lattice truss and the best surviving example of the work of Nichols Montgomery Powers, a prolific New England covered bridge builder. HAER VT-28, sheet 2, Kimberly Clauer and Naomi Hernandez, delineators, 2002.

in all parts of this extensive country."[29] The advantage of the Town lattice truss extended beyond its ease of assembly. Since it was entirely free from arch action, it could theoretically be erected on less massive and, therefore, less costly abutments. The Town lattice system was used worldwide for bridges until well into the twentieth century.[30] Of the thousands of Town-lattice covered bridges built during the historic era of covered bridge building, approximately 110 survive in the United States, primarily in the Northeast and South, with some of the finest examples located in Vermont.[31]

As early as the 1820s, there was a trend toward applying science to the technical problems associated with the nation's industrial, geographic, and economic expansion. Institutions emerged to provide specialized academic training in science and technology. Established in 1802, the U.S. Military Academy at West Point, New York, was the first institution in the United States to offer academic instruction in civil engineering using a curriculum modeled after the École Polytechnique in France. The first engineering schools were established at Norwich, Vermont, in 1819 and Troy, New York, in 1824. Curriculums included applied math and science, as well as training in the design of roads, canals, and bridges. Mechanics' institutes, such as the Franklin Institute, founded in Philadelphia in 1824, also promoted engineering knowledge, particularly among American working men. Publication of technical journals and textbooks also served to spread mathematical and scientific principles and fostered the growth of civil engineering as a profession.[32]

Stephen H. Long was one of the first bridge builders to apply mathematical theory to the practice of bridge design. Born in Hopkinton, New Hampshire, in 1784, Long was a prominent American engineer and military officer and the inventor of the Long truss. He graduated from Dartmouth College in 1809 and joined the U.S. Army Corps of Engineers in 1814. He led military surveying expeditions in the American West between 1817 and 1823 and subsequently spent several years helping to survey and build the Baltimore and Ohio Railroad. In 1829, Long built his first timber bridge over a railroad cut at Baltimore, Maryland. That structure served as the basis of a patent Long obtained in 1830 for a timber truss that introduced mathematical principles of engineering to American bridge building.[33] Prior to this, bridge builders had relied upon empirical methods. By 1836, Long had twenty-six agents in eleven states, including his brother, Moses Long; his nephew, Horace Childs; and Stephen Daniels, father of Indiana bridge builder J. J. Daniels. In addition to his army duties, Long served as a consultant to various railroads until 1856, when he was put in charge of navigation improvements on the Mississippi River. In 1861, Long was called to Washington, D.C., to serve as commander of the Corps of Engineers, a position he held until his retirement in 1863.

Figure 3.11 "Major. Stephen Harriman Long on the Rocky Mountain Expedition, 1819-1820, attributed to Titian Ramsay Peale. Courtesy of Catherine Dail Fine Art, New York.

The Long truss is a traditionally framed panel truss with paired diagonal braces and single counterbraces crossing within each panel. This design is of engineering interest because it introduced the modern concept of prestressing—the creation of permanent stresses in a structure to improve its performance under loading—achieved by driving wedges into counterbrace connections to increase rigidity. The use of counterbraces, Long explained, would result in "stiffness of structure, and exemption from trembling, springing and oscillations of every kind."[34] Some of the first truss railroad bridges in the United States used the Long truss because of its ability to carry heavy loads without excessive deflection. Although the Long truss advanced understanding of structural behavior and scientific analysis, it eventually fell out of favor because, although it eliminated some tension connections, it still required intricate framing details. None of the bridges designed by Stephen

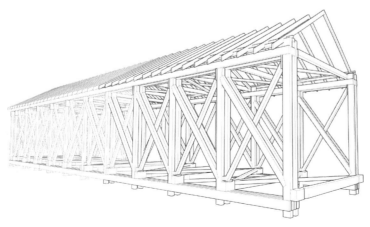

Figure 3.12 Eldean Bridge (1860) in Miami County, Ohio, is one of the best surviving examples of a Long-truss covered bridge. Built by local contractors James and William Hamilton, the bridge features wooden wedges driven between the counterbraces and lower chords to prestress the structure. HAER OH-122, sheet 2, William Dickinson, delineator, 2002.

Long survive, but eight Long trusses built during the historic era of covered bridge building are scattered throughout the eastern United States, with the purest examples having wedges acting on the counterbraces. While it is not known how many covered bridges have this feature, the Eldean Bridge (1860) in Miami County, Ohio, and Blair Bridge (1869) in Grafton County, New Hampshire, do.[35]

Millwright Peter Paddleford, born in 1785 in Littleton, New Hampshire, was a proponent of the Long truss and built several bridges of this type before developing his own truss design in the early 1830s. Paddleford built a number of significant covered bridges, including two across the Connecticut River between Vermont and New Hampshire, as well as numerous lesser-known spans in the upper reaches of those two states and in western Maine.

The Paddleford truss was a multiple-kingpost truss with long counterbraces extended over more than one panel, which helped distribute loads and increase the truss's rigidity. Although never patented, the Paddleford truss dominated covered bridge construction throughout northern New England for over half a century. This was due, in part, to the work of Peter's son, Philip H. Paddleford, who went into partnership with his father in 1835 and continued building bridges throughout his career. Of the dozens of Paddleford-truss covered bridges built during the historic era of covered bridge building, twenty-one examples survive in New England, although none are the work of the designer himself.[36]

In the 1830s, demand increased for standardized bridges that could be rapidly erected to keep pace with the growth of the nation's railroad network. This demand was a major impetus to the development of American bridge-building technology. Training in mechanics and strength of materials allowed bridge designers to understand how the various members of a bridge functioned under loading and then design them accordingly. As scientific understanding of truss action increased, the focus turned to building bridges that were not only economical but also structurally efficient.

Figure 3.13 William Howe, Otis H. Cooley, daguerreotype, 5.5 x 4.3 cm, ca. 1850. Courtesy of National Portrait Gallery, Smithsonian Institution, NPG.2008.58.

Born in 1803 in Spencer, Massachusetts, William Howe was a millwright and the inventor of the Howe truss, which was the first bridge truss type to use iron for primary structural members. In 1839, Howe built his first bridge for the Western Railroad across the Quaboag River in his hometown. The structure so impressed railroad engineer George Washington Whistler that he gave Howe the contract for the seven-span, 1,330-foot-long Western Railroad Bridge (1841) at Springfield, Massachusetts.[37] In 1840, Howe received a patent for a truss design that used adjustable wrought-iron rods (instead of wood posts) for the tension members. This arrangement overcame the inherent difficulty of creating tension connections in wood structures and allowed for easier and more efficient prestressing of the members.[38] That same year, Howe moved to Springfield, Massachusetts, where he entered the bridge-building business with his brother-in-law, Amasa Stone Jr. of

Cleveland. In 1842, Stone bought the rights to Howe's patent and formed a bridge company with railroad magnate Azariah Boody. Boody, Stone, and Company continued under various names until the late nineteenth century.[39] Howe continued to sell patent rights to companies throughout the country and received royalties that earned him a sizeable fortune.

Railroads favored the Howe-truss design because it had standardized framing connections incorporating prefabricated iron elements and could be quickly erected and easily adjusted. The American Society of Civil Engineers praised the Howe truss as "the most perfect wooden bridge ever built," adding "others have been designed of greater theoretical economy; but for simplicity of construction, rapidity of erection, and general utility it stands without rival."[40] Used extensively for railroad bridges in North America and abroad during the mid-nineteenth century, the combination wood/iron Howe truss was gradually superseded by all-metal Howe truss structures, but it remained one of the most important timber-truss types of the nineteenth century. Of the hundreds, perhaps thousands, of Howe-truss covered bridges built during the historic era of covered bridge building, about 100 examples survive—although none by Howe himself—primarily in the Midwest and Pacific Northwest. The purest examples of the widespread commercial Howe truss have cast-iron angle blocks and the standard endpost treatment of two vertical wood posts with an iron tension rod between them and wood angle blocks on the final braces.[41]

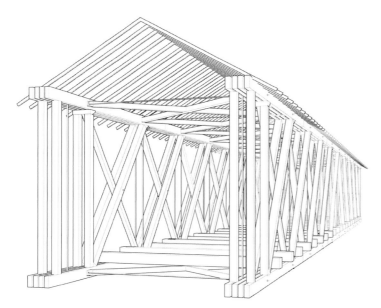

Figure 3.14 Built by Joseph A. Britton, one of Indiana's most prolific covered bridge builders, Pine Bluff Bridge (1886) in Putnam County, Indiana, is an exceptionally fine example of a timber Howe truss, featuring the cast-iron bearing blocks and standard endpost treatment that were common in late-nineteenth-century timber bridges of this type. HAER IN-103, sheet 2, Charu Chaudhry, delineator, 2002.

Railroad engineer Thomas Willis Pratt was born in Boston, Massachusetts, in 1812, where his father, Caleb Pratt, was a noted architect. After attending the Rensselaer School (now Rensselaer Polytechnic Institute), Thomas Pratt served as engineering assistant for the U.S. Army Corps of Engineers, building drydocks at Charleston, South Carolina, and Norfolk, Virginia. He subsequently was employed in the field of railroad construction, where he began designing bridges. In 1844, Thomas and Caleb Pratt obtained a patent for a combination panel truss that featured vertical wood posts at each panel point and diagonal iron rods crossing within each panel.[42] While not immediately popular for wood bridges, the design was later widely adopted in a modified all-metal version. Over the course of a career that spanned forty years, Thomas Pratt became a prominent civil engineer who supervised the construction of several major railroad lines in the Northeast and built a number of important railroad bridges. Today, he is remembered for the invention of the Pratt truss, a highly significant American bridge design, although he received few patent royalties from it.[43]

The Pratt truss reversed the configuration of the 1840 Howe truss, placing the shorter web members (verticals) in compression and longer web members (diagonals) in tension, which reduced the danger of structural failure through buckling. Developed at a time when railroads were placing new demands on bridges and the structural action of trusses was just beginning to be understood, the Pratt truss was one of several truss types that heralded the transformation from empirical to scientific bridge design. Few timber Pratt trusses were built and only one surviving example, the Sulphite Railroad Bridge in Merrimack County, New Hampshire (1896), somewhat resembles the patent. After the Civil War, the Pratt-truss design was successfully

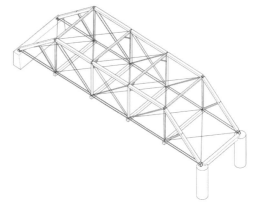

Figure 3.15 Built by the American Bridge Company in 1886, Honey Run Bridge in Butte County, California, is one of only three surviving Pratt-truss covered bridges in the United States. Invented in 1844, the Pratt truss reversed the configuration of the 1840 Howe truss to reduce the chance of structural failure through buckling. Few timber Pratt truss bridges were built, but the design was later adapted to metal-truss bridges, and it remained the standard American truss type for moderate road and railroad spans well into the twentieth century. HAER CA-312, sheet 6, Jeremy Mauro and Ben Shakelton, delineators, 2012.

adapted, with some modifications, to metal bridge building. The modified Pratt truss came to be favored for its strength and simplicity, and from the late nineteenth century well into the twentieth century, it was the standard American truss for moderate-size, metal railroad and highway spans. A few combination wood/metal Pratt-truss bridges were built and covered, which was presumably a back-formation from the all-metal version. There are two surviving combination wood/metal Pratt-truss covered bridges in California: Honey Run Bridge in Butte County (1886) and Felton Bridge in Santa Cruz County (1892).[44]

Covered Bridge Architecture

The earliest covered bridges were magnificent structures, both in terms of engineering and architecture. Financed with private capital, the early turnpike bridges were all custom-built structures, wide enough for two lanes of travel, with highly ornamented exteriors. The Schuylkill Permanent Bridge was probably one of the most extravagant, but other grand covered bridges once existed at major river crossings along the East Coast.

By 1820, covered bridges were much more common and less ornate. Covered bridges built by towns and counties were often quite plain in appearance. Architectural variations occurred, often on a regional level, reflecting the use of local materials and building traditions. For example, covered bridges in southeastern Pennsylvania often had long stone-masonry approaches and stepped gables, while many of the covered bridges in Madison County, Iowa, featured flat roofs and arched portals. Covered bridges erected by the Kennedy family of Rush County, Indiana, bore ornamental scrollwork and cornice brackets, and those built during the 1930s in Blount County, Alabama, were covered with corrugated metal roofing and siding. In Oregon, where covered bridges were built according to state-issued plans into the 1950s, each county developed its own distinctive bridge-housing style.

Because the housing was considered expendable and was expected to be periodically replaced, the majority of covered bridges were left unpainted until the mid-twentieth century. Those that were painted might be red or white, but other colors were also used. By the 1950s, Americans decided, for reasons yet unknown, that covered bridges should be red, and within two decades, approximately one-third of the covered bridges in the United States were painted that color. The term "covered bridge red" even slipped into modern advertising to market such items as paint, yarn, and wine. A popular Christmas card image of the Bedell Bridge, which spanned the Connecticut River at Newbury, New Hampshire, from 1866 to 1979, was even tinted red, although the bridge itself had never been painted.[45]

Figure 3.16 **Top Left:** 3.16a) Dreibelbis Station Bridge (1869) in Berks County, Pennsylvania, exhibits the masonry approach walls and stepped gables that were original characteristics of covered bridges in southeastern Pennsylvania. HAER PA-587-4, Jet Lowe, photographer, 2002. **Top Right:** 3.16b) Holliwell Bridge (1880) in Madison County, Iowa, exhibits the nearly flat roof and gracefully arched portals that were used in several of the county's covered bridges. HAER IA-64-27, Jet Lowe, photographer, 2004. **Left:** 3.16c) Swann Bridge (1933) in Blount County, Alabama, is clad in the corrugated metal roofing and siding adopted to house a number of the county's covered bridges in the 1930s. HAER AL-201-4, Jet Lowe, photographer, 2002.

In addition to regional architectural styles, the height of the trusses and location of the bridge deck could also dictate the bridge housing. Pony-truss (or low-truss) bridges, which were often used for shorter spans, required no overhead bracing, so each of the trusses might be individually housed (these are referred to as "boxed" trusses). Sometimes, through-truss (or high-truss) bridges were also "boxed," or housed, in a similar manner, by enclosing the trusses without adding a roof. Deck-truss bridges, in which the deck is carried on the upper chords, were typically used in locations with steeply sloping terrain, where placing the trusses below the travelled way allowed for shorter and less expensive substructure components. Timber deck-truss bridges often had a roof and siding located below the deck.[46]

Covering a wood bridge is the most reliable way to protect it from decay, but in some instances builders did away with the housing in favor of treating the timbers with chemical preservatives or protecting the upper chords with sheet metal. Non-housed timber-truss bridges share a common history with covered bridges, but very few have been preserved.[47]

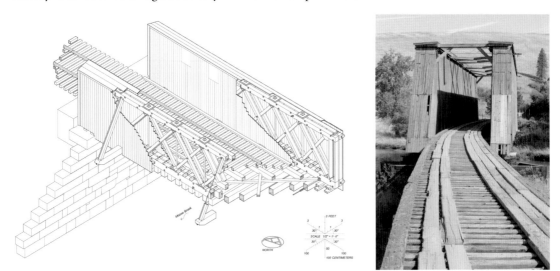

Figure 3.17 **Left:** 3.17a) The Boston and Maine Railroad used boxed pony-truss bridges for short spans well into the twentieth century. Moose Brook Bridge (1918) in Coos County, New Hampshire, was one of six surviving boxed pony-truss bridges in the United States until it was seriously damaged in an arson fire in 2004. HAER NH-48, sheet 6, Bradley M. Rowley and Anne E. Kidd, delineators, 2009. **Right:** 3.17b) The Great Northern Railway used boxed through-truss bridges for moderate spans well into the twentieth century. Harpole Bridge (1922) in Whitman County, Washington, is the last surviving boxed through-truss bridge in the United States. HAER WA-135-5, Jet Lowe, photographer, 1993.

Wood versus Iron

Throughout the nineteenth century, interest grew in a new structural material: iron. The tensile strength of iron, coupled with its resistance to fire, rot, and insects, made it an appealing material, particularly on railroads where rigid bridges that were easy to erect and maintain and capable of carrying increasingly heavy loads were desired. Between 1836 and 1839, Capt. Richard Delafield of the U.S. Army Corps of Engineers designed and oversaw construction of America's first iron bridge across Dunlap's Creek on the National Road at Brownsville, Pennsylvania. That innovative structure was an 80-foot, cast-iron arch consisting of five tubular arch rings supporting the roadway.[48] Other engineers tinkered with ideas for iron-truss bridges in the 1840s, but enthusiasm for the use of this new material in structures was tempered by periodic structural failures, which led to lingering suspicion of iron in the public mind. Some designers merely substituted iron parts directly for wood, but ignoring the differences in the structural properties of the two materials figured prominently in the 1876 collapse of an iron bridge in Ashtabula, Ohio, that killed eighty-three people.[49]

Due to these periodic failures, the adoption of iron occurred relatively slowly. As is often the case when a new building material is introduced, there were successes and failures—radical advancements and technological dead ends. As engineers worked to better understand the behavior of iron structures, bridge builders continued to alternate between wood and iron for much of the nineteenth century. For all of its benefits, iron also had its drawbacks: it was expensive, difficult to manufacture, susceptible to corrosion, and it often failed without warning. Ultimately, the advantages that iron construction afforded, combined with the disadvantages of timber construction (susceptibility to fire and rot and the need for periodic maintenance), led many engineers and public officials to view timber bridges as obsolete.

In the post–Civil War era, covered wood bridges were still economical, except for very long spans, and there were still opportunities for innovative timber-bridge builders to remain competitive, especially in regions where timber was readily available.[50] The surest route to reducing the cost of any construction is to minimize the quantity of materials that goes into it, and many timber bridges were overbuilt for the loads they carried. By employing the methods of mathematical stress analysis described by engineer Squire Whipple in his 1847 *Essay on Bridge Building*, builders could proportion structural members in the most efficient manner possible, and, in doing so, cut costs.[51] From the 1860s onward, several inventors addressed this challenge and used the advances in civil engineering to build timber bridges less expensively so they could compete with iron-bridge manufacturers.

Robert W. Smith, born in Tippecanoe City, Ohio, in 1833, was the inventor of the highly successful Smith truss. Smith was educated at home until he was 15 and only attended public school for six weeks to study geometry. He learned carpentry from his father and older brother, who were barn builders. Early in his career, Smith ran a woodworking shop and lumberyard but eventually turned his attention to bridges. In 1867, Smith patented a bridge truss that, for a short time, allowed wood bridges to successfully compete with iron ones.[52] By 1869, Smith had established the Smith Bridge Company factory in Toledo, Ohio. Bridges were prefabricated to order, shipped to their sites, and erected under the supervision of company agents. The company built hundreds of covered bridges during the 1870s and successfully made the transition to the manufacture of iron bridges. In 1890, the Smith Bridge Company ceased operations,

Figure 3.18 Portrait of Robert W. Smith. North & Oswald, Toledo, Ohio, photographers, ca. 1880. Courtesy of Miriam Wood Collection.

and the plant was sold to the Toledo Bridge Company. Of the hundreds of Smith-truss covered bridges built during the historic era of covered bridge building, twenty-three examples survive in the United States, primarily in Ohio and Indiana.[53]

The Smith truss featured parallel chords connected by a series of intersecting inclined posts and braces and was notable for being both economical and strong. Smith subsequently made several minor modifications to his design, and he received a second patent in 1869, but all Smith trusses followed the same general layout, with one, two, or three web planes, depending upon the length of the span.[54]

Other inventors followed Smith's lead, and at least two received patents that were geometrically similar to the Smith truss. In 1870, Isaac H. Wheeler of Sciotoville, Ohio, patented a modified Smith truss with offset compression members and an intermediate chord along the midline of the truss.[55] Two years later, Reuben L. Partridge of Marysville, Ohio, patented another modified Smith truss with metal bearing shoes that were intended to reduce the amount of material required for the chords.[56] Neither the Wheeler nor the Partridge trusses ever entered the mainstream of covered bridge building, but they illustrate a mid-nineteenth-century flowering of innovation in American timber-bridge design.

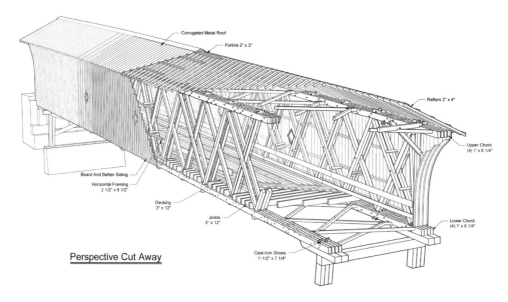

Corrugated Metal Roof

Purlins 2" x 3"

Rafters 2" x 4"

Upper Chord
(4) 1' x 6 1/4"

Board And Batten Siding

Horizontal Framing
2 1/2" x 6 1/2"

Decking
3" x 12"

Joists
3" x 12"

Lower Chord
(4) 1' x 6 1/4"

Cast-Iron Shoes
1'-1/2" x 7 1/4"

Perspective Cut Away

Figure 3.19 Built for the California Powder Works in 1872, Powder Works Bridge in Santa Cruz, California, is the only surviving example of the Smith Bridge Company's operations on the West Coast, and it represents the last effort to market timber bridges on a national scale. The 180-foot span required a heavily-built structure using three planes of web members (Smith truss, Type 4), because the bridge carried pedestrians and wagons as well as horse-drawn freight cars on a narrow-gauge railroad track until the black powder manufacturing plant closed in 1914. Today the bridge carries limited vehicular traffic within a private residential community. HAER CA-313, sheet 9, Jeremy Mauro, Ben Shakelton, and Christopher H. Marston, delineators, 2012.

Decline of Covered Bridge Building

By the 1880s, bridge builders had learned how to best utilize the strengths of iron, and the material came to dominate bridge construction. Iron and steel bridges began rapidly replacing timber bridges across the country in the last two decades of the nineteenth century. Many towns and counties debated the costs of construction and maintenance of different types of bridges and were influenced by what neighboring towns and counties were building, which were often the prefabricated metal bridges widely marketed by bridge manufacturing firms. Railroads enabled manufacturers to ship prefabricated metal bridges to distant markets and thereby compete with local builders for contracts. The cost-effectiveness of iron, and later steel, was largely responsible for the decline of timber-bridge building in the early twentieth century.

In addition, the last decades of the nineteenth century saw the rise of the Good Roads Movement, as farmers and bicyclists and, later, increasing numbers of automobile users began to agitate for paved roads and modern bridges. Most engineers viewed wood as a material outmoded for modern purposes. Lacking incentives to maintain aging timber spans, state highway departments across the country began bypassing or demolishing covered bridges and replacing them with steel and concrete structures that were wider, more open, and better suited for heavy, motorized vehicles traveling at increasingly faster speeds. Thus, during the first decades of the twentieth century, most Americans considered covered bridges neither particularly useful nor worthy of devotion; instead, they often viewed them as archaic, unsightly, and dangerous.

Figure 3.20 Modern spans replaced many covered bridges in the early twentieth century. After fifty years of service, the San Marcos River Bridge (1845) in Gonzales County, Texas, was replaced with a metal-truss span in 1904. Courtesy of Texas Department of Transportation.

Birth of a Cultural Icon

The automobile brought physical changes to the landscape and was also the means by which growing numbers of individuals experienced their rapidly changing world. In the face of the technological and industrial advances of the early twentieth century, covered bridges within pastoral landscapes generated powerful feelings of nostalgia, and public interest in these picturesque landscape features began to grow.

In the 1930s and 1940s, covered bridges reemerged in the public imagination, becoming the subject of folklore and legend. They also regularly appeared in American popular culture as nostalgic, romantic, or mysterious elements. Many examples can be found in mid-twentieth-century literature, cartoons, music, radio, film, and television. Advertisers, hoping to associate their products with positive images of an idealized America, used covered bridges to market everything from insurance and thermal underwear to cigarettes

Figure 3.21 In the late nineteenth and early twentieth centuries, advertisements were sometimes painted on the exteriors of covered bridges in prominent locations. As a consequence, the Portland-Columbia Bridge (1869) spanning the Delaware River between Pennsylvania and New Jersey was known as the "Coca-Cola Bridge" in the early twentieth century. Hurricane-related floods in 1955 destroyed the bridge. Edward Hungerford, photographer, 1916. Courtesy of Thomas E. Walczak Collection.

and beer. A number of well-known companies, including Coca-Cola, Ford, McDonald's, and Sears, used covered bridges in mid-twentieth-century advertising campaigns.

Figure 3.22 Roseman Bridge (1883) is one of nineteen covered bridges built in Madison County, Iowa, in the nineteenth century and one of only five that survive. Prominently featured in the 1995 movie adaptation of Robert James Waller's romantic novel, *The Bridges of Madison County*, the bridge has since become a popular wedding venue. HAER IA-95-5, Jet Lowe, photographer, 2004.

Beginning in the 1950s, people built small-scale covered bridges for their backyards and businesses, sometimes even demanding that "replicas" of old covered bridges be built on public roads. Curiously, while the housing of covered bridges was traditionally a practical consideration to extend the life of a timber bridge, it often became the primary focus of folk-art bridges and replicas. In many instances, the covering was merely a shed built over a concrete slab or steel-stringer bridge, creating the illusion of a covered bridge.[57]

By the 1960s and 1970s, the iconic status of the covered bridge in the American collective memory resulted in communities across the country recognizing the historical importance of covered bridges and beginning to take steps to preserve them for future generations. In the last few decades, many covered bridges have become cherished local landmarks and symbols of community pride. Although covered bridges continue to be lost to floods, fires, neglect, and vandalism, far fewer are destroyed in the name of progress than previously, and many have been the objects of intensive preservation efforts, as described in chapter 7.[58]

Historic Era of Covered Bridge Building Ends

While construction of covered bridges had virtually ceased in the rest of the country, there was a resurgence in Oregon in the first half of the twentieth century, when wartime steel shortages and the economic downturn of the Great Depression encouraged covered bridge construction in this region of abundant virgin timber. In 1915, the Oregon State Legislature passed legislation requiring that county bridges costing more than $500 be built under the supervision of the newly-formed Oregon State Highway Commission. After investigating various bridge types, state highway engineers calculated that a well-built, covered, wood bridge could last as long as a steel bridge and cost much less to build. They subsequently developed standard plans for covered bridges that were designed specifically for motorized vehicles. Over the next four decades, county engineers and road crews used these state-issued plans to build approximately two hundred covered bridges on secondary roads in western Oregon.[59]

The covered bridges designed by the Oregon State Highway Commission were wider, sturdier, and more open than their nineteenth-century counterparts, since they were built to accommodate motorized, rather than horse-drawn, vehicles. Most of these bridges used a simplified Howe truss without counterbraces. State engineers recommended the Howe truss because it required minimal steel and could be built rugged enough to meet modern load requirements. The availability of large-dimension virgin timber in western Oregon allowed builders to return to traditional timber-framing practices (for example, mortising the braces directly into the chords, rather than using angle blocks), and some bridges used hand-hewn, single-stick chords, rather than built-up plank chords.[60]

The resurgence of covered bridge building in western Oregon remained strong through the 1920s and 1930s, and lasted through the 1940s in some counties. In 1944, approximately 230 covered bridges were in use on rural roads in the state.[61] After World War II, the price of lumber and labor dramatically increased, making it comparatively less expensive to build new spans of steel or concrete. By the late 1940s, few covered bridges were being built anywhere in the United States, even in the timber-rich region of the Pacific Northwest. The historic era of American covered bridge building ended in Oregon in the 1950s.[62]

Figure 3.23 Built by the Linn County Engineering Department in 1941, Larwood Bridge is one of the best surviving examples of Oregon's standard-plan Howe trusses. HAER OR-124-13, Jet Lowe, photographer, 2004.

Revival Era of Covered Bridge Building Begins

By the time the historic era of covered bridge building ended in the Pacific Northwest, a new era of covered bridge building was beginning in the Northeast. As early as the 1930s, covered bridges were becoming tourist attractions. Growing public interest in preserving covered bridges eventually led to the building of modern copies for nostalgic reasons. This revival of covered bridge building occurred at different times in different regions of the country and followed a period generally spanning several decades when covered bridges were widely regarded as obsolete in each region. The revival-era covered bridges are distinct from their historic-era counterparts in that they were built, at least in part, for sentimental reasons, rather than purely economic ones.

The replacement Hancock-Greenfield Bridge (1937) in Hillsborough County, New Hampshire, is the first known example of a covered bridge built primarily for nostalgic reasons in the United States.[63] That bridge remained an anomaly until the 1950s, when the Massachusetts Department of Public works began replacing old covered bridges with new ones, at the urging of local communities. These early revival-era covered bridges were very different in construction and appearance from the bridges they replaced, as they were built to modern highway specifications and used timber connectors rather than traditional timber-framing techniques. As time went on, some twentieth-century timber framers began to build modern covered bridges in much the same manner as traditional ones. Built to replace an aging iron span, the Union Street Bridge (1968–69) in Woodstock, Vermont, was one of the first revival-era covered bridges to utilize traditional trusses and framing techniques. These bridges, and several others built around the same time, ushered in a revival of covered bridge building that continues today in a few scattered parts of the country.[64]

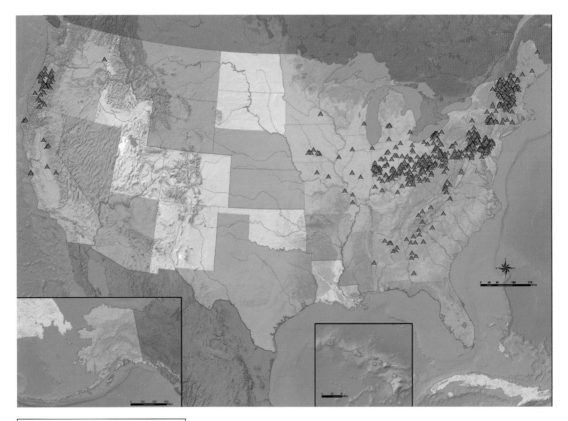

U.S. Covered Bridges

▲ Existing Covered Bridges
▬ States with Covered Bridges
▬ States with a History of Covered Bridges

Figure 3.24 The historic covered bridge era ended in the Pacific Northwest. Yet, as this map demonstrates, the vast majority of extant historic covered bridges can be found east of the Mississippi River. Map created by James Stein and Matthew Stutts, Cultural Resources Geographical Information System facility, National Park Service, 2004, 2014.

Conclusion

Covered bridges were a practical and economical engineering solution to crossing rivers in the nineteenth century; as such, they played a critical role in the growth of this nation by facilitating transportation, settlement, and commerce. They also represent a period of great technological achievement that occurred in the early to mid-nineteenth century, during which engineers and builders perfected designs for sturdy and cost-effective bridges that could span long distances and safely carry heavy, moving loads. The basic engineering principles applied during America's historic era of timber-bridge building continue to be used by engineers around the world today. Of the more than ten-thousand covered bridges that once existed throughout the country, nearly seven-hundred covered bridges built during the historic era of covered bridge construction still survive in twenty-nine states.[65] Many of those are still in use on public roads, reaffirming that these venerable structures are more than just quaint relics of a bygone era; they are an integral part of our political, social, cultural, and engineering heritage that merits preservation.

Endnotes

1 Before the nineteenth-century explosion of American covered bridge building, nearly all covered bridges were constructed in the forested regions of central Europe. American scholars have recently become aware of hundreds of ancient covered bridges in China; however, most of these bridges were built for pedestrian use, and their construction techniques and reasons for covering differ from the Western tradition. An excellent reference is Ronald G. Knapp, *Chinese Bridges: Living Architecture from China's Past* (Singapore: Tuttle Publishing, 2008).

2 This is only a rough estimate of known covered bridges that existed ca. 1870. Initial data compiled by the Covered Spans of Yesteryear project, http://www.lostbridges.org, suggests that this figure may be too low.

3 While bridges built during the more recent revival era of covered bridge construction will increasingly be regarded as "historic" as they age over time, they will remain a product of a period of covered bridge construction that was markedly different from that of their forebears.

4 In 55 BC, Julius Caesar ordered the world's first major timber bridge built across the Rhine River near present-day Koblenz, Germany. Considered a masterpiece of military engineering, Caesar's Bridge was a pile-and-beam structure estimated at between 460 and 1,300 feet long.

5 For more on the Grubenmann brothers and their bridges, see Angelo Maggi and Nicola Navone, *John Soane and the Wooden Bridges of Switzerland: Architecture and the Culture of Technology from Palladio to the Grubenmanns* (London: John Soane Museum, 2003). For a list of surviving covered bridges in Switzerland, see David W. Wright, ed., *World Guide to Covered Bridges* (National Society for the Preservation of Covered Bridges, 2009), 236–71.

6 Isaac Weld Jr. describes some of the challenges of overland travel in *Travels Through the States of North America and the Provinces of Upper and Lower Canada During the Years 1795, 1796 and 1797* (London: John Stockdale, 1807).

7 The Great Bridge (1662) across the Charles River at Boston, Massachusetts, and Sewell's Bridge (1761) across the York River at York, Maine, were notable exceptions. Both bridges consisted of a series of simple beam spans. The Great Bridge was supported by stone-filled log cribs, while the York River Bridge used timber pile trestles.

8 *The Massachusetts Spy, or, American Oracle of Liberty* (Worcester, Mass.), February 10, 1785, 3.

9 Andrea Palladio, *The Four Books of Architecture* (London: Giacomo Leoni, 1716–20), book 3, plates III–V.

10 John Bliss's 124-foot Leffingwell Bridge (1764–77) across the Shetucket River at Norwich, Connecticut, was described as being "supported by Geometry work above" and may have been the first use of the truss principle in American bridge design; however, Timothy Palmer was the first builder to use the truss in a long-span bridge. Frances Manwaring Caulkins, *The History of Norwich, Connecticut* (Norwich, Conn.: Thomas Robinson, 1845), 348, and Richard Sanders Allen, *Covered Bridges of the Northeast* (Brattleboro, Vt.: Stephen Greene Press, 1957), 12.

11 The Essex Merrimack River Bridge was considered a great engineering achievement but was denounced as a hindrance to navigation. Thus, in 1810, a novel iron chain suspension bridge designed by Judge James Finley of Pennsylvania replaced the main span. See "Essex-Merrimack Bridge," HAER No. MA-93.

12 "Description of the Essex Merrimack River Bridge," *Massachusetts Magazine*, May 1793, 1.

13 Helen Park, "A List of Architectural Books Available in America Before the Revolution," *Journal of the Society of Architectural Historians* 20, no. 3 (October 1961): 128.

Endnotes

14 Timothy Palmer built at least ten major bridges between 1792 and 1805: Essex Merrimack River Bridge (1792), Newburyport, Mass.; Andover Bridge (1793), Lawrence, Mass.; Piscataqua Bridge (1794), Newington, N.H.; Haverhill Bridge (1794), Haverhill, Mass.; Rocks Bridge (1795), West Newbury, Mass.; Little Falls Bridge (1796), Georgetown, Md.; Cornish Bridge (1796), Cornish, N.H.; Kennebec River Bridge (1799), Augusta, Maine; Schuylkill Permanent Bridge (1804), Philadelphia, Pa.; and Easton Bridge (1805), Easton, Pa. None of Palmer's bridges survive.

15 Built in 1697, the triple stone-arch Pennypack Creek Bridge is the oldest extant roadway bridge in the United States. See "Pennypack Creek Bridge," HABS No. PA-1786 and HAER No. PA-465. Quote from Richard Peters, *A Statistical Account of the Schuylkill Permanent Bridge Company* (Philadelphia: Jane Aitken, 1807), 6.

16 Fortescue Cuming, *Sketches of a Tour to the Western Country, 1807–1809* (Pittsburgh: Cramer, Spear, and Eichbaum, 1810), 25.

17 Peters, *Statistical Account*, 49.

18 Peters, *Statistical Account*, 34.

19 The writings of both Richard Peters and Owen Biddle suggest that the Schuylkill Permanent Bridge was the only covered bridge in the United States at the time of its completion. See Peters, *Statistical Account*, quote from 34, 46–51, and Owen Biddle, *The Young Carpenter's Assistant* (Philadelphia: Benjamin Johnson, 1805), 96. See also Richard Sanders Allen, "Comment and Commentary on the 'The First Covered Bridge in America,'" *Covered Bridge Topics* 11, no. 2 (Summer 1953): 4.

20 Fred Kniffen, "The American Covered Bridge," *Geographical Review* 41, no. 1 (January 1951): 119.

21 Because little was known about the structural action of trusses, early long-span timber bridges often combined trusses with arches. The ancient structural form of the arch utilizes the principle of compression to span long distances and is the only way to construct long spans of masonry. Most major bridges in Europe were masonry arches and British books available in eighteenth-century America discussed bridge building solely in terms of arch construction. In America, with few exceptions (dependent on the availability of high-quality stone), masonry bridges were too expensive and labor-intensive to build, so the arch form was adapted to less expensive timber construction.

22 Only six extant covered bridges in the United States use arch construction instead of truss construction. Three tied-arch covered bridges survive in Vermont, and three polygonal-arch covered bridges survive in Virginia; all but one of these bridges span modest distances of less than 50 feet. See, for example, "Swallow's Bridge," HAER No. VT-36 and "Sinking Creek Bridge," HAER No. VA-126.

23 Noteworthy examples of the kingpost truss include "Neal Lane Bridge," HAER No. OR-126 and "Pine Brook Bridge," HAER No. VT-37; examples of the queenpost truss include "Morgan Bridge," HAER No. VT-33 and "Flint Bridge," HAER No. VT-29; and examples of the multiple-kingpost truss include "Humpback Bridge," HAER No. VA-1 and "Taftsville Bridge," HAER No. VT-30. Additional examples of these truss types are listed in the appendix.

24 Burr's 1806 patent was lost in the 1836 U.S. Patent Office fire, but the 1817 patent was recovered. See Theodore Burr, U.S. Patent No. 2,769X, April 3, 1817. See also, Hubertis M. Cummings, "Theodore Burr and His Bridges Across the Susquehanna," *Pennsylvania History* 23, no. 4 (October 1956): 484.

25 The Edna Collins Bridge (1922) in Putnam County, Indiana, was the last Burr-arch truss covered bridge built in the United States during the historic era of covered bridge building.

26 Noteworthy examples of the Burr-arch truss include "West Union Bridge," HAER No. IN-105 and "Hyde Hall Bridge," HAER No. NY-330. Additional examples of this truss type are listed in the appendix. See also Joseph D. Conwill, "Burr Truss Bridge Framing," *Timber Framing* 78 (December 2005), 4.

Endnotes

27 The Yadkin River Bridge was replaced sometime after the Civil War

28 Ithiel Town, U.S. Patent No. 3,169X, January 28, 1820.

29 Ithiel Town, *A Description of Ithiel Town's Improvement in the Construction of Wood and Iron Bridges: Intended as a General System of Bridge-Building* (New Haven, Conn.: S. Converse, 1821), 3–4.

30 The Town lattice truss was also adapted for roof trusses, reportedly used in the Second Presbyterian Church (1835), Madison, Ind.; the First Presbyterian Church (1832), Fayetteville, N.C.; the Mormon Tabernacle (1864), Salt Lake City, Ut. (see HAER No. UT-1); and the Gov. Thomas Bibb House (1836), Huntsville, Ala. See Joseph D. Conwill, "Town Lattice Trusses by the Master Himself," *Covered Bridge Topics* 54, no. 1 (Winter 1996): 3–4; "Town Lattice Roof Trusses in Madison, Indiana," *Covered Bridge Topics* 62, no. 2 (Spring 2004): 6.

31 Noteworthy examples of the Town lattice truss include "Brown Bridge," HAER No. VT-28 and "Roseman Bridge," HAER No. IA-95. Additional examples of this truss type are listed in the appendix.

32 Lawrence P. Grayson, *The Making of an Engineer: An Illustrated History of Engineering Education in the United States and Canada* (New York: John Wiley and Sons, 1993), 24.

33 S. H. Long, U.S. Patent No. 5,862X, March 6, 1830. In most Long-truss bridges, the struts above the upper chords and below the lower chords were eliminated.

34 S. H. Long, *Description of Col. Long's Bridges, Together With a Series of Directions to Bridge Builders* (Concord, N.H.: John F. Brown Printers, 1836), 42.

35 Noteworthy examples of the Long truss include "Eldean Bridge," HAER No. OH-122 and "Blenheim Bridge," HAER No. NY-331. The latter bridge was destroyed by floods that followed Hurricane Irene in 2011. Additional examples of this truss type are listed in the appendix.

36 Noteworthy examples of the Paddleford truss include "Sunday River Bridge," HAER No. ME-69 and "Mechanic Street Bridge," HAER No. NH-45. Additional examples of this truss type are listed in the appendix.

37 The Quaboag River Bridge was replaced in 1873 with a larger Howe-truss covered bridge capable of carrying two tracks. The Western Railroad Bridge (which was left uncovered) was replaced with a covered bridge in 1855.

38 William Howe, U.S. Patent No. 1,711, August 3, 1840. Howe received another patent in 1846 and a reissue in 1850, but the design of most Howe-truss bridges was simplified from the patent drawings.

39 Victor C. Darnell, *A Directory of American Bridge Building Companies, 1840–1900* (Washington, D. C.: Society for Industrial Archeology, 1984), 25–26.

40 "Bridge Superstructure," *Transactions of the American Society of Civil Engineers* (1878), 340.

41 Noteworthy examples of the Howe truss include "Pine Bluff Bridge," HAER No. IN-103 and "Knight's Ferry Bridge," HAER No. CA-314. Additional examples of this truss type are listed in the appendix.

42 Thomas W. Pratt and Caleb Pratt, U.S. Patent No. 3,523, April 4, 1844.

43 "Pratt, Thomas Willis," in *Dictionary of American Biography*, vol. 8 (New York: Charles Scribner's Sons, 1933), 179.

44 See "Sulphite Railroad Bridge," HAER No. NH-36 and "Honey Run Bridge," HAER No. CA-312. See also Joseph D. Conwill, "Wood Copies Steel: the Modified Pratt Truss," *Covered Bridge Topics* 52, no. 4 (Fall 1994): 10.

45 Joseph D. Conwill, "The Red Covered Bridge: Fiction Affects Fact," unpublished typescript, July 26, 2004.

Endnotes

46 Snyder Brook Bridge (1918) in Coos County, New Hampshire, is one of five surviving boxed pony truss bridges in the United States; see "Snyder Brook Bridge," HAER No. NH-49. Harpole Bridge (1922) in Whitman County, Washington, is the only surviving boxed through-truss bridge in the United States; see "Harpole Bridge," HAER No. WA-133. Sulphite Railroad Bridge in Merrimack County, New Hampshire, is the only surviving deck-truss covered bridge in the United States; see "Sulphite Railroad Bridge," HAER No. NH-36.

47 There are widely scattered examples of non-housed timber-truss bridges across the United States and significant numbers are still in use in Canada.

48 See "Dunlap's Creek Bridge," HAER No. PA-72. Dunlap's Creek Bridge has been widened but is still in service.

49 David A. Simmons, "Fall From Grace: Amasa Stone and the Ashtabula Bridge Collapse," *Timeline* 6, no. 3 (June–July 1989): 34

50 Some areas of the country still had a reasonable supply of local timber, while others imported it from timber-rich regions. In some places, a strong local tradition and/or the presence of a prominent bridge builder kept covered bridge building competitive into the late nineteenth and early twentieth centuries.

51 Squire Whipple, *An Essay on Bridge Building* (Utica, N.Y.: by the author, 1847).

52 Robert W. Smith, U.S. Patent No. 66,900, July 16, 1867.

53 Noteworthy examples of the Smith truss include "Powder Works Bridge," HAER No. CA-313 and "Cataract Falls Bridge," HAER No. IN-104. Additional examples of this truss type are listed in the appendix. Also see "Structural Study of Smith Trusses," HAER No. PA-645.

54 Robert W. Smith, U.S. Patent No. 97,714, December 7, 1869. In 1967, industrial engineer and covered-bridge enthusiast Raymond E. Wilson of Swarthmore, Pennsylvania, established a classification of Smith-truss variations, based on the number and configuration of the web members. Type 1 follows the drawing shown in the 1867 patent. Type 2 follows the drawing shown in the 1869 patent. Type 3 is similar to type 2 but with extra braces in the center panel. Type 4 has double inclined posts and single braces the full length of the truss. Wilson's taxonomy is still in use today; however, it is considered by some scholars to be overly simplistic, primarily because it fails to account for a primary innovation addressed in Smith's first patent: increasing the number of web planes as span length is increased. See also discussion in chapter 5. Raymond E. Wilson, "The Story of the Smith Truss," *Covered Bridge Topics* 25, no. 1 (April 1967): 3–5; Matthew Reckard, "Robert Smith's Trusses," Second National Covered Bridges Conference, Dayton, Ohio, June 5–9, 2013, http://www.woodcenter.org/docs/dayton-conference/Reckard_Smith's%20Trusses.pdf.

55 Isaac H. Wheeler, U.S. Patent No. 107,576, September 20, 1870. One Wheeler-truss bridge survives in Kentucky, but it was substantially rebuilt in 2004; see "Bennett's Mill Bridge," HAER No. KY-49.

56 Reuben L. Partridge, U.S. Patent No. 127,791, June 11, 1872. Five examples of the Partridge truss survive in Ohio, including "Pottersburg Bridge," HAER No. OH-125.

57 Hundreds of these backyard and folk-art bridges can be found throughout the United States. Arthur F. Hammer, ed., *Romantic Shelters: A Supplement to the World Guide to Covered Bridges* (Marlboro, Mass.: National Society for the Preservation of Covered Bridges, 1989).

58 Arson is a major challenge to covered bridge preservation. Since the 1950s, nearly 200 covered bridges have been deliberately set on fire. On average, between two and five covered bridges are lost annually to arson.

59 Oregon State Highway Commission, *Second Annual Report of the Engineer of the Oregon State Highway Commission for the year ending November 30, 1915*, 53.

Endnotes

60 Some of the single-stick chords found in Oregon covered bridges are of impressive dimensions. Pengra Bridge (1938) in Lane County has bottom chords measuring 16 inches x 18 inches x 126 feet. See "Pengra Bridge," HAER No. OR-119.

61 Nick Cockrell and Bill Cockrell, *Roofs Over Rivers: A Guide to Oregon's Covered Bridges* (Beaverton, Ore.: Touchstone Press, 1978), 103. Many of those covered bridges were lost in the latter half of the twentieth century. Today, approximately forty covered bridges built during the historic era of covered bridge building survive in Oregon.

62 Joseph D. Conwill, *Covered Bridges Across North America* (St. Paul, Minn.: MBI Pub. Co., 2004), 77. Irish Bend Bridge (1954) in Benton County, Oregon, is generally considered to be the last covered bridge built during the historic era of covered bridge building. The structure was bypassed in the 1970s and moved to the Oregon State University campus at Corvallis in 1989.

63 See "Hancock-Greenfield Bridge," HAER No. NH-42.

64 Milton S. Graton, *The Last of the Covered Bridge Builders* (Plymouth, N.H.: Clifford-Nicol, Inc., 1978), 79–108; Conwill, *Covered Bridges Across North America*, 108–10.

65 Approximately 80 percent of the nation's extant covered bridges built during the historic era of covered bridge building are located in six states: Pennsylvania (27 percent), Ohio (17 percent), Indiana (13 percent), Vermont (11 percent), New Hampshire (6 percent), and Oregon (6 percent).

Chapter 4

The Engineering Design of Covered Bridges

by Dario Gasparini, Rachel H. Sangree, and James Barker;
edited by David A. Simmons and Michael R. Harrison

C overed bridges are, indeed, wonderful examples of craftsmanship, but they should also be appreciated as engineered structures. Engineers have historically contributed to their development, especially to their safety and reliability. In fact, the demand for reliable covered bridges was a driving force in the growth of the American engineering profession in the 1830s and 1840s. This chapter explores concepts and principles used in the engineering design of covered bridges in order to enhance understanding and appreciation of these iconic American structures.

The general objective of covered bridge design is to provide a cost-effective, functional, safe, and durable crossing. The siting of the bridge and the locations of piers and abutments are critical decisions of primary importance. These essential *foundation* components must be safe during extreme floods. The overall geometry of a bridge and its approaches must provide for a safe crossing. A wooden bridge must be protected from fire, water, and biological degradation to achieve durability. And, importantly, a wooden structure must be conceptualized and detailed to resist a variety of loads. It is this process of *structural design* that is the focus of this chapter. Structural design is based on the application of several important mathematical and physical concepts.

Basic Engineering Concepts

For most of human history, structures have been built on the basis of experiment and observation, or, it is said, empirically. This means that builders used "traditional proportions" established over time from observation of successful existing structures. Alternatively, for some simple structures, small-scale physical models were built in an attempt to infer the strength and stability of full-scale structures. James Finley, for example, successfully built suspension bridges in early-nineteenth-century Pennsylvania based on his observations of small-scale models.[1] Similarly, small-scale models of stone arches were built to identify potential failure mechanisms of actual arches. In general, however, it is difficult to construct appropriate small-scale physical models from which reliable predictions of forces may be made. Although many of mankind's celebrated structures were built empirically, such a design process is now understood to have a clear drawback: the safety of designs conceptualized in response to new uses or improved materials is difficult to verify prior to building the actual structure. Therefore, an empirical design process generally involves higher risk and expense. An alternative, called the *engineering* design method, emerged in the early nineteenth century. This new method was made possible by a centuries-long gradual understanding of significant engineering concepts as well as through the transformative work by French engineer Claude-Louis-Marie-Henri Navier in the 1820s.

The essential concepts for structural design are those of force, moment of a force, and equilibrium; elasticity and strength of materials; and geometric compatibility between member deformations and joint movements in a structure, described in further detail below.

Force, moment of a force, and force equilibrium — The concept of *force* developed from observation of natural phenomena, including the weights of objects, the action of simple mechanisms such as the lever, the fluid effect of buoyancy, the existence of friction, and the motion of bodies. Isaac Newton defined a force as the causative action for a change in momentum of an object or for an acceleration of a mass. Acceleration has an

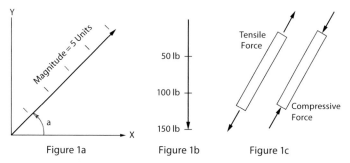

Figure 1a   Figure 1b   Figure 1c

Figure 4.1 Forces having magnitude and direction can be represented by vectors. In figure 1a, the force has a component in the Y direction and a component in the X direction. Figure 1b is a vector representation of the weight of a 150-lb person acting in a downward direction. In covered bridges, axial forces are tensile or compressive, depicted in figure 1c. Unless otherwise noted, all diagrams in this chapter were drawn by Dario Gasparini and Pavel Gorokhov.

associated *direction* and its causative action, the force, must have the same direction. A force is, therefore, a quantity that has both size, or magnitude, and a direction. Such a quantity may be defined using the mathematical concept of a *vector* and may be depicted by an arrow as shown in figure 4.1a. The direction of a force in a plane may be defined by an angle, *a*, with respect to a reference axis and the tip of the arrow. The length of the arrow represents the size, or magnitude. Force magnitudes are given as multiples of standard units such as the pound (lb), or the Newton (N).

In the context of covered bridge trusses, the primary forces in the members are generally aligned with the longitudinal axes of the members. Such *axial* forces are said to be *tensile* or *compressive*, as shown in figure 4.1c.

A body in a plane can have acceleration in the vertical and horizontal directions as well as *rotational* acceleration about an axis perpendicular to the plane of the body. A simple example is the rotation of a wheel about its axle. The causative action for rotational acceleration is called the *moment of a force* or simply the *moment*. The magnitude of the moment of a planar force about an axis perpendicular to its plane equals the force magnitude multiplied by the perpendicular distance from the line of action of the force to the axis (figure 4.2).

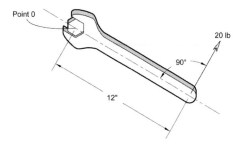

Figure 4.2 The action of loosening a bolt with a wrench is an example of the moment of a force. In this case, the moment of the 20-pound force about the point, or axis, 0 is 20 pounds x 12 inches = 240 pounds-inch.

Objects not accelerating nor at rest can have forces acting on them, but the *net* or *resultant* forces must be zero. When this is the case, the body is said to be in *equilibrium*. A two-dimensional or planar structure, such as a bridge truss, must satisfy three independent equilibrium requirements in order to remain at rest: the sum of the forces in the horizontal direction must be zero; the sum of the forces in the vertical direction must be zero; and the sum of the moments about any axis perpendicular to its plane must also be zero (figure 4.3).

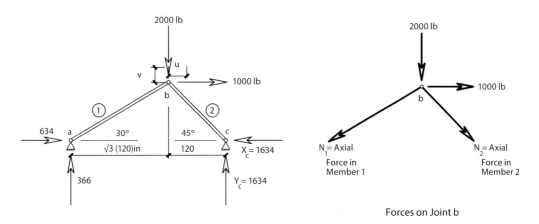

Figure 4.3 This two-member truss demonstrates equilibrium. The truss shown is subject to a horizontal force of 1,000 pounds and a vertical force of 2,000 pounds acting at joint b. Since the truss is at rest, the reactive forces at supports a and c must be such that the resultant force in the horizontal direction on the entire truss is zero, and, independently, the resultant force in the vertical direction must also be zero. The member axial forces, N1 and N2, may be determined by invoking equilibrium at joint b.

This equilibrium requirement also applies to any discrete part of a structure as well as to points on a structure. The *method of joints*, whereby engineers isolate each joint in a truss and calculate the forces acting on those points, is a fundamental application of equilibrium principles in both structural engineering generally and bridge design specifically.

Elasticity and strength of materials — All materials and structural members deform when forces are applied. This is evident when stretching a rubber band or when compressing a spring. In 1678, Robert Hooke made the important observation that for many materials the deformation is *linearly proportional* to the applied force. Figure 4.4 shows a specimen with an initial length L and cross-sectional area A subjected to an applied axial tensile force N. The force or load divided by the cross-sectional area is called *stress*, and the elongation e divided by the initial length is called *strain*. For many materials the strain is linearly proportional to the stress. The slope of the stress-strain curve, denoted by E, is called the *modulus of elasticity*, or *Young's modulus*.[2] The term *linear elastic* is used to define a material whose stress-strain behavior is linear and that has an unloading curve that coincides with its loading curve.

In the experiment illustrated in figure 4.4, the applied stress may be increased until the material ruptures or fails. The magnitude of the stress that causes rupture is called the *strength* of the material. A basic criterion of structural design is that the stresses in completed structures should be well below the strengths of the materials used.

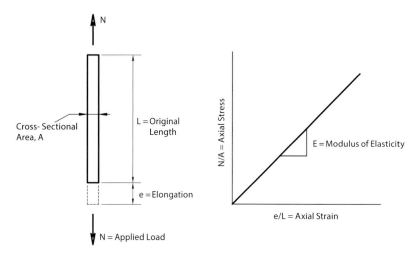

Figure 4.4 Left: 4.4a) represents a tensile test to determine the mechanical properties of material; the force N divided by cross-sectional area A is called *stress*, while the amount of elongation (e) divided by the original length(L) is called *strain*. Right: 4.4b) is a graph representing linear stress-strain behavior where E defines the modulus of elasticity of a material.

Geometrically compatible member axial deformations and joint movements — Another independent concept used in engineering design is that the deformations of members of a structure must be geometrically consistent, or *compatible*, with the movements or displacements at various points in a structure. Geometric compatibility requirements were studied extensively in the eighteenth century, primarily in the context of calculating work done by forces.[3] Equations stating geometric compatibility requirements depend on whether the movements of a structure are small or large. Commonly, the movements that occur when loads are applied to a structure are small relative to the structure's dimensions. For these common cases, the compatibility equations are linear, and the structure is said to be geometrically linear. The nature of geometric compatibility equations may be illustrated by considering the two-member truss in figure 4.5. The applied loads cause changes in member lengths, or axial deformations, denoted by e_1 and e_2. These deformations, in turn, produce movements, or displacements, of joint b, denoted as u and v. The member axial deformations and the joint displacements must satisfy two linear equations derived from geometry in order to be compatible.

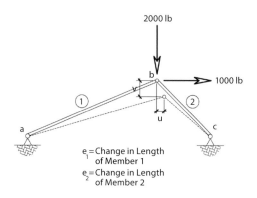

Figure 4.5 Applied loads cause changes in member lengths and movements of joint *b*, denoted by *u* and *v*. The dashed lines indicate the displaced position of the truss.

By the end of the eighteenth century, the concepts of force equilibrium, linear elasticity, and geometric compatibility had been known for over 100 years. But a method for using these three *independent* requirements to predict the effects of loads on structures had not been defined. Such a synthesis occurred early in the nineteenth century and was largely the work of one individual, Claude-Louis-Marie-Henri Navier.

The Transformative Work of Navier

Claude-Louis Navier (1785–1836) was a professor at the *École Nationale des Ponts et Chaussées* in Paris, the pre-eminent engineering school of the time. He first published his lectures in an 1826 book titled *Résumé des leçons* that included extensive data on the mechanical properties of materials, important theoretical developments on beams and trusses, and discussions of specific designs. Navier assembled experimental data from a variety of leading European engineers, including Jean Rondelet, John Rennie, Thomas Tredgold, Jean-Rodolphe Perronet, Giovanni Poleni, Marc Seguin, Jean-Marie-Constant Duhamel, Thomas Telford, Georges Louis Leclerc Buffon, William Henry Barlow, and Guillaume Henri Dufour. Navier's book contained data on the modulus of elasticity of stone, brick, cast iron, wrought iron, iron wire, and wood, including "le pin d'Amerique [American pine]." In addition, Navier considered strengths of *members*, specifically beams and columns, where buckling was an important consideration, and proposed *allowable stresses* for various materials.

Figure 4.6 Bust of Claude-Louis-Marie- Henri Navier, sculpted by Henri Cros in 1885. Courtesy of École Nationale des Ponts et Chaussées.

Navier's theoretical developments focused on the theory of beams and the theory of trusses. In the context of trusses, he gave explicit solutions for forces in the members of an asymmetric kingpost truss subject to a vertical load as shown in figure 4.7. He determined the effects of the load through a process now known as *structural analysis*. The simple kingpost truss is said to be *statically determinate* because the forces in the members may be determined using only equilibrium equations. The significance of Navier's solution, together with knowledge of member strength,

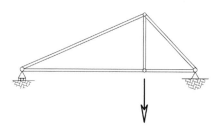

Figure 4.7 An asymmetrical kingpost truss studied by Navier.

was that an engineer could size wood members in such a way that stresses were at *allowable values*, well below strength levels. The *structural analysis* process moved structural design practice away from empirical methods. By 1826, an engineer could reliably size the members of a kingpost truss for any span and load.

Furthermore, Navier derived an explicit solution for the forces and displacements of the three-member truss shown in figure 4.8. This truss was significant because it was *statically indeterminate*; its member forces could not be determined using only equilibrium equations. Navier combined the three conditions of force equilibrium, linear elasticity, and geometric compatibility to arrive at a set

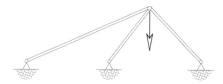

Figure 4.8 A statically indeterminate three-member truss studie by Navier

of equations that could be solved for the joint displacements and member forces. It is said that Navier defined a *mathematical model* of the truss in the sense that the set of equations modeled the mechanical behavior of the actual truss. Navier's formulation required solving a set of two simultaneous linear algebraic equations, a task easily done manually, and it was almost surely the first linear elastic structural analysis of a statically indeterminate structure. But, as the number of joints in a truss increased, the number of simultaneous linear algebraic equations quickly increased to the point where a manual solution became impractical. Therefore, the full power of Navier's formulation was not realized until the late 1950s or early 1960s, when computer programs for structural analysis were first developed.

Navier's most influential contribution to wooden-truss bridge design came from his observation that a parallel chord truss stiffened by diagonals functioned effectively as a beam. The calculations builders used to determine stresses in beams could therefore be adapted to ascertain the maximum forces in the chords of single-span trusses. He determined that the stiffness of a parallel chord truss was proportional to the area of the chords multiplied by the square of the distance between them. This observation enabled engineers to safely size the chords in parallel-chord trusses for any span and load, as depicted in figure 4.9.[4]

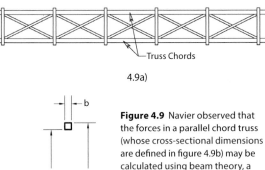

Figure 4.9 Navier observed that the forces in a parallel chord truss (whose cross-sectional dimensions are defined in figure 4.9b) may be calculated using beam theory, a methodology he devised. He proved that the stiffness of such a truss was proportional to the area of the chords multiplied by the square of the distance between them.

Navier's contributions to structural analysis transformed structural design itself. His work enabled engineers to define mathematical models of structures, to compute the effects of loads, and, together with data on material and member strength, to size members by limiting stresses to safe, allowable values. Navier's paradigm is still used in structural design today.

Navier's advances were transferred to America very quickly. A young engineer named Stephen Harriman Long, who graduated from Dartmouth College in 1809, published an article in *The Port Folio* in 1825 that cited Navier as well as Jean-Nicholas-Pierre Hachette's *Traite elementaire des machines*, demonstrating that Long had read the most recent developments in French engineering science.[5] In 1829, Long sized the chords of the wooden-truss Jackson Bridge, carrying the Washington Road over the Baltimore and Ohio Railroad, using Navier's beam analogy, almost surely the first American use of this new development. Long's truss design for this bridge, which he patented in 1830, was quickly and widely adopted.[6]

Long published a booklet in 1830 describing the Jackson Bridge and giving instructions to builders using his patent. He revised these instructions in 1836 when he published another booklet describing his patent in greater detail. The latter contained remarkable tables providing truss depths and cross-sectional areas of all members for twenty spans ranging from 55 feet to 300 feet. The areas of the chords in Long's book were consistent with Navier's analysis of a parallel-chord truss as a beam, showing that Long understood and applied Navier's theories.[7]

Instructors at West Point used French engineering education as their model. It is likely Navier's lectures were known at West Point shortly after their 1826 publication, if not before. Dennis Hart Mahan graduated first in his class from West Point in 1824 and became an assistant professor at the academy that same year. In 1826, he sailed for France to study at the military school for engineers and artillerists at Metz. He returned to teach at West Point in 1830 and remained there his entire life.[8] Mahan included many of Navier's ideas in his 1837 textbook, *An Elementary Course of Civil Engineering for the Use of the Cadets of the United States Military Academy*. Mahan commented in the book's introduction that Navier's name "is connected, either as author or editor, with the ablest works on the subject under consideration that have appeared in France within the last twenty years; and the best counsel that the author could give to every young engineer is to place in his library every work of science to which M. Navier's name is in any way attached." The mechanics portion of Mahan's text considered many of the same examples and provided the same solutions as those found in Navier's *Résumé des leçons*. Specifically, Mahan gave the solution for the forces in a kingpost truss and stated Navier's analogy of a parallel-chord truss as a beam, actually using one of Navier's figures. Mahan did not repeat Navier's analysis of a statically indeterminate truss, perhaps because he recognized the practical limitations of applying Navier's formulas to trusses with many more joints.[9]

Although Navier did permanently change the way engineers designed structures, his work was only a start. There has since been a continuous line of contributions to mathematical modeling of structures and understanding of structural behavior, progress in structural engineering knowledge that continues today. In addition, it should be emphasized that Navier's contributions were primarily in structural analysis, which is only one step in the structural design process.

Structural Design of Bridges

The bridge design process has evolved over time but there are basic design considerations that have remained the same. The design process begins by prescribing functionality requirements that set the width, span, clearances, abutment elevations, and other geometric features. Design loads must then be defined, which normally include the estimated self-weight, or, in engineering usage, *dead load*, and transient, or *live*, loads, such as people, vehicles, snow, and wind. (It should be noted that wind causes primarily horizontal, or *lateral*, forces on the sides of a covered bridge.) Selecting the magnitudes of design live loads can be a source of conflict or disagreement among participants because of the uncertainty in the actual load magnitudes that may occur and the tradeoff between design loads and the cost of a bridge. In general, the larger the design loads the greater the cost of a bridge. Engineers refer to larger loads, which are less likely to occur, as being more *conservative*. Current design load magnitudes are generally prescribed by legal documents, or *codes*, but these standard loads were only defined in the United States beginning in the late 1870s.

The next step in the design process is to conceptualize a structural system that can safely carry the design loads. This includes a floor system, a system for lateral loads, and the principal trusses for the dead and live gravity loads. Because of their primary responsibility for safety, engineers generally do not favor conceptual designs that are inconsistent with their understanding of structural behavior or that are difficult to model mathematically. This may explain why Navier barely referenced the famous—and complex—European covered bridges at Schaffhausen and Wettingen and why he never discussed the very successful and widely used Town and Burr designs, which were surely known to him. As part of the conceptual design, suitable materials must also be selected. Structural design then generally enters a cyclic, or *iterative*, process of mathematical modeling of the structure and loads, structural analysis to determine the effects of the loads, and checks on whether acceptance criteria on strength, stiffness, and stability are met. Concurrently, the all-important connections must be designed and detailed. Each of these steps involves concepts that shed light on engineering structural design and therefore are described in more detail in the following sections.

Selecting Design Loads

Pioneering builders of covered bridges, like Timothy Palmer, Lewis Wernwag, and Theodore Burr, did not know the superimposed loads that their bridges could safely carry because mathematical techniques for predicting the effects of loads had not been developed. With the introduction of structural analysis techniques in the late 1820s, engineers were able to define explicit design loads and to size members to safely carry the effects of these loads.

Covered bridges, of course, have to be able to support their own weight, called the *dead load*. Estimating dead load is a simple but critical and laborious task that requires calculating the volumes of the various materials in the bridge and then multiplying the volumes by their corresponding unit weights. A much more challenging task is to define imposed or moving loads, called *live loads*. Depending on the type of covered bridge, moving loads could include pedestrians, livestock, carriages, freight wagons, or trains. Engineers assumed such loads primarily caused downward, gravitational forces. Other actions normally considered in structural design were wind-induced pressures and snow loads. Although earthquakes are typically considered today, nineteenth-century engineers thought of them as "acts of God," along with extreme floods, and did not expect the structures to survive without significant damage or even collapse.

Wagons, animals, and pedestrians crossing covered bridges moved too slowly to cause significant acceleration responses, so nineteenth-century engineers treated such loads as *static* rather than *dynamic*, even though they represented people or vehicles in motion. Engineers of that era also ignored forces created by changing temperatures (thermal forces), as the coefficient of thermal expansion for wood parallel to its grain was so low. In modeling static loads, engineers needed to decide whether the loads acted as a *concentrated force* at a single point on a bridge, or as a *distributed force* over a given area, as shown in figure 4.10. For example, even though individuals in a crowd cause gravity forces at their specific locations, the entire crowd is generally regarded as a uniformly distributed load over a particular area.

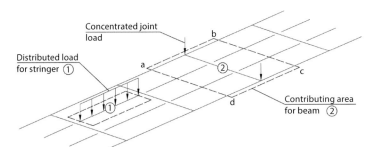

Figure 4.10 Typical bridge floor framing is shown with concentrated loads, distributed loads, and contributing area. A distributed load is usually allocated to specific members using the geometric concept of *contributing area*. In this example, crossbeam 2 in the diagram is assumed to carry the entire distributed load over the contributing area defined by points *a-b-c-d*.

Another important decision that engineers had to make when selecting design loads was where along a span to place a heavy concentrated load, such as a heavily-loaded wagon or the engine of a train. This decision required predicting the effects of the concentrated load in all members for all the possible positions of the load. In general, a load position that caused the greatest effect, or force, in one member was different from the load position that caused the greatest effect in another member.

An even more fundamental judgment required deciding which loads should be assumed to act concurrently, or *in combination*. For example, it is intuitive that the dead load should always be included in combination with a live load. But should wind-induced forces be assumed to act concurrently with distributed live loads, given that each design magnitude had a low probability of occurrence? These assumptions are now largely prescribed by design codes—which did not exist in the early nineteenth century—but initially required engineering judgment.

The last step in modeling a load was the all-important decision on the *magnitude* to be used. Large, very conservative magnitudes resulted in designs that were safer but could entail costs that were excessive. Conservative thinking on loads was intimately related not only to safety but also to cost. Engineers generally defined load magnitudes that were well above average, although the actual probability of exceeding them was unknown. Today, engineers call such design loads *working loads*.

Some of the issues involved in the evolution of load modeling are illustrated with a review of the early development of design live loads for suspension bridges, specifically the work by Navier on defining design loads for the *Pont des Invalides*, a suspension bridge over the River Seine. His 1823 report on theoretical developments related to suspension bridges included a detailed description of his logic for defining uniformly distributed design live loads.[10] He considered three load scenarios:

1. an orderly crowd of men, women, and children modeled as three 65-kilogram persons per square meter, or a uniformly distributed live load of 195 kg/m^2;

2. a cavalry troop traversing the span, a load he estimated to be 130 kg/m^2 by considering the actual weights of horses and cavalrymen and the areas they occupied; and

3. two lines of wagons carrying building stones, each weighing 8,400 kg and pulled by four horses, which also produced a uniformly distributed load smaller than that caused by a crowd. (He recognized that heavier wagons existed but stated that it was unlikely to have two lines of such wagons on the span simultaneously.)

Based on these three scenarios, Navier designed the bridge to support a uniformly distributed live load of 195 kg/m^2 (40 lb/ft^2). In 1826, Guillaume Henri Dufour and Marc Seguin, two pioneering French suspension bridge designers who also had to make decisions on design live loads, commented on Navier's logic and decision. Dufour stated that such a load seemed unnecessary "except for small bridges . . . and for those large bridges in very populous capital cities . . . everywhere else probability should govern decisions so as not to succumb to exaggerated expense." Dufour explicitly stated that loads were *random* and recommended that designers decide on loads that had an acceptable and consistent probability that they would not be exceeded. Dufour understood that the probability of having a uniform load of 195kg/m^2 over the entire area of a small bridge in an urban setting was much greater than the probability of having the same load over the entire area of a large bridge in a rural setting, and he consequently objected to using the same design load in both cases. Marc Seguin, who echoed Dufour's thoughts, reduced his live load estimate to 183 kg/m^2 for his famous Tournon-Tain suspension bridge, while Dufour used an even lower distributed live load of 154 kg/m^2 for his Saint Antoine Bridge.[11]

British engineers deduced their own design live loads. Thomas Telford used an effective distributed load of only 54 kg/m^2, or 11 lb/ft^2, for his renowned Menai Straits Bridge of 1826, but other British engineers, whose logic is unknown, typically used a live load of 70 lb/ft^2, which was considerably greater than Navier's.[12]

Stephen Long was likely the first American covered bridge builder to explicitly state a design live load. He used a live load of 120 lb/ft² in his 1836 booklet to compute axial stresses in bridge chords. He proportioned chord areas so that the maximum chord stresses were one-half of the minimum wood strength (assumed to be 4,000 psi). Long apparently computed this design load, three times Navier's load, using the weight of two trains on a bridge. Although Long used very large, uniformly distributed live loads, he "allowed" relatively high axial stresses, equal to one-half of his assumed minimum compressive wood strength.[13]

D. H. Mahan's 1837 book provided no guidelines for design live loads. Influential New York engineer Squire Whipple felt it proper to consider "the whole area of the roadway, covered with men, which is about 100 lbs. to the square foot, as the greatest load to which the bridge can be exposed." Herman Haupt stated without explanation that "the greatest variable load is generally considered as caused by a crowd of people, and is estimated at 120 lbs. per square foot."[14] Such a load seems to have been a maximum live load used by early engineers for road bridges.

By 1888, American engineer J. A. L. Waddell recommended a more measured approach, as illustrated by table 1. Waddell defined three classes of "ordinary" highway bridges. "Class A" included urban bridges with continuous heavy loads; "Class B" comprised urban bridges with occasional heavy loads; and "Class C" included country road bridges. In addition, Waddell defined live loads for joists, floor beams, beam hangers, and hip verticals as "one hundred (100) pounds per square foot for bridges of Classes A and B, and eighty (80) pounds per square foot for Class C." Waddell's categorization of bridges and distinction between bridges of different lengths (and different surface areas) reflected the assessment made by Dufour and Seguin. He thought that the loadings on larger bridges and those in rural areas could be reduced without fear that they would be exceeded under ordinary circumstances.[15]

Span in feet	Moving load per square foot of floor			
	Class A	Class B	Class C	Class D
0 to 50	100	100	80	65
50 to 100	100	95	80	60
100 to 150	95	90	75	55
150 to 175	90	85	75	50
175 to 200	85	80	70	---
200 to 225	80	75	65	---
225 to 250	75	70	60	---
250 to 275	70	65	55	---
275 to 300	65	60	50	---
300 to 350	65	55	45	---
350 and over	65	55	40	---

Table 1: Waddell's uniformly distributed live loads for bridges, from J. A. L. Waddell, *General Specifications for Highway Bridges of Iron and Steel*, 2d ed., page 25.

In northern climates, engineers also designed for the imposed weight of snow. The main questions regarding snow were its unit weight, the accumulated depth, and variations due to the pitch, or slope, of various roof surfaces. John C. Trautwine measured snow unit weights and performed experiments with snow accumulation on a variety of roof surfaces and slopes, publishing the results in the 1872 first edition of *The Civil Engineers' Pocket-Book*. His trials "showed the wt. of freshly fallen snow to vary from about 5 to 12 lbs per cub. ft.; apparently depending chiefly upon the degree of humidity of the air through which it had passed." In the United States, he suggested, "the allowance for snow should not be taken at *less* than 12 lbs; or the total for snow and wind, at 20 lbs." The 1904 edition of the *Pocket-Book* noted, "The snow load, in States north of lat. 35°, may be taken as varying (chiefly with latitude) from 10 to 30 lbs. per sq. ft. of horizontal projection of roof surface." Today, engineers still use the concept that snow load is applied to the horizontal projection of a roof.[16]

The steady evolution toward bridge design specifications that began in the early nineteenth century with wooden trusses reached its culmination in the third quarter of the century through the design of iron railroad bridges. For railroad bridges, the principal loading was obviously not from crowds or snow but from the weights of the engines, tenders, and loaded cars. Their dramatic increase from the 1830s through the nineteenth century made it essential to prescribe safe loads as part of the bridge design specifications. In the early 1870s, various bridge companies, such as the Phoenix Iron and Bridge Works, began specifying bridge capacities. Important changes in the definition of train design loads originated with Louis Bouscaren's 1875 specifications for the Newport and Cincinnati Bridge over the Ohio River of the Cincinnati Southern Railway, as shown in figure 4.11.[17]

CINCINNATI SOUTHERN RAILROAD BRIDGE ACROSS THE OHIO RIVER.

Figure 4.11 The specifications for the Newport and Cincinnati Bridge designed by Louis Bouscaren for the Cincinnati Southern Railway and completed in 1877 were instrumental in establishing national bridge design standards. From *Illustrated Business Directory and Picturesque Cincinnati, 1883* (Cincinnati, Ohio: Spencer & Craig Printing Works, 1883), 76. Courtesy of Ohio History Connection.

About this time, engineers recognized that rapidly moving trains caused some acceleration responses and inertia forces in a bridge. A train could be a *dynamic* rather than a *static* load, requiring the addition, in Bouscaren's terms, of "ten to thirty percent" to the stresses computed from static load and bridge models. Called an *impact factor*, it and Bouscaren's prescribed axle loads (figure 4.12) became permanent changes in bridge specifications still used to this day.

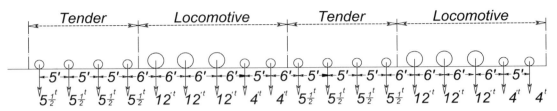

Figure 4.12 Bouscaren prescribed for the first time that a train must be modeled as a set of moving axle point loads, here given in *tons*. Engineers had to consider *all* possible positions of the point loads in order to determine the greatest effect (force) in each member. Adapted from Thomas Lovett, *Report on the Progress of Work, Cost of, Etc., of the Cincinnati Southern Railway* (Cincinnati, Ohio: Wrightson & Co., Printers, 1875), 25.

The collapse of the all-iron Howe-truss railroad bridge at Ashtabula, Ohio, on December 29, 1876, accelerated the process of developing "model" or national specifications, especially for railroad bridges. Perhaps the most widely adopted specifications in America were those written by Theodore Cooper, an early version of which appeared in *Engineering News* in 1879. Cooper's specifications followed Bouscaren's lead in requiring a moving axle load model for trains.[18]

The forces induced on bridges by strong winds were less understood and more difficult to model. Navier's 1826 *Leçons* gave no guidelines on wind; he merely stated that wind forces and their effects could not be accurately predicted. As wind blows over a bridge, it creates pressures perpendicular to surfaces that vary from point to point depending on the shape of the bridge, the direction of the wind, and the wind's turbulence. Nevertheless, the overall stability of a bridge generally depends

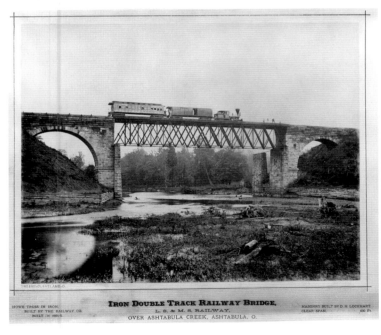

Figure 4.13 Amasa Stone was a highly accomplished railroad contractor of traditional combination wood and iron Howe trusses. After building several Howe trusses with cast-iron webs, he experimented with a Howe design that substituted wrought-iron I-beams for the wooden diagonals. Completed in 1865, the Ashtabula Bridge collapsed during a blizzard in December 1876, resulting in one of the nation's deadliest bridge disasters. A broken cast-iron bearing block was identified as the immediate cause of the collapse. Thomas T. Sweeny, photographer, 1865. Courtesy of Ohio History Connection.

on some average pressure over the entire exposed surface of the structure, not on peak pressures at a few locations. The main discussion in the nineteenth century focused on determining reasonable values for this average pressure that could be used in designing bridges and checking their stability.

John Smeaton's *An Experimental Enquiry Concerning the Natural Powers of Water and Wind to Turn Mills*, published in 1760, and Julius Weisbach's *Principles of the Mechanics of Machinery and Engineering*, first published in an American edition in 1848, were the two principal scientific references on fluid pressures used by nineteenth-century structural engineers. Smeaton's publication contained a table that correlated wind velocity to wind pressure. Smeaton's data went as high as 100 mph, as shown in table 2. Because such velocities seemed extreme, bridge engineers typically used design wind pressures between 30 lb/ft^2 and 50 lb/ft^2.[19]

Wind velocity (mph)	Wind pressure (psf)	"Common appellations of the force of winds."
30	4.429	"High winds."
40	7.873	"Very high."
50	12.3	"A storm or tempest."
60	17.715	"A great storm."
80	31.490	"An hurricane."

Table 2: Selected wind velocities with their corresponding wind pressures as given by John Smeaton in his 1760 study of wind and water power. Based on John Smeaton, *An Experimental Enquiry Concerning the Natural Powers of Water and Wind to Turn Mills, and other Machines, depending on a Circular Motion* (London: [s.n.], 1760), table VI, page 68.

The collapse of the Firth of Tay high-level bridge in Scotland on December 28, 1879—almost exactly three years after the Ashtabula Bridge failure—during a windstorm focused international attention on design wind loads. Nonetheless, other than personal experiences, observations, and preferences on design wind pressures, no advances in modeling occurred. There was general agreement that, given the rare occurrence of large wind pressures, an increase in allowable stresses of between 25 percent and 33 percent was necessary for wind loads. It probably represented an economizing effort to minimize increases in member sizes due to wind.

In summary, a necessary step in the engineering design process required imagining loading scenarios and mathematically modeling the loads. The examples of floor live loads and wind loads show their inherently uncertain or random nature. As a consequence, engineers typically defined—and still do define—simple static models with magnitudes that were well above average, even when faced with the unknown probability of exceeding these loads. Very conservative, highly improbable design loads generally led to safer structures, but they could also result in greater, and possibly prohibitive, costs. Despite inherent uncertainties and some inconsistencies, simple load models allowed engineers to achieve designs with acceptable safety and reliability.

Structural Materials

Alongside developing load scenarios, engineers had to select appropriate structural materials for the various bridge components. Wood was the primary material of covered bridge construction. It formed the load-bearing structure as well as the distinctive siding and roofing that protected the structure from deterioration. Selecting the right wood required careful consideration of the strength, weight, resistance to decay, workability, and cost of the woods available. Early-nineteenth-century builders tended to use regional timber species. In New England, spruce and eastern white pine grew abundantly and were frequently used in covered bridges. Eastern white pine, a light but reasonably strong species, also grew in Michigan and Wisconsin and was favored in the Midwest, where white oak and poplar were common. Later, as railroads allowed more economical long-distance shipment, southern pine was adopted as a strong and cheap alternative throughout the nation. Noted Indiana bridge builder J. J. Daniels purchased hundreds of acres of Georgia forest to provide a reliable source of southern pine for his business. Douglas fir, the great western building timber, formed the covered bridges of Oregon, Washington, and California, but it was not used east of the Great Plains during the nineteenth century.

When a tree is first cut, it has a high moisture content and is said to be *green*. Green wood shrinks as it dries, so cut lumber today is typically prepared for use by seasoning it or drying it in a kiln. Even after seasoning, wood remains hygroscopic and continuously absorbs or desorbs water vapor as the humidity and temperature of its environment change. Wood, therefore, constantly experiences moisture-induced strains. The mechanical properties of wood strongly depend on its moisture content, and these mechanical properties typically degrade as moisture content increases. While some historic wooden truss designs, such as Long and Howe trusses, were routinely built using green timbers, nineteenth-century builders well understood that seasoned lumber produced more stable and long-lasting results.

Covered bridge builders also understood that the mechanical properties of wood varied depending on the presence of knots, checks, shakes, and other flaws. This variability necessitated the use of allowable stresses that were small fractions (usually one-fifth to one-tenth) of measured strengths to keep the probability of having under-strength members acceptably small. Old-growth timber, from which many covered bridges were historically fabricated, was noteworthy for the absence of most flaws.

Early-nineteenth-century builders and engineers possessed a wealth of practical knowledge about wood and wood science. Thomas Tredgold's comprehensive *Elementary Principles of Carpentry*, published in England in 1820 and in the United States in 1837, provides a good window on the extent of that knowledge. The book covered wood science, mechanical properties, fabrication technology, common structural forms, and structural design guidelines. It discriminated among various wood species, distinguished between heartwood and sapwood, prescribed proper felling, sawing, and seasoning practices, and discussed decay and decay prevention. Tredgold provided extensive data on the mechanical properties of wood such as the modulus of elasticity, crushing strength, and the tensile or "cohesive" strength in the axial and radial directions. The woods Tredgold discussed included North American white pine, yellow pine, and the wood from a then "unknown species . . . discovered in the northwest coast of America by Mr. David Douglas."[20]

Tredgold described wood framing techniques for floors, roofs, domes, and bridges and illustrated appropriate designs for mortise and tenon joints, scarf joints, and tension splices. He cautioned that "the effects of shrinkage and expansion should be considered in the construction of joints," specifically noting that swelling could cause splits and that shrinkage tended to loosen bolts. He also considered the strength of columns and beams and suggested that allowable stresses should be one-fourth of measured strengths. Tredgold's data was invaluable to any engineer undertaking the design of covered wooden bridges.[21]

Stephen H. Long's 1830 directions to the builders of the Jackson Bridge provide a complementary contemporary perspective on wood use in bridges:

> The timber best adapted to the construction of a Frame Bridge is White Pine. The qualities which entitle it to this distinction are, its lightness, stiffness, and exemption from the ravages of worms, insects, &c. Cypress, Yellow Pine, White Cedar, Hemlock, Poplar, and Chestnut, are to be regarded as among the most valuable substitutes afforded within the limits of the United States. Yellow, or hard Pine, is probably better adapted for the necessary keys and wedges than any other material; but when those are not to be had, White Ash, White Oak, Locust, or Chestnut, may be used to advantage. The timber employed, especially in the frame-work of the Bridge, should be perfectly sound, free from sap, knots, shakes, splits, twists, and all other defects calculated to impair its strength, tenacity, and durability; and should be of the character denominated "quartered timber," or timber cut through, and deprived of, the heart or pith.[22]

Long's remarks reveal the clear contemporary understanding that flaws significantly lowered the strength of wood. Similarly, Squire Whipple's 1847 treatise *A Work on Bridge Building* included an extensive discussion of the shear strength of wood.[23]

Today, it is well understood that wood is a biopolymer consisting mostly of cellulose, which is hydrophilic, and lignin, which is relatively hydrophobic. Largely because of its particular cellular microstructure, the mechanical properties of wood at a given point depend on the direction of applied stresses and strains. Wood strength, stiffness, and many other properties are significantly greater in the axial (parallel-to-the-grain) direction than in the radial (perpendicular-to-the-grain) and tangential directions. Wood is also a *viscous* material; if a constant stress is applied to wood, the strain increases with time. This phenomenon, called *creep*, generally causes wood structures to deform over time. It also causes changes in member forces in statically indeterminate trusses over time.[24]

By 1830, iron was an essential component of covered bridges as well. The physical and mechanical properties of cast iron were well known in the early nineteenth century. In his *Practical Essay on the Strength of Cast Iron and Other Metals*, first published in 1822, Thomas Tredgold provided data on the modulus of elasticity, tensile strength, and compressive strength of cast iron, among other materials. His principal finding was that the tensile strength of cast iron was much smaller than its compressive strength, a fact that led cast iron to be used for compression members but not for tension members. Cast iron was also used for beams, but only with great care. "With regard to cast iron," Whipple later wrote, "it is not economical to employ it to sustain tension, and whenever it may be exposed to that action, I would not rely on it for more than about 4,000 lbs. to the square inch." Cast iron was most commonly used in wood bridges for the nodes (shoes) on Howe trusses.[25]

The relatively high carbon content of cast iron lowered its melting temperature and facilitated casting, but it also contributed to the material's low tensile strength. A process for removing carbon and other elements from iron was invented by Henry Cort in 1784, which involved oxidizing out the impurities in a special furnace called a puddling furnace and then hot working the metal in a rolling mill to increase its strength—particularly its tensile strength. This process also lent the metal excellent resistance to corrosion. The final product of Cort's process was *wrought iron*, and wrought-iron components came into common use in covered bridges for tension rods, such as those in Howe trusses, and diagonal braces and counterbraces, such as those in wooden Pratt trusses.[26] Wrought iron has a fibrous microstructure as shown in figure 4.14.

	Carbon	Silicon	Sulfur	Phosphorus	Manganese
Pig iron	3.5–4.25	1–2	0.30–0.1	0.50–1.00	0.25–1.00

Table 3: Chemical composition of pig and wrought iron (percent by weight). The pig iron from a smelting furnace, while consisting mostly of the element iron, also contained carbon and other elements. Adapted from M. O. Withey and James Aston, with F. E. Turneaure, ed., *Johnson's Materials of Construction*, 5th ed. (New York: John Wiley & Sons, 1919), 545.

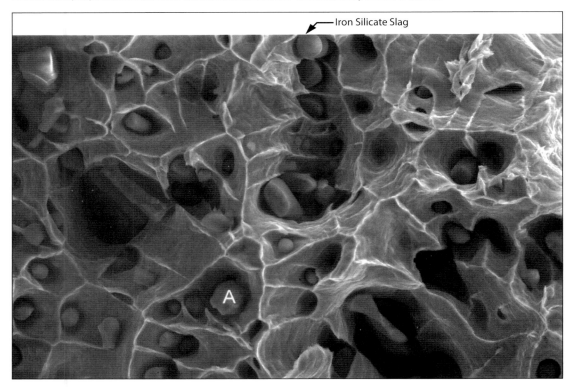

Iron Silicate Slag

Figure 4.14 Wrought iron was the final product of changes affected in iron by heating in a puddling furnace and then hot working. Table 3 demonstrates that the puddling process removed most of the carbon in the iron and bound the silicon, manganese, and phosphorus within the slag phase, an important chemical change that, together with the rolling process, gave wrought iron its unique microstructure and character. The rolling process created slag fibers—whose microstructure is shown in this scanning electron microscope image of a wrought-iron fracture surface—that are aligned with the rolling direction. The phase marked "A," which has a sharp fracture surface, is slag. The presence of slag fibers gave wrought iron both its excellent resistance to corrosion and its ease in being cut by threading machines. The slag fiber also allows a simple physical test for identifying wrought iron. A specimen suspended for a half hour in a solution of nine parts water, three parts sulfuric acid, and one part hydrochloric acid will etch wrought iron deeply and unevenly, producing a rough, fibrous, "woody" surface. Courtesy of Professor Gerhard Welsch, Case Western Reserve University.

Wrought iron was supplanted by steel at the end of the nineteenth century, and it is now an archaic material, no longer made in industrial quantities. Because of this, wrought-iron components add much to the historic fabric of many wooden covered bridges.

Structural design criteria

After deciding on design loads and choosing the proper structural materials, an engineer's design process set structural design criteria. This meant deciding how the bridge was to perform under various loading conditions. The general objective of structural design was to create a durable bridge that safely carried the design loads without excessive displacements. The principal structural design criteria were strength and stability, stiffness, and durability. A structural designer had to assure that every member and every connection, as well as the bridge as a whole, had adequate strength and remained stable. Any member could fail in a variety of ways, such as from excessive axial forces (figure 4.15a), moments (figure 4.15b), or shears (figure 4.15c).

Members not only had to have adequate strength, they also had to be properly connected so that loads were transferred to the abutments. Compressive axial forces could cause an initially straight member to become unstable; a member could bend or *buckle*, as shown in figure 4.16.

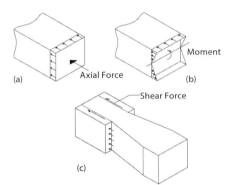

Figure 4.16 Member buckling from a compressive force.

Figure 4.15 Three common modes of failure.

The compressive stress that caused buckling depended on the member's end connections and the material's modulus of elasticity. It was also an inverse function of the square of the member's *slenderness ratio*, defined as:

$$\frac{\text{length of member}}{k \, (\text{smallest cross} - \text{sectional dimension})}$$

In the above equation, k is a constant, approximately equal to 0.3 for rectangular sections. Lattice truss diagonals were often relatively slender and were able to carry only limited compressive forces before buckling occurred. It was also possible for the entire compressive chord of a truss to become unstable and move horizontally as shown in figure 4.17. This phenomenon is today called *lateral instability*. Both member buckling and lateral instability of compressive chords had to be anticipated and prevented.

A bridge could be stable and have adequate strength, but it could also be too flexible, such that the imposed gravity loads caused excessive vertical displacements or deflections, as shown in figure 4.18. Such a bridge is today said to have insufficient *stiffness* and to not meet *serviceability* requirements. Predicting displacements mathematically required significant computations, a level of engineering science not achieved until the 1870s. As a consequence, historic covered bridge designers depended on the empirical knowledge of prior bridges that had proven to have adequate stiffness.

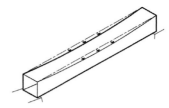

Figure 4.17 Lateral instability of a top chord.

Most importantly, covered bridge designers needed to devise systems and details that delayed degradation and the consequent loss of strength. The wooden structural framework had to be protected from fungal and insect attack and from wetting and drying cycles resulting from direct exposure to rain and snow. Designers then conceptualized a structural system that met the various design criteria.

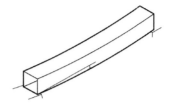

Figure 4.18 Excessive vertical displacement or sag in a bridge.

Conceptual structural design

Covered bridges could be built as *through, pony,* or *deck* types, as shown in figure 4.19. The individual trusses in the rare wooden pony trusses were often *housed*, although without a roof over the roadway. The type chosen depended largely on the topography and the bridge span. For all types, a principal

Figure 4.19 Historic examples of through, pony, and deck trusses include: **Top Left:** 4.19a) Dover Toll Bridge, a Howe through truss, carrying a train across Great Bay in Dover Point, New Hampshire, prior to being covered (stereograph by H. Copeland, 1873); **Top Right:** 4.19b) a Howe pony truss on the Portland and Ogdensburg Railroad in Crawford Notch through the White Mountains in New Hampshire (stereograph by B. W. Kilburn, ca. 1870); and **Left:** 4.19c) an uncovered Howe deck truss on the Troy and Greenfield Railroad (stereograph by Horton & Wise, undated). All stereograph halves courtesy of a private collection.

design parameter was the *depth-to-span ratio,* which strongly affected the stiffness of a bridge. This ratio typically ranged from one-fifth to one-tenth. Once a depth-to-span ratio was chosen, a designer conceptualized systems that satisfied the design criteria for all the considered loads, effectively visualizing "paths" by which the applied loads were transferred to the abutments. Often, a designer conceptualized a three-dimensional bridge as an assembly of two-dimensional, or planar, components, each performing separate functions. For example, for the dominant gravity dead and live loads, a designer visualized the vertical sides of a bridge, as shown in figure 4.20, to be the principal components that carry the vertical loads to the abutments.

The two vertical sides must generally be subdivided or *trussed* using a variety of patterns, such as those shown in figures 4.20a, b, and c. (The most widely used trusses are described in further detail in chapter 5.) It was important to distinguish whether a particular trussing pattern was statically determinate or indeterminate. Statically indeterminate trusses often had "main diagonals" and "counter diagonals" in an X pattern. If a truss was statically indeterminate, a state of prestress could be induced, for example, by driving wedges or tightening nuts on threaded iron rods. Such a state of pre-stress could increase the stiffness of a bridge. In theory, in a statically determinate truss, if one member failed, the entire truss failed. Conversely, the failure of a single member in a statically indeterminate truss did not necessarily lead to failure of an entire truss.

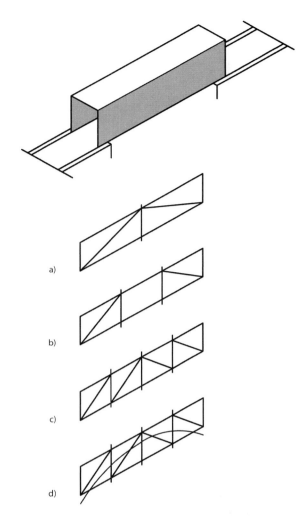

Figure 4.20 The vertical sides of a bridge are the principal components for carrying gravity loads, with a variety of truss types shown. Before the mechanical properties of trusses became well understood and had established reliabilities, it was common to add arches as shown in (d), with the arch and truss each carrying a fraction of the gravity load.

Conceptual design also required accounting for wind loads. Common systems devised to resist lateral wind forces are shown in figure 4.21. The floor of a typical covered bridge, as previously shown in figure 4.10, was conservatively assumed *not* to be part of the wind load resisting system. It was designed only to transfer local floor gravity loads to the lower chords of the vertical trusses. The various members were sized to carry the loads within their contributing areas.

Figure 4.21 To transfer horizontal or lateral wind forces to the abutments, designers conceptualized and designed horizontal trusses and two-dimensional, or *plane*, frames as shown here. The horizontal trusses are at the plane of the floor and at the plane defined by the two top chords. For pony-type bridges, it was not possible to carry wind load and stabilize the top chord through a horizontal truss, so *outriggers* were installed. Examples of bracing include **Top Left:** 4.21a) horizontal lateral bracing to resist wind on the West Union Bridge (1876), Parke County, Indiana, HAER IN-105-13, James Rosenthal, photographer, 2004; **Middle:** 4.21b) Portal frames to transfer loads taken by the top chord on the Flint Bridge (1874), Orange County, Vermont, HAER VT-29-5, Jet Lowe, photographer, 2003; **Bottom L:** 4.21c) outriggers to stabilize top chords on the Beaverkill Bridge (1865), Sullivan County, New York, HAER NY-329-10, Jet Lowe, photographer, 2003.

A bridge's self weight, or dead load, could create a downward vertical displacement, so designers generally designed the deck with a small upward displacement, called *camber*, which ideally was equal but opposite to the self-weight displacement (figure 4.22).

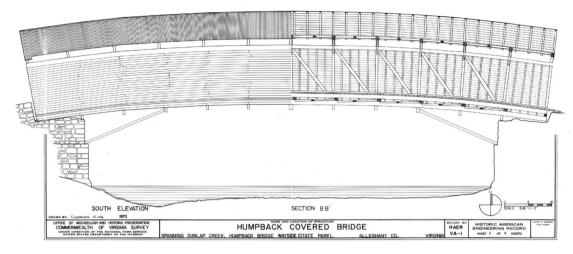

Figure 4.22 The necessary camber for a bridge was generally achieved by making each top chord panel length slightly longer than the corresponding lower chord panel length. For example, if the lower chord panel length was 120 inches, the corresponding upper chord panel length was approximately 120.125 inches. The exact length increment was determined mathematically by considering the truss to be part of a circular arc. The Humpback Bridge, shown here, displays a 4 percent camber. HAER VA-1, sheet 2, Charles King, delineator, 1970.

Durability was, of course, an all-important design criterion involving wood choice and the appropriate siding and roofing, carefully detailed to protect the ends of a bridge. Significantly, roofs and siding were always viewed as expendable protection for the all-important trusswork and floor systems. Their eventual replacement was expected during the service life of a bridge, and failure to maintain the coverings has long been a primary reason for the deterioration and loss of covered bridges. Occasional modern attempts to preserve the siding and roofing as elements critical to the significance of historic bridges fly in the face of the builders' intent.

Mathematical modeling and structural analysis

After a design is conceptualized, engineers proceeded with the step that was begun by Navier: estimating the forces in all parts of a bridge caused by the design loads in a process known as *mathematical modeling and structural analysis*. Although by 1826 Navier had applied equilibrium to determine forces in simple kingpost trusses and had postulated an analogy that enabled estimation of forces in truss chords, structural analysis for more complicated truss forms developed slowly over the course of the nineteenth century. In fact, the engineering science of computing forces in all members of statically determinate trusses only became widely taught and applied in the 1870s, and computing forces in statically indeterminate wood trusses remains an uncertain process to this day.

Equilibrium equations at joints may be solved either algebraically or graphically, using geometry. During the nineteenth century, graphical methods were seen as simpler and more efficient and offered a visual error check not available through algebra. Some methods of graphical analysis were known in France as early as 1725 and were used by engineers in America during the first half of the nineteenth century. The earliest American publication to show a graphical method appears to have been the first American edition of English engineer Thomas Tredgold's *Elementary Principles of Carpentry*, published in Philadelphia in 1837. Tredgold demonstrated how to find the resultant force on an inclined member using the *parallelogram of forces*, a theorem whose proof was credited to Daniel Bernoulli in 1726.

Tredgold illustrated the method with a simple diagram (figure 4.23a) accompanied by this explanation:

> Let AC represent the magnitude and direction of a force, acting on the body C, and BC the magnitude and direction of another force, also acting on the body C. Then to find the resultant, draw bB parallel to AC; and Ab parallel to BC; join bC, which represents the resultant required.[27]

Using the example of a kingpost truss, Tredgold illustrated how the parallelogram of forces could be used to analyze a statically determinate truss by calculating the components of axial force in each truss member (figure 4.23b). This is the same problem solved analytically by Navier in his *Résumé des leçons*, only now solved geometrically.

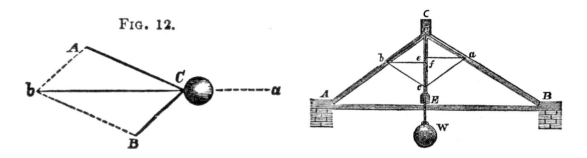

Figure 4.23 Left: 4.23a) Tredgold's illustration for finding the resultant of two forces graphically. **Right:** 4.23b) A kingpost roof truss used by Tredgold to demonstrate the parallelogram of forces. [Note: *C* added at top of kingpost.] In this diagram, the magnitude of the weight *W* is known and represented graphically by the length of *Cc*. Lines *ac* and *bc* are drawn parallel to members *AC* and *BC*, respectively; the lengths of *ac* and *bc* then represent the magnitudes of axial force in members *AC* and *BC*, respectively. Likewise, the horizontal line *bf* represents the horizontal component of force in *BC* as well as the thrust at B, and the horizontal line *ae* represents the horizontal component of force in *AC* as well as the thrust at A. The axial tensile force in member AB equilibrated the outward thrusts of AC and BC. From Thomas Tredgold, *Elementary Principles of Carpentry* (Philadelphia: E. L. Carey and A. Hart, 1837), Plate II, Fig. 11, art. 25, and Plate I, Fig. 4, art. 17.

American civil engineers Squire Whipple and Herman Haupt presented methods similar to Tredgold's in publications dating to 1847 and 1851. Graphical methods of analysis gained further popularity after the appearance of Karl Culmann's *Die Graphische Statik* in 1864, followed by works by American engineers Augustus Jay Du Bois, Charles Ezra Greene, and Henry T. Eddy in the 1870s.[28] In fact, Du Bois pointed out in 1875 that drawing the parallelogram of forces was unnecessary. It was much simpler, and just as accurate, to draw the forces (such as *ac* and *bc* in figure 4.23b) head to tail, with the resultant line drawn from the head of the first force to the tail of the last force being the line necessary to close the polygon, and therefore enforce equilibrium. Du Bois defined the *force polygon* as "the polygon formed by the successive laying off of the lines parallel and equal to the forces."[29] Squire Whipple was aware of this simplification much earlier, demonstrating use of the force polygon in his 1847 publication to graphically find the compressive force in the top chord of a truss (figure 4.24).

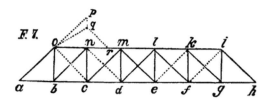

Figure 4.24 Whipple used a force polygon to find the compressive force in member *o-n*. From Squire Whipple, *A Work on Bridge Building: Consisting of Two Essays, the One Elementary and General, the Other Giving Original Plans and Practical Details for Iron and Wooden Bridges* (Utica, N.Y.: H. H. Curtiss, Printer, 1847), 12.

The *method of joints* is the algebraic counterpart of the force polygon, based on satisfying the three equations of equilibrium at every joint in a truss. Although Whipple did not name this method explicitly, it is clear that he used it in conjunction with the force polygon to determine the forces in a truss.

In addition to promoting the use of force polygons, Du Bois and Greene both presented the idea of the *equilibrium polygon*, a curve used to graphically represent the change in bending moment along the length of a beam. Shear and moment diagrams, derivatives of the equilibrium polygon, are instrumental in structural analysis today (figure 4.25).

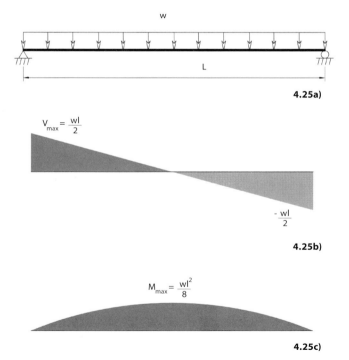

Figure 4.25 Graphical representation of the external forces and internal shears and moments in a simply-supported beam under uniform loads. The shear diagram (4.25b) demonstrates the change in shear V due to load w along the length of the beam; and the moment diagram (4.25c) demonstrates the change in bending moment M due to load w along the length of the beam.

Used in concert with Navier's beam analogy, such graphical representations of moment and shear in a beam could be used to calculate stresses in the chords and web members throughout the length of a truss. Using Navier's beam analogy to relate moment and chord force was described earlier in this chapter, but the analogy could be extended to calculate forces in the web members of the truss as well. Shear forces work to displace the top and bottom chords with respect to one another; it is the role of the web members to resist that relative displacement by developing tensile and compressive stresses. For a uniformly loaded beam with simple supports, shear force is highest at the ends of the beam and zero at the midpoint (figure 4.25). For a multiple-kingpost truss of the same length, the axial force in each diagonal truss brace is proportional to the shear force in the beam at the same location along the span, which means that the axial forces in the diagonal braces at the truss ends are higher than the axial forces in the diagonal braces near midspan of the truss (figure 4.26). With this understanding, braces could be sized to meet particular allowable stresses, though typically they were all the same size, which was dictated by the maximum axial force at the truss ends.

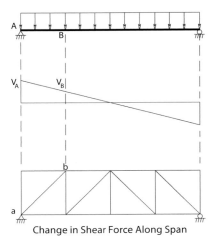

Change in Shear Force Along Span

Figure 4.26 In a uniformly loaded beam, the shear forces increase linearly from midspan to the supports. In a truss, shear forces are carried mainly by the diagonals; therefore the forces they carry also increase from midspan to the supports.

Stephen Long, who used Navier's beam analogy to size chord members, did not reveal in his writings whether he extended the analogy to size his braces and counterbraces. However, Haupt did so in 1851 when he demonstrated the use of the beam analogy to calculate axial force in the web members of a Town-lattice truss, described in his calculations for the Cumberland Valley Railroad Bridge.[30]

Mathematical modeling and structural analysis continue to be essential steps in the structural design of bridges, although the modeling has become substantially more complex since the development of structural analysis computer programs. Nevertheless, the most widely used tool still remains the first one formulated by Navier for the statically indeterminate three-member truss: linear elastic structural analysis (aka linear elastic finite element analysis), which will be discussed shortly.

Whether by algebraic or graphical means, bridge engineers used the mathematical modeling tools developed by Navier and those who came after him to estimate truss-member forces so that they could size the components of their bridges to perform within safe limits. In his *Résumé des leçons*, Navier introduced the idea that the allowable stress of wood in compression should be one-fifth its compressive strength. The ratio of actual strength to allowable stress came to be called the factor of safety. Tredgold collected and published the results of experimental work performed by Peter Barlow and numerous others and recommended a safety factor of four, while Mahan provided general values for allowable stresses in tension and compression only, invoking the safety factor of five suggested by Navier.[31] Numerous other sources between 1837 and 1908 published allowable stress values for different species of wood in tension, compression, bending, and shear; these published values often disagreed with each other.[32] It was not until 1934 that standard values were published for engineers' use in the *Guide to the Grading of Structural Timbers and the Determination of Working Stresses*. This publication not only standardized the allowable stresses used in design; it also provided a quantitative method for decreasing allowable stresses to account for knots and other natural defects in the wood.[33]

Foundations

To this point, the discussion of engineering issues has focused on the bridge itself, the superstructure. The engineering issues involved with the design of foundations, piers, and abutments were historically a vital part of bridge design and also worthy of consideration. For many covered bridges, the substructure cost more than the timber span it supported. In fact, most covered bridges were built through two separate contracts, one for the substructure masonry work and another for the truss fabrication. Shallows in large streams, islands, and rock outcroppings determined a bridge's location and road alignment and could lead a builder to construct several shorter spans instead of fewer longer ones. Where bedrock lay close to the surface, foundation construction could be easy and durable. In the absence of surface bedrock, a raft of heavy timbers, placed as deep below ground level as money and equipment would allow, served as a base for the foundation stonework. Because floodwaters could undercut a raft, this foundation type was best used where abutments could be set back from the channel and where there was less chance of the channel meandering.

Figure 4.27 Erecting piers in the mid-nineteenth century for a multi-span bridge across the Merrimack River in Haverhill, Massachusetts. Half of a stereograph courtesy of a private collection.

Deeply driven timber piles provided a more reliable foundation base than rafts, especially when used beneath piers in a channel. In the nineteenth century, straight tree trunks were the only piles available. These were pounded vertically into the ground, below the level desired for the foundation. A solid raft was installed atop the piles, and the masonry rose from there. When placed below the water table, timber piles and rafts did not decay.

Bridge piers and abutments were typically built of stone before the turn of the twentieth century, when concrete was more widely used. The best type of stonework was ashlar masonry, that is, cut stone blocks laid in regular courses. Less finished abutments and piers used irregularly sized and shaped stones. There was wide variation in stone dimensions, finishes, and mortar joints; for example, dry-laid large, flat stones formed the base for many bridges in the Northeast. Stone substructures were, in general, highly durable and were frequently reused when covered bridges were replaced. Many more survive today than is usually recognized. Often later topped with reinforced-concrete caps, they lie beneath more recent spans, continuing to support and carry traffic far beyond the lifespan that their builders envisioned.

Mortar provided uniform bearings for all types of masonry, reducing stress cracking and prolonging the life of the structure. The earliest builders used lime mortar, a combination of lime, sand, and water that gained strength by absorbing atmospheric carbon dioxide as it cured. Lime mortar dissolves in water, however, and is not suitable for masonry exposed to water. An important improvement in mortar occurred during the construction of the Erie Canal in New York in 1820, when Canvass White, an engineer working on the canal, identified a limestone near the canal route that, when processed, produced a waterproof hydraulic cement superior to any then in use. White's cement, which he patented, revolutionized the construction of masonry exposed to water. It was used to create "hydraulic mortars" that were not only durable in water but actually gained strength with exposure to water. An English mason, Joseph Aspdin, recognized that a hydraulic cement could be produced by firing and grinding a suitable combination of limestone and clay. He patented his process in 1824 and called his product "Portland cement." By the 1880s, Portland cement had replaced natural hydraulic cements in America; to this day it remains the most widely used cement in mortar. The two very different types of mortar, their many formulations, and the many ways they can be finished—indented, flat, protruding, rounded, or pointed—have led to wide-ranging opinions how best to build bridge substructures in stone.

The choice of truss affected the sizes and details of abutments and piers. A Burr-arch bridge required unique, angled bearing surfaces—often called "skewbacks"—in the faces of the abutments to receive the ends of the arch rings. Loading in a Town-lattice truss, however, was spread over multiple interlaced systems of diagonal boards instead of being concentrated at any single point. The abutments for Town lattices had to extend back along the line of the lattice far enough to receive the load from each diagonal system, a distance that could be as much as 20 feet, and piers had to be wide enough to receive the load from as many of the diagonal systems as possible. This explains why major Town-lattice trusses, such as the Cornish-Windsor Bridge, extend a substantial distance beyond the face of their abutments and need particularly wide piers. The interdependence of superstructure and substructure made selecting the optimal bridge style more complex than simply selecting the least expensive truss type.

Figure 4.28 Examples of bolster beams and skewbacks. **Left:** 4.28a) Bolster beam detail on Hall Bridge, Windham County, Vermont, installed by Graton Associates in 1982. HAER VT-40-7, Jet Lowe, photographer, 2009. **Right:** 4.28b) Cast-iron skewback and rod tying the Burr arch into the limestone abutment of J. J. Daniels's West Union Bridge (1876), Parke County, Indiana. The arches bear on an inclined bearing surface called a skewback. HAER IN-105-11, James Rosenthal, photographer, 2004.

Although the adjustable bearings that accommodate expansion and contraction on metal bridges were not needed on timber trusses, the chord timbers of covered bridges were placed on bearing beams of a durable species like white oak to raise them several inches above the stone abutments. This helped insulate the truss timbers from rainstorm splash and condensation. These bearing timbers (or bolster beams) were easily replaced if they deteriorated. Many early covered bridges also employed inferior arch braces that acted in compression, much like an arch, to decrease the tensile forces in the lower chords.

Joinery

The strength and durability of a wooden bridge was intimately linked to the quality of the connections used to fasten its structural members together. America's early bridge builders adopted simple wood trusses such as the kingpost and queenpost, which had been used for centuries in roofs and bridges in Europe. Eighteenth- and early-nineteenth-century roof trusses, such as those illustrated in Peter Nicholson's *The Carpenter's New Guide* (1793) and Owen Biddle's popular *Young Carpenter's Assistant* (1805), primarily used traditional mortise and tenon joinery, sometimes combined with reinforcing wrought-iron straps. As builders sought to span longer distances, carry heavier and faster moving live loads, and incorporate greater resistance to the elements, they adopted more innovative truss forms and, correspondingly, more innovative joinery.[34]

Relatively simple truss forms such as the kingpost, queenpost, and multiple kingpost relied on diagonal braces to transfer axial forces from the top chords of a bridge to the bottom chords—following Navier's beam analogy, the diagonal braces served to resist shear forces. Generally, these braces were framed into the posts, either using mortise and tenon joints or by notching the post through its entire depth and fitting the end of the brace into the notch.

Many builders preferred framing the braces into full-depth notches because the mortise and tenon joint presented certain shortcomings when used in bridges. It was expensive, requiring skilled craftsmen to make precise cuts. Poorly constructed joints were easy to hide, and even the best joints were susceptible to rot from water infiltration. As Robert Fulton observed, "Hitherto, in bridges not covered from the weather, the immense quantity of mortices and tenons, which, however well done, will admit air and wet, and consequently tend to expedite the decay of the weak parts, has been a material error in constructing bridges of wood." Additionally, cutting tenons in the ends of compression members also reduced the amount of bearing area available.[35]

Because braces were oriented to remain in compression under a uniform load, the brace-to-post connections had to transfer compressive forces only. Most early carpentry manuals did not provide details for brace-to-post connections, but Thomas Tredgold's *Elementary Principles of Carpentry* illustrated several for use in roof trusses. The different connections reproduced in figure 4.29 illustrate a detail common to simpler truss forms: a bearing surface on the post perpendicular to the direction of the wood fibers in the brace. To provide this surface, the top and bottom of the post had to be much wider than the rest of the post, requiring the removal of a significant amount of material along the length of the post. Both Tredgold and Dennis Hart Mahan stressed the importance of providing such a bearing surface. If it could not be achieved, Tredgold suggested cutting the end of the brace so that only a portion of it bore on the post in a direction perpendicular to its fibers.

Not all builders followed this suggestion. Theodore Burr suggested that braces "may be put into the corners where the posts are united to the chord and crown plates without tenon or mortise by cutting the angle of the ends of the brace to correspond with the lines of the chords, plates and kingposts, allowing the angle to be partly on each as may suit, in equal proportion is best, or by square or shoulders with tenon and mortise."[36]

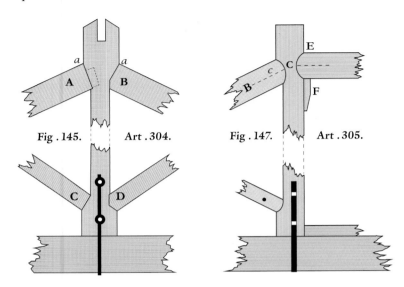

Figure 4.29 Tredgold's 1837 volume included examples of brace-to-post connections with both **Left:** 4.29a) traditional and **Right:** 4.29b) rounded ends. Tredgold (and Mahan) proposed using rounded surface joints so that, as the truss settled, the joint simply rotated like a ball in a socket. The labor involved in forming them likely made them unpopular, and, indeed, they are unknown in any American bridge. Still, their existence illustrates that the short-comings of traditional framing were already understood, leading bridge builders to search for better methods. From Tredgold, *Elementary Principles of Carpentry*, Plate XXII.

A significant weakness associated with traditional brace-to-post connections was that, over time, truss settlement caused the braces to rotate, leading to an uneven distribution of pressure across the connected surfaces. To compensate for this, Tredgold suggested that the joint between the central post and the diagonals be left a little open, "so that when the roof settles it may not bear upon the acute angle." (See the top joints in figure 4.29a.)[37]

As the need for longer trusses emerged, so too did the need for counterbraces to resist the shear forces caused by moving live loads. Counterbraces were the diagonal members whose orientation was opposite to that of the braces. Under a uniform (dead) load, counterbraces experienced only tension forces; since none of the traditional brace-to-post connections could effectively transfer tension forces between a wood counterbrace and wood post, the counterbrace was essentially ineffective unless called into action by a moving live load (figure 4.30). In addition, timber shrinkage and bridge settlement increased the axial compressive forces in the braces and tended to loosen the

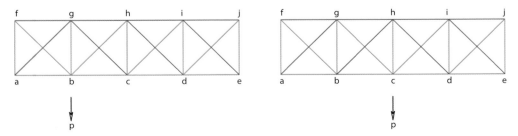

Figure 4.30 The sense of the forces in the diagonals can change for different positions of a live load. With the live load at point *b*, the force in member *gc* is compression; when the live load moves to point *c*, the force in member gc is tension.

counterbraces, making them ineffective. So, while early builders understood that counterbraces were necessary to increase the stiffness of a truss (and both Timothy Palmer and Theodore Burr used counterbraces in their early long-span bridges), they were rarely employed in simpler truss forms because builders lacked effective means for positively connecting them to the posts.

Builder Lewis Wernwag recognized the shortcomings of mortise and tenon joinery and the problems created by timber shrinkage at the turn of the nineteenth century. He went to special lengths to prevent dry rot, hoping to forestall these problems in both his famous 1812 design for the 340-foot Fairmount Bridge near Philadelphia, known as the Colossus, and his bridge crossing the Delaware River between New Hope, Pennsylvania, and Lambertville, New Jersey. By sawing the timbers through the heart, Wernwag exposed any defects. He used iron links and screw bolts to provide air space between the bridge components. In addition, Wernwag minimized mortise and tenon connections, and, as shrinkage appeared in the bridge, the timbers could be screwed closer together.[38]

Instead of mortise and tenon joints for the diagonal-to-post connections of his bridge crossing the Delaware River, Wernwag placed cast-iron shoes on the lower chords at each panel point; the posts were positioned in the middle of the blocks while angled bearing surfaces were provided on each side for the braces and counterbraces. A bridge company official insisted that the design "guards more effectually against decay, perhaps, than any other." To counteract sagging, Wernwag installed wrought-iron rods parallel to each counterbrace that could be tightened as the wood dried.[39]

Stephen Long revolutionized long-span truss construction with his 1830 patent in which counterbraces were prestressed in every panel by driving wooden wedges between the counterbraces and chords, thus eliminating the need to provide a positive connection between the counterbraces and the posts. As described in chapter 5, if a bridge built to Long's design sagged due to shrinking timbers, the counterbraces would lose some of their compressive force but still retain enough compression to remain in place and effective. As the bridge sagged over time, the wedges could be further driven in to increase the compressive force in the counterbraces.

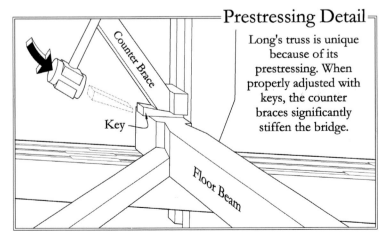

Prestressing Detail

Long's truss is unique because of its prestressing. When properly adjusted with keys, the counter braces significantly stiffen the bridge.

Counter Brace

Key

Floor Beam

Figure 4.31 Long's prestressing technique allowed counterbraces to be effectively incorporated into a truss, but it required an innovative connection between the diagonal and the post, including wooden wedges which were driven below the counterbrace to induce compression in the member. HAER OH-122, detail from sheet 6, William Dickinson, delineator, 2002.

Despite Long's innovative method of prestressing, his design still required laboriously cutting daps (notches) in the verticals and the top and bottom chords. William Howe's second 1840 patent, however, simplified the prestressing process by replacing vertical wood posts with threaded wrought-iron rods, which could be tightened (post-tensioned) to maintain compression in the braces and counterbraces,

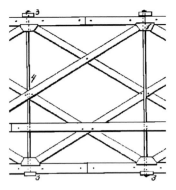

Figure 4.32 An interior panel from Howe's second 1840 patent, showing the angle blocks at each panel point, through which the iron rods passed, and to which the braces and counter-braces abutted. U.S. Patent No. 1,711, August 3, 1840.

thereby counteracting the effects of long-term increases in strain. Oak angle blocks, through which the threaded rods passed, replaced traditional joinery for the brace and counterbrace connections at the panel points. Eventually, Howe switched his angle blocks from wood to cast iron, like Wernwag's in the Colossus.[40]

Caleb and Thomas Pratt patented another version of the prestressed truss in 1844, this time replacing wood braces and counterbraces with wrought iron. They achieved prestressing by tightening the diagonal members so that they carried tension forces, which put the wood vertical posts in compression. The braces and counterbraces were connected to the panel points through wood blocks positioned above the top chord and below the bottom chord; they passed through these blocks and were secured with nuts. The system was susceptible to local crushing of the wood chord members at the connection points from the prestressing force in the diagonal members.[41]

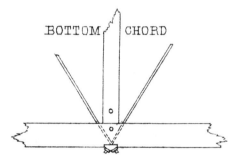

Figure 4.33 Typical connection between iron rods and lower chord in a Pratt truss. From Herman Haupt, *The General Theory of Bridge Construction* (New York: D. Appleton and Co., 1851), Plate 6

In a through truss, floor beams transfer floor and live loads to the lower chords at each panel point, and these loads are in turn transferred to the posts. Like brace connections, the post-to-lower-chord connections used in early American bridge trusses were adapted from traditional roof trusses, in which the posts were connected to the lower chords by mortise and tenon joints. Mortise and tenon joints alone were incapable of transferring tension forces from the chords to the posts; therefore, treenails were driven through the lower chords and the post tenons to connect them (figure 4.35a). The capacity of these connections depended on the strength of the treenails, and, as early as 1837, Dennis Hart Mahan observed that overstressing of mortise and tenon joints was common due to the "practice among workmen to make the hole in the tenon [for the treenail] nearer to the surface than that through the mortise, for the purpose of making a close joint." He thought the technique "very pernicious," as it placed "a great strain on the pin, and on the side of the tenon hole, which might cause one or the other to give way, if an additional strain were to take place, arising from any motion of the two beams."[42] Early builders commonly supplemented the treenails in mortise and tenon joints with iron U-straps in spans over 30 feet.

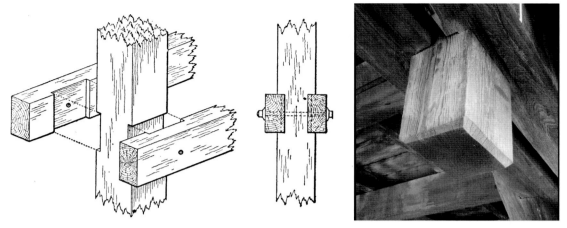

Figure 4.34 Typical detail of a double-notched post connection. **Left:** 4.34a) From Henry Jacoby, *Structural Details, or Elements of Design in Heavy Framing* (New York: J. Wiley & Sons, 1909), 135. **Right:** 4.34b) Detail of Leatherwood Station Bridge (1899), in Parke County, Indiana, HAER IN-40-15, Ed Sels, photographer, 1979.

Mortise and tenon joinery fell out of favor in roof trusses about 1840, and Mahan's *Elementary Course of Civil Engineering* suggests a similar timeline for changes in bridge truss joinery. The first edition describes fastening the foot of a kingpost "by a stirrup of iron, or by a tenon and mortise." The third edition, published in 1846, instructs builders instead to make the connection with "a bolt, an iron stirrup, or a suitable joint."[43]

Mahan's "suitable joint" was likely the double-notched joint shown in figure 4.34a, commonly seen in most surviving covered bridges. Like the mortise and tenon before it, the double-notched connection was susceptible to damage from shrinkage. Stephen Buonopane, in his 2010 study of Smith-truss connections completed for the HAER program, observed that the shear strength in the connection was often compromised by a partial cleavage crack that initiated in the corner of the post notch in line with the would-be shear plane. The crack likely began as the post attempted to shrink toward its centerline. The shrinkage was opposed, however, by a force stemming from the friction between the bottom of the lower chord and the top of the post notch (figure 4.35b).[44]

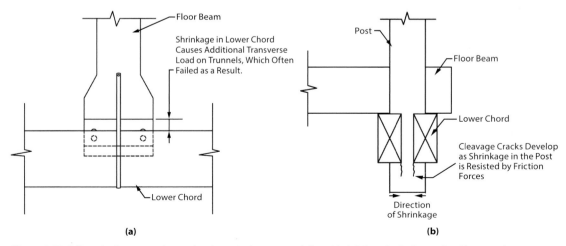

Figure 4.35 Failures in the post-to-lower-chord connection may result from (a) shrinkage in the lower chord in a mortise and tenon connection and (b) shrinkage in the post in a double-notch connection.

As bridge spans exceeded the length of available timber, the chords had to be fabricated from shorter members, often called string pieces, which were connected together through tension splices. Tension splices were most often employed in lower chords, but Long described continuous spans which required tension splices in the top chords over the piers. Tension splices, no matter how well designed, inherently reduced the strength of bridge members. Herman Haupt conservatively suggested in 1851 that lower chords consist of four parallel beams, with the necessary splices staggered in such a way that only a single splice occurred at the center of any one panel. Long suggested three string pieces, with the two exterior pieces spliced at the same location along the span, alternating with the location of the interior splice. He noted that the exterior pieces, which together made up twice the area of the interior piece, should be continuous for as long as possible at the center of the bridge, where tension in the lower chord was greatest.[45]

Bridge builders often used splices such as the fishplate joint and the scarf joint that were common in wood shipbuilding. The fishplate joint (figure 4.36) minimized the removal of material from the chord member by incorporating a piece of timber bolted to one or both sides of the string pieces being spliced. Long specified this type of splice in his 1830 patent, illustrating both wood and iron fishplates. When made of wood, the fishplates were cut with notches to fit into corresponding notches on the string pieces. Thus, the tension force in one side of the string piece was transferred to the other side via the shear and bearing strength of the notches in the fishplate and the string piece, as well as the tensile strength of each cross-section. The strength of the joint also depended on clamping bolts to prevent rotation in the eccentrically loaded splices; without the clamping bolts, the fishplate would flex and fail. Tredgold cautioned bridge builders not to rely too heavily on bolt strength, for, as timbers shrank, the clamping force of the bolts diminished as did the friction between the connected pieces. If the joint relied too heavily on a small diameter bolt, the bolt would crush the timber, causing "the joint to yield." He suggested that dependence on the bolts be lessened "by indenting the parts together . . . or by putting keys in the joint."[46]

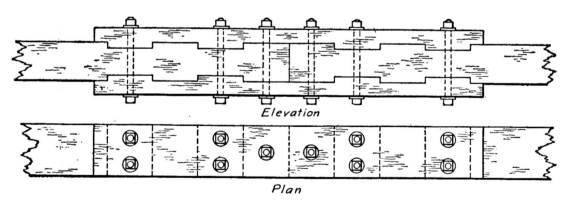

Elevation

Plan

Figure 4.36 Tabled fishplate joint. From Jacoby, *Structural Details*, 91.

Where a fishplate joint used exterior pieces to transfer the tension force between string pieces, a scarf joint relied only on notches cut into the ends of the two chord members being joined. Tredgold noted that because making a scarf required removing at least half the cross-sectional area of each timber being joined, these joints were more vulnerable to tension rupture than fishplate joints. Therefore, he advised that scarf joints should only be used "wherever neatness is preferable to strength." As in fishplate joints, clamping bolts were required in scarf joints to prevent excessive flexural stresses from developing in the string pieces.[47]

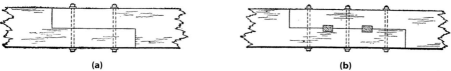

Figure 4.37 (a) Half-lapped scarf joint, (b) with keys. From Jacoby, *Structural Details*, 125.

Figure 4.38 (a) Straight tabled scarf joint, (b) with key. From Jacoby, *Structural Details*, 126

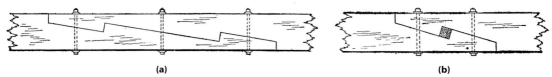

Figure 4.39 (a) Oblique tabled scarf joint (b) with key. From Jacoby, *Structural Details*, 127.

Ithiel Town's lattice trusses were constructed entirely of wood, yet they avoided both mortise and tenon joints and tension splices, relying instead on lapped joints connected by treenails to transfer loads between members. Town instructed builders of his truss design to use round, 1-1/2 inch diameter seasoned treenails cut from white oak, with three to four treenails per joint. Town claimed that the redundancy of having a considerable number of connections transferring shear forces from the chords through the lattice into the abutments was "a very important advantage over any other mode."[48]

Town's lower chords were built up from two beams, approximately 3 to 3-1/2 inches thick by 10 to 11 inches wide, with joints staggered along their length. Treenail connections between the chords and the lattice members were so regularly spaced that creating tension joints in the lower chords was unnecessary. Historic preservation engineer David Fischetti has suggested that treenails both united the chords and lattice together and allowed for "load sharing within the individual chord sticks to provide continuity through joint locations."[49]

Herman Haupt acknowledged that the force in the diagonal ties and braces in a Town-lattice truss was difficult to estimate correctly. The ability of Town's treenail connections to transfer loads depended on the treenails' strength in bearing perpendicular to grain, in horizontal shear, and in bending, as well as the strength of the lattice members in bearing on end grain. Civil engineer Lewis M. Prevost noted in the 1840s that the lattice members were known to split at their ends as a result of the treenails bearing on end grain. Squire Whipple thought the treenails themselves, not the lattice members, limited the strength of the connections, since their lateral strength was less than the strength of the end grain of the lattice members through which they passed.[50]

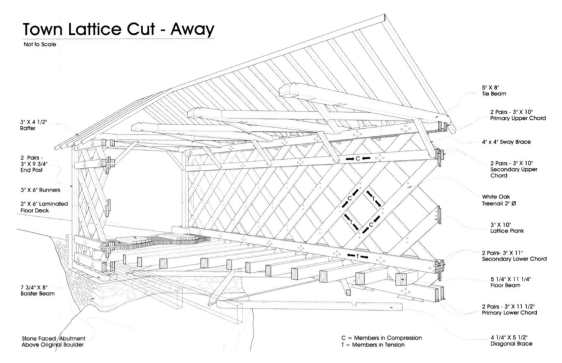

Town Lattice Cut - Away
Not to Scale

5" X 8"
Tie Beam

2 Pairs - 3" X 10"
Primary Upper Chord

4" x 4" Sway Brace

2 Pairs - 3" X 10"
Secondary Upper
Chord

White Oak
Treenail 2" Ø

3" X 10"
Lattice Plank

2 Pairs- 3" X 11"
Secondary Lower Chord

5 1/4" X 11 1/4"
Floor Beam

2 Pairs - 3" X 11 1/2"
Primary Lower Chord

4 1/4" X 5 1/2"
Diagonal Brace

3" X 4 1/2"
Rafter

2 Pairs -
3" X 9 3/4"
End Post

3" X 6" Runners

2" X 6" Laminated
Floor Deck

7 3/4" X 8"
Bolster Beam

Stone Faced Abutment
Above Original Boulder

C = Members in Compression
T = Members in Tension

Figure 4.40 Treenail connections on the Town lattice of Nichols Powers's Brown Bridge (1880), Rutland County, Vermont. Four treenails per joint were used on the primary and secondary upper chords, while two treenails were adequate on the typical lattice connections. HAER VT-28, sheet 6, Naomi Hernandez, delineator, 2002.

After 1830, the construction of heavy timber roof trusses was outpaced by light wood roof trusses, as stick framing became a more economical type of building construction. The economy came, in part, from the reduced skill needed for light wood frame construction. Light wood roof trusses did not require—nor could they accommodate—traditional wooden joinery; as a consequence, metal dowel-type connectors and, later, metal plates, replaced such detailing. Covered wooden bridges continued to be built using traditional methods and traditional joinery, particularly in rural areas, where heavy timbers and skilled craftsmen were available, but at a reduced rate. Even when new covered bridges are constructed, it is more common to see modern engineered solutions to either reduce the number of connections needed (such as glued laminated lower chords to eliminate the need for traditional tension splices) or to simplify the bridge's construction and maintenance.

Present-Day Engineering Design and Covered Bridges
By the 1830s, American bridge builders, benefiting from the work of Navier, had begun incorporating the science of structural engineering into their work. Some, like Stephen Long, had the advantage of formal education, but many learned their trade while working on that great engine of innovation, the American railroad. Understanding the evolution of their engineering knowledge is vital to appreciating and preserving innumerable historic covered bridges. This greater historical awareness has also informed a new era of covered bridge building, so that covered bridge construction is no longer a lost art.

Over time, standards and codes have been developed that prescribe loads, design procedures for wood, safe bridge geometries, and other safety features. These regulatory standards constrain the design of new covered bridges far beyond those with which nineteenth-century bridge designers and builders worked. Moreover, the design process now includes more stakeholders with different views of the cultural role of covered bridges, appropriate materials, structural forms, and appearance. Structural engineers need to be responsive to this variety of viewpoints while designing bridges that meet all safety requirements. Creating a responsive engineering design for a new covered bridge requires a deep understanding of historic designs.

The Federal Highway Administration's *Covered Bridge Manual* and David Fischetti have presented case studies of new covered bridge designs.[51] Many more new covered bridge designs will be found in the portfolios of engineering firms that specialize in heavy timber framing and covered bridges.

In addition to designing new covered bridges, structural engineers are commonly called upon to assign live-load capacities and to design rehabilitations, or interventions, for existing bridges. These tasks are arguably more challenging than designing new bridges because they require an appreciation for and an understanding of the historic engineering designs and the processes that resulted in the construction of these bridges. The structural assessment of a standing structure by engineers includes the condition of a bridge's materials, connections, vertical- and lateral-load carrying systems, floors, bearings, and foundations. The most widely used tools are inspection and analytical modeling, but the engineer's toolkit also features non-destructive testing and ad hoc load testing. Considerable uncertainty often remains following an assessment, and load ratings must necessarily be conservative, since the methods used have not been calibrated by actual strength tests in the field.

Whether designing a new bridge, load rating an existing bridge, or designing a rehabilitation, the main tool used by structural engineers is *linear elastic finite element analysis* (LEFEA) of mathematical models of a bridge. If material properties are conservatively estimated and the strengths of the connections are assured, then a design procedure based on LEFEA leads to a bridge strength that is greater than the loads the bridge was designed to support. Because LEFEA does not estimate the actual strength of a bridge or its subsystems, the reliability of a design cannot be estimated. In general, engineers to this day are not able to precisely predict the strength of statically indeterminate wood trusses. Linear elastic structural analysis involves working with significant uncertainties, especially when engineers use it to assess historic covered bridges for rehabilitation. To start, the material elastic properties of a bridge's structural components are usually uncertain, as are the initial member stresses induced during fabrication and erection. The time-dependent stress/strain behavior of wood can cause a redistribution of forces in statically indeterminate trusses that is difficult to account for, and even the inevitable minor foundation settlements can influence forces in wood bridges. Finally, the modeling of connections is difficult and produces highly uncertain results. These issues combine with uncertainty in the loads to make the results of linear elastic analyses highly approximate. Perhaps the most significant limitation of LEFEA is that it provides only a lower-bound estimate of the strength of a bridge, and even this estimate is generally uncertain because connection strength rather than member strength can determine the capacity of a bridge.

The historic period of covered bridge construction in America was a time of innovation and creativity. Capitalizing on the vast woodlands native to the country, bridge builders, intent on providing strong, durable bridges as economically as possible, devised a wide range of structural systems. Various designs adjusted to and reflected the needs and constraints of regional and local conditions. It was also an era when American engineers began the development of scientific methods for bridge design, and many covered bridges played key roles in the refinement of that process.

The increasing sophistication of bridge design coincided with the growth of American railroads, and covered bridges provided an economical and efficient design choice as these lines expanded across the nation. Because of this early adoption, covered bridges—which are now exclusively linked with highways—were important elements in the innovations fostered by civil engineers working for the railroads. Since so few railroad covered bridges remain today, it is easy to overlook their critical place in the gradual professionalization of American engineering.

Beyond this purely historical perspective, an appreciation of the engineering heritage and thought processes that resulted in the completion of these bridges is important as a guide for those planning historic preservation projects. Judgments on the proper technique for a restoration or rehabilitation of a historic bridge must start with an understanding of the original decisions made in the creation of that structure. Every historic project administrator must gain a respect for the men who designed and built America's covered bridges. And that respect begins with a thorough understanding of the thought processes that went into the creation of a covered bridge, thought processes we label historic engineering concepts.

Endnotes

1 Eda Kranakis, *Constructing a Bridge: An Exploration of Engineering Culture, Design, and Research in Nineteenth Century France and America* (Cambridge, Mass.: MIT Press, 1997).

2 Thomas Young, *A Course of Lectures on Natural Philosophy and the Mechanical Arts*, 2 vols. (London: J. Johnson, 1807).

3 See for example Lorenzo Mascheroni, "Nuove ricerche sull' equilibrio delle volte," *Biblioteca Scelta di Opere Italiane Antiche e Moderne* 236 (1829).

4 D. A. Gasparini and Caterina Provost, "Early Nineteenth Century Developments in Truss Design in Britain, France and the United States," *Construction History* 5 (1989): 22.

5 Stephen H. Long, "Railways and Canals," *Port Folio* 276 and 277 (May and April 1825), 353.

6 Stephen H. Long, "Description of a Patent for Certain Improvements in the Construction of Wooden or Frame Bridges," *Journal of the Franklin Institute* 5, no. 4 (April 1830): 231–35. This article was republished in Stephen H. Long, *Description of the Jackson Bridge together with Directions to Builders of Wooden or Frame Bridges* (Baltimore: Sands & Neilson, 1830).

7 Long, *Description of the Jackson Bridge*; Stephen H. Long, *Description of Col. Long's Bridges, Together With a Series of Directions to Bridge Builders* (Concord, N.H.: John F. Brown Printers, 1836).

8 George W. Cullum, *Biographical Register of the Officers and Graduates of the U.S. Military Academy at West Point . . .* , vol. 1 (New York: D. Van Nostrand, 1868), 256–57.

9 Dennis Hart Mahan, *An Elementary Course of Civil Engineering for the Use of the Cadets of the United States Military Academy*, 1st ed. (New York: Wiley and Putnam, 1837), quote from p. vii.

10 C. L. Navier, *Rapport à Monsieur Becquey . . . et mémoire sur les ponts suspendus* (Paris: L'Imprimerie Royale, 1823); Stephen Buonopane and David Billington, "Theory and History of Suspension Bridge Design from 1823 to 1940," *Journal of Structural Engineering* 119, no. 3 (March 1993): 954–77.

11 Tom F. Peters, *Transitions in Engineering: Guillaume Henri Dufour and the Early 19th Century Cable Suspension Bridges* (Boston: Birkhäuser Verlag, 1987), 111.

12 Peters, *Transitions in Engineering*, 111.

13 Gasparini and Provost, "Early Nineteenth Century Developments," 28–30; S. H. Long, *Rail Road Manual, or a Brief Exposition of Principles and Deductions Applicable in Tracing the Route of a Rail Road* (Baltimore: Wm. Wooddy, Printer, 1828).

14 Squire Whipple, *A Work on Bridge Building Consisting of Two Essays, the One Elementary and General, the Other Giving Original Plans and Details for Iron and Wooden Bridges* (Utica, N.Y.: H. H. Curtiss, Printer, 1847), 83; Herman Haupt, *The General Theory of Bridge Construction* (New York: D. Appleton and Co., 1851), 99.

15 J. A. L. Waddell, *General Specifications for Highway Bridges of Iron and Steel*, 2d ed. (Kansas City, Mo.: Selden G. Spencer, 1889), 25.

16 John C. Trautwine, *The Civil Engineer's Pocket-Book* (Philadelphia: Claxton, Remsen & Haffelfinger, 1872), 519; idem, *The Civil Engineer's Pocket-Book* (New York: Wiley, 1904), 713.

17 G. Bouscaren, *Report on the Progress of Work and Cost of Construction of the Cincinnati Southern Railway* (Cincinnati: Wrightson & Co., 1878).

Endnotes

[18] Theodore Cooper, "General Specifications for Iron Bridges," *Engineering News* (May 31, 1879), 174–75.

[19] John Smeaton, *An Experimental Enquiry Concerning the Natural Powers of Water and Wind to Turn Mills, and other Machines, depending on a Circular Motion* (London: [s.n.], 1760), 67–68; Julius Weisbach, *Principles of the Mechanics of Machinery and Engineering,* edited by Walter R. Johnson, 2 vols. (Philadelphia: Lea and Blanchard, 1848–49).

[20] Thomas Tredgold, *Elementary Principles of Carpentry* (Philadelphia: E. L. Carey and A. Hart, 1837), 245.

[21] Tredgold, *Elementary Principles of Carpentry*, 172.

[22] Long, *Description of the Jackson Bridge*, 9.

[23] Whipple, *Work on Bridge Building*, 95–98.

[24] Lorna J. Gibson and Michael F. Ashby, *Cellular Solids: Structures and Properties* (Cambridge: Cambridge University Press, 1999).

[25] Thomas Tredgold, *Practical Essay on the Strength of Cast Iron and Other Metals* (London, 1822); Whipple, *Work on Bridge Building*, 59.

[26] R. A. Mott, *Henry Cort, The Great Finer: Creator of Puddled Iron* (London: Metals Society, 1983).

[27] Tredgold, *Elementary Principles of Carpentry*, 13.

[28] Whipple, *Work on Bridge Building*; Haupt, *General Theory of Bridge Construction*; Karl Culmann, *Die Graphische Statik* (Zurich: Verlag Von Meyer & Zeller, 1864); Augustus Jay Du Bois, *The Elements of Graphical Statics and Their Application to Framed Structures* (New York: John Wiley and Sons, 1875); Charles E. Greene, *Graphics for Engineers, Architects, and Builders: A Manual for Designers, and a Text-Book for Scientific Schools, Trusses and Arches Analyzed and Discussed by Graphical Methods* (New York: John Wiley and Sons, 1879); Henry T. Eddy, *New Construction in Graphical Statics* (New York: D. Van Nostrand, 1877); Stephen P. Timoshenko, *History of Strength of Materials* (New York: McGraw-Hill Book Company, 1953). Dr. Frank Rausche translated the works of Culmann for Dario Gasparini.

[29] Augustus Jay Du Bois, *The New Method of Graphical Statics* (New York: D. Van Nostrand 1875), 11; Whipple, *Work on Bridge Building*, 12.

[30] Haupt, *General Theory of Bridge Construction*, 237–41.

[31] Tredgold, *Elementary Principles of Carpentry*, 40; Mahan, *Elementary Course of Civil Engineering*, 39.

[32] See, for example, Whipple, *Work on Bridge Building*; Haupt, *General Theory of Bridge Construction;* Augustus Jay Du Bois, *The Strains in Framed Structures* (New York: John Wiley and Sons, 1883); Milo S. Ketchum, *The Design of Highway Bridges and the Calculation of Stresses in Bridge Trusses* (New York: Engineering News Publishing Co., 1908).

[33] T. R. C. Wilson, *Guide to the Grading of Structural Timbers and the Determination of Working Stresses*, Miscellaneous Publication No. 185 (Washington, D. C.: U.S. Department of Agriculture, 1934).

[34] Llewellyn Edwards, *A Record of History and Evolution of Early American Bridges* (Orono, Maine: University Press, 1959); Jan Lewandowski, et al., *Historic American Roof Trusses* (Becket, Mass.:

Endnotes

Timber Framers Guild, 2006); Peter Nicholson, *The Carpenter's New Guide* (London: J. Taylor, 1808), plate 42.

35 Robert Fulton quoted in Ithiel Town, "A Description of Ithiel Town's Improvement in the Construction of Wood and Iron Bridges: Intended as a General System of Bridge-Building . . . ," *American Journal of Sciences and Arts* 3, no. 1 (New Haven, Conn.: S. Converse, 1821): 165.

36 Tredgold, *Elementary Principles of Carpentry*, 163; Mahan, *Elementary Course*; Burr quote from Edwards, *Record of History and Evolution of Early American Bridges*, 51.

37 Tredgold, *Elementary Principles of Carpentry*, 162.

38 Lee H. Nelson, *The Colossus of 1812: An American Engineering Superlative* (New York: ASCE Press, 1999), 32.

39 Nelson, *Colossus of 1812*, 38.

40 Robert Fletcher and J. P. Snow, "A History of the Development of Wooden Bridges," *American Society of Civil Engineering Proceedings* 53 (1932): 1455–98.

41 Dario Gasparini and David Simmons, "American Truss Bridge Connections in the Nineteenth Century. I: 1829–1850," *Journal of Performance of Constructed Facilities* 11, no. 3 (August 1997): 119–29.

42 Quote from Mahan, *Elementary Course*, 107.

43 Mahan, *Elementary Course*, 1st ed. (1837), 164; Mahan, *Elementary Course*, 3rd ed. (1846), 177.

44 Stephen Buonopane, "Structural Study of Smith Trusses," HAER No. PA-645, 2010.

45 Long, *Description of Col. Long's Bridges*, 30-31; Haupt, *General Theory of Bridge Construction*, 116.

46 Tredgold, *Elementary Principles of Carpentry*, 157.

47 Tredgold, *Elementary Principles of Carpentry*, 157.

48 Ithiel Town, *A Description of Ithiel Town's Improvement in the Construction of Wood and Iron Bridges* (New Haven: S. Converse, 1821), 163.

49 David Fischetti, *Structural Investigation of Historic Buildings: A Case Study Guide to Preservation Technology for Buildings, Bridges, Towers, and Mills* (Hoboken, N.J.: John Wiley and Sons, 2009), 217.

50 Haupt, *General Theory of Bridge Construction*; Lewis M. Prevost, "Description of Howe's Patent Truss Bridge," *Journal of the Franklin Institute* 3, no. 5 (May 1842): 289–92; Whipple, *Work on Bridge Building*, 97.

51 P. C. Pierce, R. L. Brungraber, A. Lichtenstein, and A. Sabol, *Covered Bridge Manual*, publication no. FHWA-HRT-04-098 (U. S. Department of Transportation, Federal Highway Administration, Turner-Fairbank Highway Research Center, April 2005); Fischetti, *Structural Investigation of Historic Buildings*.

Chapter 5

The Development of the American Truss

by Dario Gasparini, Rachel H. Sangree, and Matthew Reckard;
edited by David A. Simmons

The sixteenth-century Italian architect Andrea Palladio is generally credited with developing the structural form known as the truss, which is a simple framed structure composed of straight members connected together to act as a single rigid body. The simplest possible truss is a triangle, and any truss is essentially an assemblage of connected triangles. A discussion of the most important truss systems used by American wooden-bridge builders follows.

Early Truss Forms

Truss bridges in America developed gradually from simpler structural forms. The simple beam bridge set on piles was the most common waterway crossing used in seventeenth- and eighteenth-century America. Examples include the Charles River bridge built in 1660, a bridge erected in 1792 over the Merrimack River, and another that crossed the Mohawk River in 1795. Early bridge historians suggested that these structures were modeled after the famous ancient bridge built over the Rhine in 55 BC on Julius Caesar's orders, but it is more likely that carpenters simply applied their general knowledge of construction to create these practical forms. The drawbacks with this type of bridge were that ice flows and high water could "quickly carry it seaward in little pieces." Nevertheless, simple beam bridges are still in use today, though they are normally reserved for spanning small waterways in rural areas.[1]

Figure 5.1 Roman Bridge over the Rhine. From Thomas Pope, *A Treatise on Bridge Architecture* (New York: A. Niven, 1811), 40. Courtesy of George Peabody Library, The Sheridan Libraries, Johns Hopkins University.

To extend the length of a simple beam bridge, inclined struts were sometimes installed between the abutment faces and the bottom of the beam, effectively shortening the span length of the simple beam. Early-nineteenth-century civil engineer Dennis Hart Mahan described several methods for executing this form while minimizing stresses at the point of contact between the strut and the beam, including proposing the addition of a "straining beam" between the ends of the struts (figure 5.2a). This form also had an ancient precedent, having been used by Palladio for his 1569 bridge at Bassano (figure 5.2b). Col. Enoch Hale reportedly built the first strutted beam bridge in the United States in 1785 over the Connecticut River at Bellows Falls, Vermont.[2]

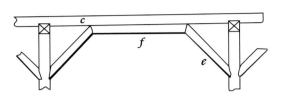

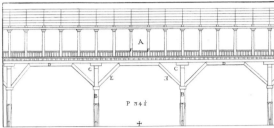

Figure 5.2 Left: 5.2a) Illustration of a longitudinal beam *c* strengthened with the use of corbels *e* and a straining beam *f* from Dennis Hart Mahan, *An Elementary Course of Civil Engineering* (New York: Wiley and Halstead, 1857), 176; **Right:** 5.2b) Palladio's Bridge at Bassano, from Andrea Palladio, *The Four Books of Architecture* (reprint, New York: Dover Publications, Inc., 1965), third book, plate VI.

Despite the innovation of Hale's bridge, placing struts below the deck of a bridge was often impractical because it left them vulnerable to damage from waterway debris and decay from exposure. Furthermore, struts provided limited opportunities for increasing the length of a crossing. The next logical step was to shift the struts and the straining beam to a position above the deck. Kingpost and queenpost trusses—the "royal family" trusses as they were called by historian Richard Sanders Allen—had long been used in roof construction before being adopted by bridge builders. Both forms employed a "suspension piece" to support the deck; the kingpost used a single, central suspension piece for spans between 20 and 30 feet (figure 5.3), and the queenpost extended that span length by using dual suspension pieces with a straining beam between (figure 5.4).[3]

Under an evenly distributed load (e.g. when the self-weight or "dead" load was more or less evenly distributed to each panel point), the king- and queenpost bridges transferred loads to the abutments through tension in the posts and lower chord, compression in the braces, and, in the case of the queenpost truss, the straining beam (figures 5.3a and 5.4a). Live loads caused a similar distribution of axial forces in the kingpost (figure 5.3b), as there was only one lower panel point between supports—at midspan—for live load to be transferred from the road surface to the truss. In the queenpost, on the other hand, the existence of two panel points meant that live load was transferred to the truss asymmetrically, causing shear deformation in the traditionally open center panel; for this reason, Mahan suggested that bracing be provided in the center panel for queenposts of longer spans.[4] Assuming that the center panel braces could resist

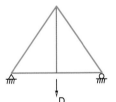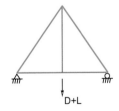

Figure 5.3 Axial forces that develop in a kingpost truss resulting from **Left:** 5.3a) dead load and **Right:** 5.3b) dead load and live load. Red indicates compression, blue indicates tension.

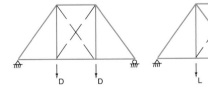

Figure 5.4 Axial forces that develop in a queenpost truss from **Left:** 5.4a) dead loads and **Right:** 5.4b) an asymmetric live load. The center panel braces in 5.4b) were suggested by Mahan in 1857 to resist panel shear caused by the asymmetric live load. Red indicates compression; blue indicates tension; and black dashes indicate zero force, assuming that the brace-to-post connection is unable to transmit tension forces.

only compressive forces (reliable tension connections were difficult to construct), an asymmetric live load would produce compression in one brace and no force in the other (figure 5.4b).

The simple kingpost form could be expanded into a multiple kingpost to span longer distances. The Humpback Bridge in Alleghany County, Virginia, was built in 1857 with a span of 85 feet 10 inches (see figure 4.22 in chapter 4). This remarkable length was achieved both by a significant amount of camber as well as below-deck struts supporting the outer panels of the lower chord. In general, the greater number of brace-to-post connections in multiple-kingpost trusses, which were normally constructed using traditional mortise and tenon joinery, led to greater flexibility in these bridges as the members shrank and the joints loosened over time.

In addition, an absence of counterbraces in a multiple-kingpost truss did not provide the stiffness necessary to resist the shear caused by moving live loads (figure 5.5). Figure 5.5b, like figure 5.4b, assumes that no tension force may be developed in the braces. Success in long-span bridge construction required innovative truss forms that utilized arches and counterbraces to reduce the effects of shrinkage and creep and to stiffen the truss against moving live loads.

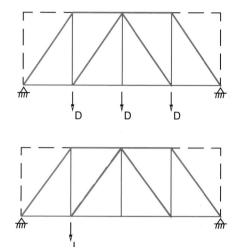

Figure 5.5 Axial forces that develop in a king post truss resulting from **Top:** 5.5a) dead load and **Above:** 5.5b) dead load and live load. Red indicates compression, blue indicates tension, and black dashes indicate zero force.

Burr-Arch Truss

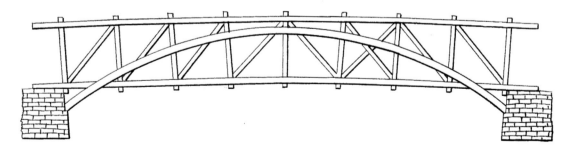

Figure 5.6 Theodore Burr, drawing from U. S. Patent No. 2,769X, April 3, 1817.

Several early bridge builders, both European and American, recognized the strength of a bridge form that combined an arch with a truss. The Grubenmann's Wettingen Bridge of 1764–66, Timothy Palmer's Permanent Bridge of 1805, and Lewis Wernwag's "Colossus" of 1812 all employed some combination of arch and truss to provide the necessary strength and stiffness for a wide river crossing. Theodore Burr was the first to patent such a form. Burr took out two patents in his lifetime, one in 1806 (no. 662X) and one in 1817 (no. 2,769X); both patents were destroyed in the patent office fire of 1836, but the 1817 patent drawing (figure 5.6) was recovered. Prior to settling on his 1817 patent, Burr spent several years experimenting with various truss forms. Among them was the 175-foot Waterford Bridge, built in 1804 across the Hudson River between Waterford and Lansingburgh, New York (figure 5.7). The bridge consisted of a parallel-chord truss with braces and counterbraces in each panel connected to a superimposed arch springing between the abutments. Around the same time that Burr was working on the Waterford Bridge, he erected a bridge over the Delaware River near Trenton, New Jersey, that suspended the deck below tied wooden arches using iron chains (figure 5.8). The Trenton Bridge was replaced in 1876 but was much respected and discussed by contemporary engineers. Burr's Mohawk River Bridge at Schenectady, New York, built in 1808, was an experiment with a wooden suspension form (figure 5.9). While the bridge stood until 1873, significant deflections became a problem after only twenty years, and additional piers were needed to support the bridge at the middle of each span.[5]

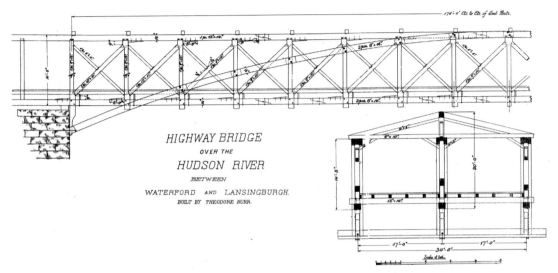

Figure 5.7 Burr's bridge across the Hudson River between Waterford and Lansingburg, New York. From Theodore Cooper, "American Railroad Bridges," *Transactions of the American Society of Civil Engineers 21* (July–December 1889): plate VI.

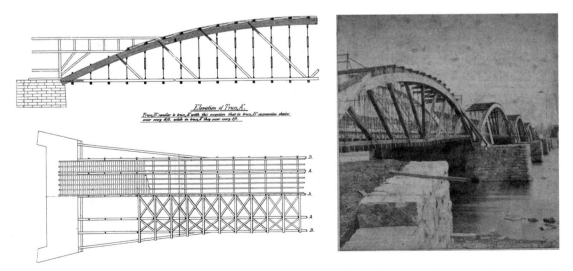

Figure 5.8 Burr's bridge across the Delaware River south of Trenton, New Jersey. **Left:** 5.8a) From Cooper, "American Railroad Bridges," plate VII; **Right:** 5.8b) half of an undated stereograph of the multi-span Burr arches of the Trenton Bridge, courtesy of a private collection.

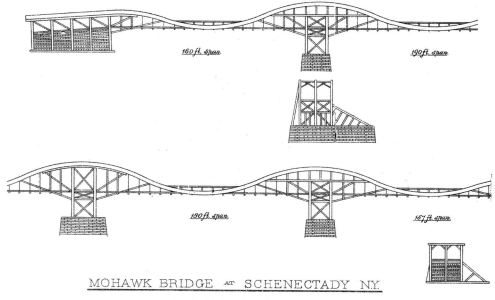

MOHAWK BRIDGE AT SCHENECTADY N.Y.

Built by Theodore Burr.

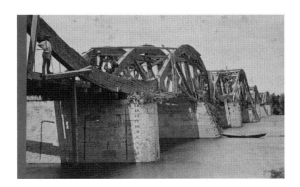

Figure 5.9 Burr's bridge across the Mohawk River at Schenectady, New York. **Top:** 5.9a) From Cooper, "American Railroad Bridges," plate VII; **Left:** 5.9b) stereograph half by Henry Tripp, photographer, ca. 1871, courtesy of a private collection.

The success and simplicity of the Waterford Bridge likely led Burr to adopt it as his signature form. In 1814, Burr began a two-year period of prolific bridge construction across the Susquehanna River. Bridges constructed included Northumberland-to-Sunbury (1814), McCall's Ferry (1815), Columbia-Wrightsville (1815), Berwick (1815), and Harrisburg (1816). Unfortunately, only the Northumberland and Harrisburg bridges withstood the river's power; McCall's Ferry Bridge was taken down by ice just three years after it was built. Columbia-Wrightsville Bridge was destroyed in an 1832 flood, and the Berwick Bridge met a similar fate in the winter of 1836. The collapse of McCall's Ferry Bridge must have been devastating to Burr, for its long span exceeded by 20 feet Lewis Wernwag's legendary "Colossus," constructed across the Schuylkill River in 1812—and so named because of its extraordinary span length (340 feet!) for its time.[6]

No practical means of analysis for this highly indeterminate truss form existed during Burr's time. Modern engineering studies suggest that most Burr-arch trusses were designed so that each system—arch and truss—could support the entire dead load. Nineteenth-century engineer Herman Haupt examined the load-sharing between a Howe railroad truss and its superimposed arch and concluded that "it will generally happen that after a bridge has been a long time in operation, the two systems bear very unequal portions." If the truss itself was not constructed to allow for adjustment, he went on, "the arch almost always sustains the whole weight of the bridge, and its load."[7] Modern analysis confirmed Haupt's claim that, over time, creep, shrinkage, and the loosening of the truss joints would result in an increased reliance on the arch to support all of the dead load. However, the truss had a much larger role to play in supporting the dead load during and just after construction, and the initial distribution of dead load between truss and arch was primarily determined by the method of construction selected by the builder.[8] Burr's 1817 patent description, as recorded by Llewellyn Edwards, may shed some light on the method of construction he followed.

> Both the chord and crown plates may be of two pieces, each embracing the kingpost between them, and are put together by lock-work or they may be single and put together by tenons and mortises or partly on the one plan and partly on the other, as may suit the builder. When put together put in the kingpost or diagonal braces. They may be put into the corners where the posts are united to the chord and crown plates without tenon or mortise by cutting the angle of the ends of the brace to correspond with the lines of the chords, plates and kingposts, allowing the angle to be partly on each as may suit, in equal proportion is best, or by square or shoulders with tenon and mortise. After this is done and the bridge is so far raised, attach cross beams on the chords and on the crown plates as horizontal braces, either by iron bolts, spikes or by mortises and tenons so as to keep the bridge from any side sway or lateral motion. There may be two, three or more ribs, segments or sections to make the bridge of any width required for carriage ways and foot walks . . . the arches are the last principal timbers that are to be raised; they may be notched a little where they cross the chords and where they cross the kingposts and braces, if thought best, but seldom necessary on the posts or braces. The arches may take their rise from below the chord, or at the chord line, as may be required to give the direct curve and to rise to the top of the crown plate or towards it, and even above it in very long spans if desired and may be double or single, if double one arch on each side of the kingpost and braces; they are put on so as to leave the kingpost between the arches when double, if they are left single to be put on that side of the kingpost that suits best.[9]

Burr's patent description left out specific details on removing the scaffolding supporting the bridge during construction. American civil engineer Herman Haupt understood the implications of timing this step.

> If, for example, a truss be constructed, and the false works removed before the introduction of the arches, if the latter be bolted to the posts, the weight of the whole structure is sustained by the truss itself, and the arches will not bear a single pound, unless they are called into action by an increased degree of settling in the truss. . . .

> Again; if we suppose the arches to be connected with the truss before the removal of the false works, and the joints be equally perfect in both systems, there is a prospect of a more nearly uniform distribution of the load; but even in this case, we cannot tell what portion is sustained by each system, because this will depend upon their relative rigidity.[10]

Both methods described by Haupt were used in the nineteenth-century construction of Burr-arch trusses in Indiana. J. J. Daniels, who built the Jackson Covered Bridge in Parke County, adopted the first method described by Haupt; the Kennedy family, who built Kennedy Bridge in Rushville and Forsythe Bridge in the vicinity of Moscow, Rush County, adopted the second method.[11]

A letter Burr wrote to Reuben Fields in 1815 about the construction of McCall's Ferry Bridge suggested that Daniels' method of allowing the truss to settle under dead load before completing the arch followed Burr's methods more closely than did Kennedy's. In the letter, Burr indicated that after constructing the truss, he erected the ends of the arch where they sprang from the abutment faces. While the constructed portions of the arch were connected to the truss, the arch itself was left open in the center of the span. Burr then "cut off the scaffold posts at the bottom, some more some less, from one to twelve inches" so that the truss would settle to a predetermined camber and, as it did, it would "bring the whole arch to its perfect height and curve." In the final step, which completed the bridge, Burr "united the centre" of the arch, thus enabling the arch to fully share any increase in dead load with the truss.[12] Following Burr's method, the initial distribution of dead load between the arch and truss was likely more balanced than Daniels's, but less so than Kennedy's, demonstrating yet one more possibility for the initial distribution of dead load demands. No matter which method was used to construct the Burr-arch truss, Haupt's assertion that continued settlement of the truss led to the arch supporting the majority of the dead load later in the life of the bridge remained true.

The interaction between the arch and the multiple-kingpost truss is a curious one, as both systems may be used to resist uniform dead loads over the life of the bridge, but neither system is stiff enough to effectively resist asymmetric, concentrated (live) loads, particularly not the arch (figure 5.10). Thus, the two systems—arch and truss—must work together to support the live load. A modern-day likeness to the Burr-arch truss, which also requires the interaction of two systems to support the live load, is the deck-stiffened arch. David Billington, professor emeritus from Princeton University, described the role of the deck in this system as providing "such a great resistance that, in effect, as the arch tries to lift on the right [due to the live load on the left], the deck reacts and produces forces in the vertical members that push the arch back down, thus drastically reducing the deflection and producing nearly uniform forces on the arch."[13] The stiffening truss in the Burr-arch truss performs a similar function to the deck described by Billington: while the left side of the truss may be affected by the asymmetric live load producing tension in the diagonal braces, the right side is not. Its braces are in compression as a result of the live load, providing additional stiffness with which to prevent the upward defection of the arch (figure 5.10).

Figure 5.10 Deflected shape of an arch under a concentrated live load force applied near the quarter-point of the span. Image generated in Mastan-2 by Rachel Sangree, 2014.

While the Burr-arch truss performed well and was widely constructed, it did have some drawbacks; namely, it required large timbers and skilled craftsmen to construct intricate traditional timber joinery. And the arches, while providing a critical function, were a challenge to maintain as they were the closest members to the waterway and were therefore vulnerable to decay and flood damage. The next significant truss design was patented by an architect who was aware of these problems and sought to provide an alternative to Burr's popular form.

Town Lattice Truss

Following the award of a patent to the well-known New England architect Ithiel Town in 1820, wooden lattice trusses became a standard in American bridge building. As a result, lattice trusses, whether they followed Town's patent or not, are often called Town lattices. In fact, most of the wooden lattice trusses in America probably were built following Town's 1820 and 1835 patents, which featured lattices and horizontal chords of 3 x 10 inch or 3 x 12 inch wooden planks and treenails to connect the members. Other lattice forms, patented and constructed in the United States and abroad by others, will be discussed later.

Ithiel Town completed his first significant work of architecture—Center Church in New Haven, Connecticut—in 1814. Briefly diverging from architecture, Town joined fellow New England architect Isaac Damon in 1816 to build Burr-arch truss bridges over the Connecticut River at Springfield (1816), Northampton (1817), and Hartford (1818). The Hartford Bridge, with its counterbraces and superimposed arches, resembled Burr's Waterford Bridge, completed in 1804.[14]

Town's experience constructing the Burr-arch trusses over the Connecticut River left him critical of the technology:

> The original mode of using the arch, by Burr, Wernwag, Field, and many others, it must be admitted, had the very important advantage of sustaining the most important portions of the strain, in the direction of the length of the materials, as in the arch-pieces, which, indeed, were the main support of the structure. In these constructions, in which the arch is so conspicuous for the strength and beauty of the superstructure, (for beautiful, it must be admitted the arch is, when applied with good taste,) there seem to be evils too great to be overcome, by the most profound science, or the most refined practical experience in execution.[15]

Town identified four issues. First, the cost of these bridges was so great that they could be justified only in the most exceptional cases. Second, the horizontal thrust of the arches increased the size and cost of abutments; additionally, Burr-arch trusses required such large timbers that they were susceptible to dry rot. Finally, the bases of the arches extended below the bridge floor into the abutments, leaving these critical members subject to weathering and decay.

After completing the Connecticut River bridges, Town spent time building bridges in the Carolinas, possibly experimenting with an improved form. Some of his works include the Yadkin River Bridge (1819), the Cape Fear Bridge (1820), and the South Yadkin River Bridge (1825).[16] Town was residing in Fayetteville, North Carolina, when he received his first patent on January 28, 1820. This patent (figure 5.11) described the principles of his truss:

Suppose a vertical plane against the side of which are placed the sides of a number of equal and similar flat pieces of timber or other substances of suitable dimensions in such manner as that they shall be parallel to each other, say between two horizontal lines in the plane and inclined so as to make an angle with the horizontal lines of about 45° or any angle that may be necessary for a brace (as they do the office of a brace) after which place another series of timbers or other substances of equal dimensions, distance apart and inclination to the horizontal lines in the same manner and between the same

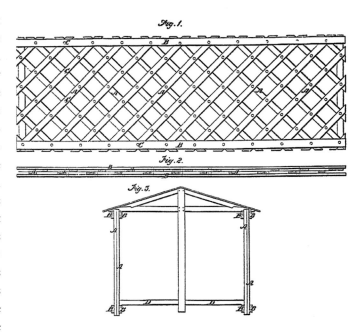

Figure 5.11 Ithiel Town, drawing of a single lattice truss accompanying U.S. Patent No. 3,169X, January 28, 1820.

parallels into equal diamonds and half diamonds. Hence the longer the pieces are in proportion to the distance between them, the smaller will be the diamonds the more times each piece in one series will be crossed by those of the other series, consequently the greater number of joints, and therefore the more strength and less strain upon each joint when weight or power is applied.[17]

The undeniable advantages the Town lattice truss possessed over the Burr-arch truss included its simple, repetitive form, relatively light timbers, and the absence of any traditional joinery. Furthermore, the arrangement of lattice members and their connection with treenails eliminated the need for an arch. The Town lattice, however, had its own share of problems. Lewis Prevost, a civil engineer operating in Massachusetts, observed that the truss tended to settle over time, a condition caused both by crushing of the treenails, which were loaded perpendicular to the direction of grain, and the tendency of the lattice members to split near their ends.[18] Prevost also noted that contact between adjacent lattice members accelerated decay. Carl Culmann, who published a German paper on American bridges following an 1849–50 tour of the United States, was also critical of the Town lattice's use of "wooden nails," calling them a "poor means of attachment."[19]

Herman Haupt provided a detailed review of the Town lattice in his 1851 book, *The General Theory of Bridge Construction*, although he did not use Town's name. While Haupt praised the truss for its simplicity of form and economic use of material, he thought it should be limited to light loads and small spans. A significant problem was the truss's tendency to warp, which Haupt compared to a thin, unsupported plank of wood loaded on its narrow face. A beam loaded in this way fails due to what is called lateral torsional buckling: the top of the beam is in compression and buckles out of the plane of bending (laterally) while the bottom of the beam is in tension and thus not subjected to buckling. This unbalanced loading between the top and bottom of the beam causes rotation in addition to translation (see figure 4.17 in chapter 4). Haupt noted that a second defect common to the Town truss occurred at the lattice ends. The shear forces at the ends of a bridge were at a maximum value, but the outermost lattice members were truncated and did not span between the top and bottom chords. To provide sufficient shear resistance, Town lattice bridges had to be extended well past the face of the abutments. Instead of extending the lattice, it was common to provide bolster beams—short wooden beams that extended toward mid-span under each lattice end. Like Haupt, Theodore Cooper criticized Town trusses in his 1889 survey of American wooden trusses, noting that the "thinness of the web system" allowed warping and that, through time, the trusses "became very flexible, owing to the want of rigidity of the treenail connections."[20]

Robert Fletcher, a professor of civil engineering at Dartmouth College, and J. P. Snow, a consulting engineer who specialized in railroads, were champions of the Town lattice truss, and Snow constructed many of them on the Boston and Maine Railroad. Both men took exception to Cooper's remarks regarding the lattice truss in their 1932 *History of the Development of Wooden Bridges*, arguing that the omission of effective transverse bracing details from many published drawings of Town lattice trusses would naturally have led to unsatisfactory warping "and getting out of line." In contrast, Fletcher and Snow presented a Town lattice truss cross-section with transverse bracing added that was similar to the Howe trusses built on the Boston and Maine (figure 5.12b).[21]

Town himself recognized the shortcomings in his 1820 patent. In 1835, he was awarded a second patent for a double-lattice truss with additional chords intended to stiffen the truss

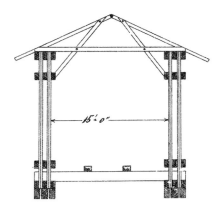

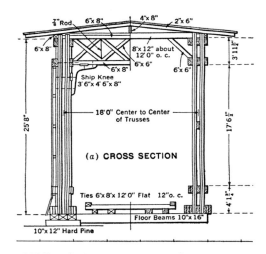

Figure 5.12 Town lattice truss cross-section from **Top:** 5.12a) Cooper "American Railroad Bridges," plate X; **Above:** 5.12b) Robert Fletcher and J. P. Snow, "A History of the Development of Wooden Bridges," Paper No. 1864, *Transactions of the American Society of Civil Engineers* 99 (1934): 334.

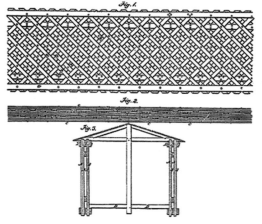

Figure 5.13 Drawing accompanying Town's 1835 patent for "An Improved Lattice Truss."

and decrease its tendency to warp (figure 5.13). It was, he asserted, "an entirely different bridge—one in which the materials are so arranged as to produce far greater strength, rigidity, and permanence, in proportion to the quantity of materials, and to be far more secure against its trusses twisting, leaning sideways, or curving in the direction of their length."[22]

The double-lattice truss was typically used on railroad bridges. The Boston and Maine Railroad used the Town lattice design extensively, even through the turn of the twentieth century, but lattice trusses were also built on the Philadelphia and Reading Railroad and the New York and Harlem Railroad.[23] Yet, even the double lattice had its critics. Herman Haupt, in particular, devoted a good deal of space to criticizing them in his *General Theory of Bridge Construction*:

> Whilst the weight of the timber from the ties and braces has been doubled, the cross-section of the chords has been only increased one-half. A great load of unnecessary timber is placed in the centre, where any weight acts with the greatest leverage, and produces the greatest strain. It is probable that this truss, as usually constructed, possesses less absolute strength with a given quantity of material than any other in common use.[24]

Modern engineers have echoed Haupt's sentiment that "unnecessary timber" lay at the center of the bridge.[25]

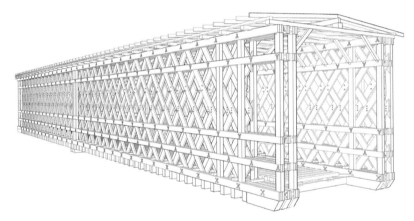

Figure 5.14 J. P. Snow built the double-web Town lattice Contoocook Bridge (1889) in Merrimack County, New Hampshire, one of eight surviving covered railroad bridges. HAER NH-38, sheet 1, Amy James, delineator, 2003.

Other Lattice-Type Bridges in the U.S. and Abroad

Town was more of a salesman than a builder, spending a great deal of time promoting his truss with his famous pitch, "Built by the mile and cut off by the yard." Royalties paid to Town for constructing a bridge based on his patent were a dollar a foot—unless someone was caught building the bridge

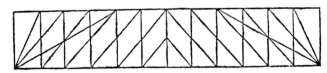

Figure 5.15 Herman Haupt's concept to improve the lattice truss was to eliminate warping by orienting the members vertically rather than at an angle. Haupt's truss design, from *The General Theory of Bridge Construction* (New York: D. Appleton and Co., 1851), 153.

without paying, in which case the royalties were doubled. Town's ability to promote his design may have overshadowed other lattice-type bridges that were built in the nineteenth century. Maine bridge engineer and historian Llewellyn Edwards claimed that an unknown builder constructed several similar bridges over Otter Creek in Vermont in 1813, predating Town's patent and even

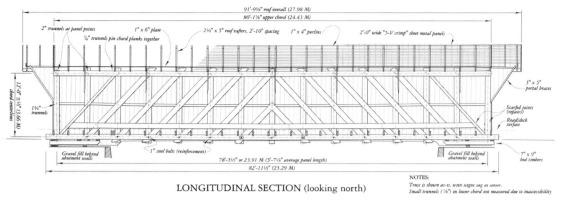

91'-9⅝" roof overall (27.98 M)
80'-1¼" upper chord (24.43 M)
2" trunnels at panel points
1" x 6" plate
2½" x 5" roof rafters, 2'-10" spacing
1" x 4" purlins
2'-0" wide "5-V crimp" sheet metal panels
⅞" trunnels pin chord planks together
3" x 5" portal braces
Scarfed joints (repairs)
Roadd[e]ck surface
1¾" trunnels
12'-4" 4/- (3.66 M) chord planks
Gravel fill behind abutment walls
1" steel bolts (reinforcement)
78'-5½" or 23.91 M (5'-7¼" average panel length)
82'-11½" (25.29 M)
Gravel fill behind abutment walls
7" x 9" bed timbers
LONGITUDINAL SECTION (looking north)
NOTES:
Truss is shown as-is, with slight sag at center.
Small trunnels (⅞") in lower chord not measured due to inaccessibility.

Figure 5.16 The only surviving historic Haupt truss is the Bunker Hill Bridge in Catawba County, North Carolina. HAER NC-46, sheet 3, Richard K. Anderson, Jr., delineator, 2004.

his experimentation with the lattice form. Herman Haupt patented a version of a lattice truss in 1839 to eliminate warping by orienting the ties vertically rather than at an angle (figure 5.15). Most of the diagonal members also met at the end "post," concentrating the reaction force rather than distributing it as in the Town lattice. The Bunker Hill Bridge in North Carolina is the only surviving example of Haupt's "improved" lattice truss (figure 5.16). New England bridge builders Bela Fletcher and James Tasker built two variations of Town's lattice in 1866 by using 6 x 8-inch timbers for the lattice, notched and bolted together, rather than Town's 3-inch planks. One of their bridges was the Pompanoosuc Village Bridge in Windsor County, Vermont; the other, which currently holds the record for the longest historic covered bridge in the United States, is the Cornish-Windsor Bridge between the towns of Cornish, New Hampshire, and Windsor, Vermont (figure 5.17). Still, testifying to Town's influence and ability as a salesman, the bridge is often referred to as a Town lattice truss.[26]

Figure 5.17 A detail of the squared-timber lattice truss on Bela Fletcher and James Tasker's Cornish-Windsor Bridge (1866). The 6 x 8-inch timbers were connected at each joint by a notch and a single bolt instead of a pair of treenails. HAER NH-8-10, Jet Lowe, photographer, 1984.

While timber lattice bridges like Town's were built extensively in the United States, where timber was plentiful and cheap, Europeans built lattice trusses (called lattice girders or trellis girders) from iron. George Smart patented an iron lattice truss in England in 1822, just two years after Town's single timber lattice, but there is no record of an iron lattice being constructed using Smart's design.[27] Instead, Sir John Benjamin MacNeill is credited with introducing the iron lattice to the British Isles in the early 1840s, building an 84-foot iron lattice over the Dublin and Drogheda Railway at Raheny, near Dublin, Ireland, and later a 140-foot iron lattice over the Royal Canal at Dublin to carry the Dublin and Drogheda Railway. Moorson built another well-known iron lattice truss for the Birmingham and Gloucester Railway. Several mid-nineteenth-century British authors credited Town with the original lattice truss, but this may be a result of Town's travels through Europe in 1829, during which he "seized the opportunity to publicize his 1820 patent truss," carrying with him copies of his 1821 pamphlet.[28]

Analysis of Lattice Trusses

Town provides no guidance in his pamphlets as to how a builder might analyze one of his lattice trusses. In 1839, he reproduced, almost word for word, a description prepared by Olinthus Gregory in 1825 on the use of a scale model to predict the strength of a full-sized structure. While Gregory referred to "Mr. Smart's Patent Mathematical Chain Bridge," Town eliminated any reference to George Smart. Town's description was not original, but it is likely he used models to assess the strength of his patent bridges, having sent Eli Whitney one such scale model around the time of his first patent. Gregory explained that strength does not scale 1 to 1 to size. That is, if the length of the bridge is n times the length of the model (and all of the other dimensions are also scaled by the same value n), the weight of the bridge will increase as 1 to n^3 while the resistance of the parts will only increase as 1 to n^2. Thus, a scale factor existed and had to be accommodated. William Humber's 1857 volume on iron bridges noted tests in Germany which had used scale models to compare the behavior of iron lattice girders to plate girders.[29]

Squire Whipple's seminal 1847 volume on bridge building included a comparative analyses of a panelized truss with counterbraces (what he called a "cancelled truss") and a lattice truss (a "double cancelled truss"), illustrated in figure 5.18. His analyses used equilibrium methods and applied a moving live load to determine the maximum effect of a concentrated force placed at different panel points. He determined that a lattice truss was slightly more efficient, and also noted that it relied more heavily on members in compression than in tension, a preferred system for a wooden truss.[30]

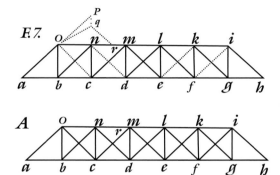

Figure 5.18 Figures accompanying Whipple's analysis of **Top:** 5.18a) a "cancelled truss" and **Above:** 5.18b) a "double cancelled truss." From Square Whipple, *A Work on Bridge Building* (Utica, N.Y.: H. H. Curtiss, Printer, 1847), 12 and 14.

Herman Haupt's 1851 volume provided an analysis for a lattice truss built for the Cumberland Valley Railroad across the Susquehanna River at Harrisburg, Pennsylvania. The analysis considered the lattice braces terminating at nodes A, b, c, d, e, f, and g, which were all directly supported and thus resisted half the weight of the truss (figure 5.19). Using trigonometry and proportioning the brace forces such that the brace terminating at A carried a maximum force and the remaining supported braces carried some fraction of A, Haupt calculated the maximum force in the end brace to be approximately one-fifth of the total reaction force distributed over nodes A through g, approximately 13,125 pounds.[31]

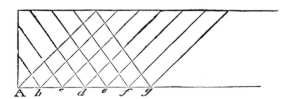

Figure 5.19 Haupt's illustration accompanying his calculations for the maximum force in a lattice brace. From Haupt, *General Theory*, 241.

British engineer William Humber's book on cast- and wrought-iron bridges demonstrated the variation in force in the lattice members due to the combination of a uniformly distributed dead load and a moving live load. He described the calculations for an iron lattice, but the principle was the same for a lattice of wood. His diagram of force variation (figure 5.20) combined the force due to a uniformly distributed dead load (shown below line *AB*) and the force due to a moving, uniformly distributed live load (shown above line *AB*). The sum of both values was indicated at discrete locations along the beam by dashed lines (*mn*).[32]

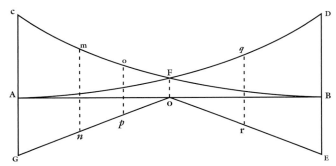

Figure 5.20 A graphical representation of the axial force in lattice members caused by a uniformly distributed dead load (diagram below AB) and a moving, uniform live load (diagram above AB). From William Humber, *A Practical Treatise on Cast and Wrought Iron Bridges and Girders* (London, 1857), 96.

Both Burr and Town developed and patented successful truss forms that were widely adopted in covered bridges throughout the United States, but, still, neither form provided effective counterbracing to stiffen the truss under moving live loads, nor were their designs capable of being adjusted as wood viscosity and shrinkage caused the truss to settle over time. Further, for long spans, even the Town lattice required a supplemental arch—whose ends, just as in the Burr-arch truss, suffered from accelerated decay and degradation. The next two highly successful truss designers, Stephen H. Long and William Howe, addressed all of these issues, each one innovating a truss form using the concept of prestressing.

Stephen H. Long's Trusses

Army engineer Col. Stephen H. Long's interest in bridge design apparently began in 1828 after his appointment to the board of engineers for the pioneering Baltimore and Ohio Railroad (B&O). It extended to the early 1840s, when he received orders to coordinate navigation improvements on the Mississippi, Missouri, Arkansas, and Ohio rivers. Long's accomplishments over the course of his extraordinary engineering service to the country included writing a seminal manual on railroad design, making improvements in locomotive design, and inventing improved wood-truss bridges.[33]

The "Jackson Bridge" and Long's 1830 Patent

Long designed a new truss bridge in 1828–29 for the B&O, but instead of using it on the main line, officials relegated it to carrying a highway over the right-of-way. He named the bridge "Jackson Bridge" in honor of President Andrew Jackson because his first assignment in 1816 was in the general's southern division and perhaps because Jackson supported Long's territorial explorations. Long received a patent for his bridge design in March 1830. He published three brief articles in the *Journal of the Franklin Institute* in 1830, which, along with his patent description, provide an understanding of his innovations. The bridge was covered and built "on the Washington road, about 2 ¼ miles from Baltimore at its intersection with the Baltimore and Ohio Railroad at an elevation 40 feet above the latter. The length or span of the bridge is 109 feet, its width from out to out 24 feet, and its height from bottom to top of its posts, 14 feet." The bridge was probably very similar to that shown in figure 5.21, which is taken from his patent application. Long explicitly stated that the "upper arch braces" specified in his patent description were not used in the Jackson Bridge, and it seems, with one known exception, they were never used in any bridge built to this design because of the practical problems they created for cladding the bridge with wood.[34]

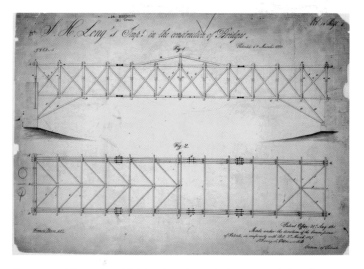

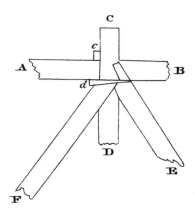

Figure 5.22 Long truss connection detail, showing the diagonals prestressed by a wooden wedge *d*. From S. H. Long, *Description of Col. Long's Bridges, Together with A Series of Directions to Bridge Builders* (Concord, N. H.: John F. Brown, Printer, 1836), plate II, p. 4.

Figure 5.21 Watercolor of Col. Stephen H. Long's elevation and plan of Jackson Bridge, 1830. Courtesy of National Archives and Records Administration, Cartographic and Architectural Branch, College Park, Md.

One of the important innovations Long claimed in his patent was the use of counter diagonals prestressed by the insertion of wooden wedges, as seen in figure 5.22. The wedges introduced compression in both diagonals, eliminating the need for tension connections at their ends. Under the action of a moving vertical load, *both* diagonals were active and contributed to the stiffness of the bridge. The ability to re-drive the wedges—thus retightening the bridge—meant that builders could use unseasoned, "green" timbers for construction. All the timber in the Jackson Bridge, except

Figure 5.23 Left: 5.23a) Detail view of one of the wedges hammered into the base of each counterbrace on the Eldean Bridge. William G. Keener, photographer, 1998. Courtesy of Ohio History Connection. **Right:** 5.23b) Interior elevation of Eldean Bridge's Long truss. The wedge connection details are out of view, just below the deck. HAER OH-122-14, Jet Lowe, photographer, 2002.

the keys, was white pine, "with no other seasoning than what it might have acquired in six weeks, during which time the work was in progress, having been framed and raised in that time by six workmen only." Long's design used neither treenails, as in Town's lattices, nor a supplementary arch, as in Burr's designs. Moreover, the forces in the members were principally in the axial direction (along the grain), with minimal bending. Another of Long's patent claims involved the method of splicing the lower tension chords; he patented both iron and wooden fish plates. Most significantly, Long used French engineer Claude-Louis Navier's analogy (see chapter 4) to size the chords of the Jackson Bridge, becoming the first American engineer to explicitly state the *capacity* of his design: "Agreeably to the most approved rules for computing the strength of similar structures, it will sustain, on every square foot of its floor, in addition to its own weight, at least 120 pounds, or equally distributed over the entire surface of its floor, about one hundred and ten tons weight."[35]

Because his design approach was based on engineering analysis, Long was able to compute and publish a table in August 1830 that prescribed chord areas and the corresponding load capacities for a set of simple spans. In the same article, Long attempted to explain the behavior of the prestressed counter and main diagonals, arguing that the stress "to which the truss frames are subjected, by the heaviest load that is admissible upon the bridge, is no greater than that exerted upon it without any load at all."[36] This was only true for the counters that shared in carrying live load until all the pre-compression was relieved and they became loose. A gravity live load did increase the compressive force in the main diagonals.

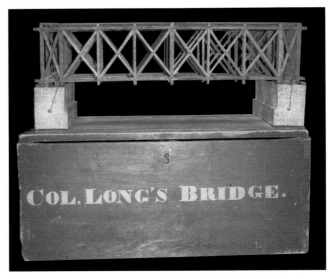

Figure 5.24 One of the original models of the Long truss, used by Stephen Long's agents to sell his bridge. Displayed at the New Hampshire Antiquarian Society in Hopkinton. Francesco Lanza, photographer, 2003.

Although the B&O chose not to build any railroad bridges using Long's design, the Jackson Bridge was a very important success. Through it, Long convinced his two colleagues on the B&O, William Gibbs McNeill and George Washington Whistler—both of whom became influential chief engineers for other railroads—of the merits of his design. In 1832, three Long bridges, two measuring 70 feet and one measuring 100 feet, were built to carry trains of the Baltimore and Susquehanna Railroad. These were probably the first wooden-truss bridges to carry railroad loads in the nation. The testimonials appended to Long's 1836 pamphlet demonstrate the spread and influence of Long's technology throughout the Middle Atlantic and New England states. Thomas Hassard received the rights to build Long-truss bridges in Maryland and built nineteen of the type for the Paterson and Hudson, Baltimore and Susquehanna, Boston and Providence, and Boston and Worcester railroads up to 1836. Long appointed his brother Moses Long as a "general agent"; Thomas Hassard and Benjamin Franklin Long, another brother, as "special agents"; and twenty-three other men as "subagents" to promote his design. The subagents included Long's relatives Horace, Enoch, and Warren Childs of Henniker, New Hampshire. Moses Long promoted the design by mailing broadsides.[37]

Long's design performed well and was widely accepted by railroads, but it required attentive, knowledgeable maintenance as wood viscosity, shrinkage, and vibration created the need to periodically retighten the wedges. Perhaps the weakest aspect of Long's design was its vertical wooden tension members. The gravity loads from the floor beams had to be transferred into the vertical tension posts at cutouts or shoulders, resulting in shear stresses along the dotted lines in figure 5.25 that could cause structural failure as the wood degraded over time. William Howe addressed this weakness in his 1840 patent.

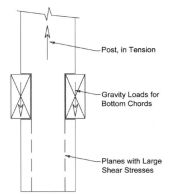

Figure 5.25 The transfer of tension forces into the vertical members that extended beyond the lower chord of Long's 1830 patent truss resulted in a detail that was highly susceptible to shear failures.

Long's 1836 Patent and Pamphlet

Long returned home to Hopkinton, New Hampshire, in 1835 and evidently spent some time thinking and writing about bridges. He was awarded a new patent on January 23, 1836 (having received other patents in 1832 and 1833), and published a pamphlet on bridges, which was republished in Philadelphia in 1841. Instead of a new design for the principal load-carrying trusses, Long's 1836 patent proposed a system for preventing out-of-plane movements of chords. Long emphasized that his object was to "produce and ensure *lateral* stiffness or inflexibility in wooden or frame bridges." Long must have observed out-of-plane buckling of truss top chords and recognized the importance of precluding such failures. His patent was probably the first awarded for a system to provide lateral stiffness in wooden bridges.[38]

Long's pamphlet described his 1830 and 1836 patents, summarized writings previously published in the *Journal of the Franklin Institute*, and provided a "series of directions to bridge builders." He also commented on gains in structural efficiency from truss designs with chords that were continuous rather than interrupted over interior piers. Long called such continuity "double action" and correctly noted that such continuity placed the top chords in tension and the bottom chords in compression at intermediate supports. He advocated making the end spans three quarters the length of the interior spans. Long repeated statements from his August 1830 *Journal of the Franklin Institute* article that the use of prestressed diagonals eliminated increases in the forces from live loads in the diagonals. Again, this observation was only true for the counter diagonals. His guidelines for raising a bridge and installing the wedges suggested that "the workmen begin at the extremities of the span, and proceed towards the center, taking care to drive them as hard as they may be driven, with an axe or sledge weighing 4 or 5 pounds."[39]

The unique element of Long's pamphlet was his series of tables prescribing member sizes for truss bridges with spans between 55 and 300 feet. These tables extended and elaborated on the table published in August 1830. Long used Navier's analogy and limited the maximum stresses in the chords to 2,000 pounds per square inch, half the assumed minimum wood strength, under an extremely large, uniformly distributed live load of 120 pounds per square foot. Carl Culmann first observed this fact in his extended paper on American bridges published following his 1849–50 U.S. tour, an observation that was reaffirmed by new research in the 1980s. Interestingly, Culmann felt that the allowable stress of 2,000 pounds per square inch was "set somewhat too high." It forced Long, Culmann opined, "to assume this abnormally large random loading of 120 pounds per square foot, which in reality can never be present."[40]

Long's 1839 Bridge Patents

Long was awarded two additional bridge patents on November 7, 1839. An extended, eight-page discussion of the patents appeared that year in the *Journal of the Franklin Institute*, and a brief description followed several years later. The details of the "Wooden-Framed Brace-Bridge" patent are largely incomprehensible. The bridge resembles Long's 1830 design but with added arch-like braces, lattice-like member sizes, diagonals connected by treenails, and no wedges for prestressing. Long's motivation for the design is difficult to discern, especially since his other patent, issued at the same time, retained the use of wedges and the prestressing concept. Long may have wanted builders who added arch-like braces to his 1830 system to pay him royalties. Alternatively, he may have observed owners failing to maintain trusses built according to his 1830 patent design, leading to the counter diagonals becoming loose and ineffective.[41]

The second November 1839 patent was for a "Wood-Framed Suspension Bridge" and had diagonals with tension connections that were pretensioned by driving wedges between the posts and the chords (figure 5.26). This placed the diagonals in tension and the vertical members in compression, the reverse of his 1830 truss. The difficulty of achieving good tension connections with treenails made the design impractical for wood, although Long included the possibility of using iron for the design. A second concept included in this patent was the use of variable panel widths, which decreased from mid-span to the abutments, in an attempt to equalize forces in the diagonals. While this approach was theoretically correct, the extra detailing and inherent construction challenges made the concept impractical. Nonetheless, the two concepts demonstrated Long's understanding of truss behavior and prestressing.

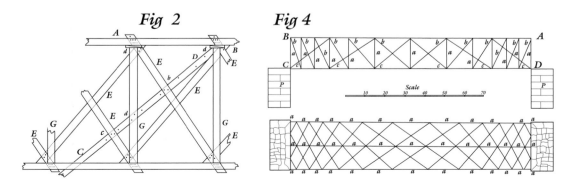

Figure 5.26 Details from Col. Stephen H. Long, drawing accompanying U.S. Patent No. 1,397, November 7, 1839. Note wedges at the top of the vertical members in fig. 2 and the decreasing panel widths in fig. 4.

Long's Contributions

As the first American engineer to use and disseminate the theoretical developments of Navier, Long's advancement of American truss design was seminal. His 1830 and 1839 patents defined the two basic designs for parallel-chord trusses. His contributions, however, are not widely recognized because of the rapid changes that occurred in material technology between 1840 and 1870. By substituting iron vertical members for wood, William Howe's 1840 patent facilitated prestressing and eliminated the main weakness in Long's trusses, quickly making Long's 1830 design obsolete. Thomas and Caleb Pratt's 1844 patent made Long's first 1839 design practical through the use of iron diagonals and counters.

The most thoughtful scholarship on Long's work was written by his German contemporary, Carl Culmann, following the latter's American tour. Culmann read Long's 1841 booklet but never met the American. The only Long bridges he examined in person were some railroad bridges in Georgia "that were close to collapse," apparently from lack of maintenance. Culmann devoted many pages of his paper to analyzing Long's designs and included two full plates with nineteen drawings containing numerous important details. In addition, Culmann reproduced portions of Long's tables and proved that Long calculated chord forces using Navier's analogy. He showed that chord areas for the entire range of spans were such that the maximum normal stress was 2,000 pounds per square inch for a uniformly distributed live load of 120 pounds per square foot. Culmann also recognized the differences between Long's 1830 and 1839 patents and admired Long's stiff patented lateral bracing system. He also found problems with Long's designs, noting that the wedges were soon loose and that the use of treenails in the 1839 patents was a "very poor means of attachment." Ultimately though, Culmann described Long as "surely one of America's most intelligent and well-educated engineers, and bridge construction in this country owes much to him. It can be gleaned from his designs that he was well aware of the effects of various forces in the interior of the structure, and knew how to deal with each of them in a suitable manner."[42]

Culmann observed that Long's trusses fell from favor with American railroads as iron and steel construction replaced wood and as newer truss designs by Howe and Pratt became prominent. Long's contributions were further obscured by the American transition in the 1870s to statically determinate forms without counter-diagonals for both Howe and Pratt trusses. As a result, most twentieth-century commentators did not give Long as much credit as Culmann had and failed to place Long's designs in the context of Howe and Pratt trusses. The comments of the late bridge historian John G. James are the most unfair. He wrote that Long "produced a stream of patents and pamphlets which have left his name far more well-known in bridge history than his engineering activities justify." Claiming it was "difficult to see that Long contributed anything of material value to wooden truss development," James also demeaned Long's patent enforcement against Nathaniel Rider, who had simply copied Long's first 1839 patent (no. 1,397). Apparently not comprehending the effects of prestressing in two of Long's patents, James was baffled by how Long intended to insure that the members in his trusses performed in accordance with his patent designs. Most egregiously, James completely ignored the significance of Long's tables. James's opinions on Long's contributions were a great injustice and damaging to an understanding of American wooden-truss bridge history.[43]

The Howe Truss

The arrangement of members shown in figure 5.27 is known as a "St. Andrew's cross." Because it resembles a Howe truss, it is logical to consider this ancient form first. Marc Seguin used the St. Andrew's cross design shown in figure 5.27 as a stiffening truss in his Tournon-Tain suspension bridge in 1824, sixteen years before the Howe patent.[44] The nut below the floor beam was used to pre-compress the diagonals and "tighten" the truss. Described and illustrated by European engineers in the 1820s, the design was used in other French suspension bridges, most notably by Joseph Chaley for his 1834 Grand Pont Suspendu at Fribourg, Switzerland. Chaley's stiffening truss was described in an 1835 issue of the *Journal of the Franklin Institute*: "On both sides . . . are strong oaken balustrades, made in the form of St. Andrew's cross, the height of which is four feet."[45] John Roebling likely came to know Seguin's stiffening truss design from Carl Berg's 1824 book *Der Bau der Hangebrucken aus Eisendraht*, which was available during his studies in Germany. Roebling's competitor, Charles Ellet, studied suspension bridges in

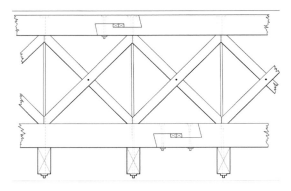

Figure 5.27 St. Andrew's cross truss. Redrawn from Marc Seguin, *Des ponts en fil de fer*, 2d ed. (Paris: Chez Bachelier, Libraire, 1826), figure 9, plate 2.

France from June 1830 to 1832 and became a strong advocate of them. Ellet's 1839 pamphlet on suspension bridges commented on Navier's 1823 analysis of suspension bridges and on those bridges at Tournon-Tain and Fribourg; furthermore, his 1840 and 1841 designs for suspension bridges at St. Louis and Philadelphia both made use of St. Andrew's cross trusses. This clearly shows that American suspension-bridge designers knew of the St. Andrew's cross truss design before the Howe patent.[46]

American engineers embraced wood trusses, especially Long's truss, for railroad bridges. In 1840, while the Western Railroad (later the Boston and Albany Railroad) was being built from Springfield, Massachusetts, to the state line at West Stockbridge, William Howe was apparently motivated to design a new truss, superior to Long's, to compete for the lucrative business of building bridges. Howe received two patents in 1840. The first, no. 1,685 (figure 5.28), was an entirely wooden truss that used wedges, but in a different manner from Long's design. The drawing shows diagonals spanning two panels, as defined by the vertical members.[47] The second patent, no. 1,711 (figure 5.29), was Howe's design for a combination wood-iron truss. In place of wedges, it used tightening nuts on threaded vertical iron rods to post-tension the structure.

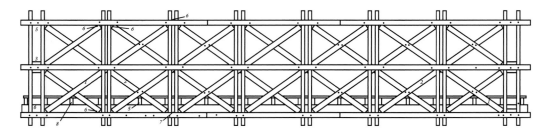

Figure 5.28 Redrawn from William Howe, drawing accompanying U.S. Patent No. 1,685, July 10, 1840.

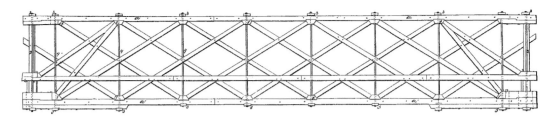

Figure 5.29 William Howe, drawing accompanying U.S. Patent No. 1,711, August 3, 1840.

Howe's solitary claim in patent no. 1,711 was the combination of iron bolts and wooden blocks "against which the braces and counter braces abut, so as to cooperate in increasing the camber to any desired extent." The text for this patent referred to the "truss-frame" of his earlier patent but indicated that it had been "deemed expedient to separate it therefrom, and make it the subject of a distinct patent." By adding vertical iron rods, Howe eliminated the principal weakness of Long's design and made truss tightening much easier. Howe's design made Long's obsolete, even though the behavior of the two trusses, with diagonals spanning only one panel, was essentially the same.[48]

Setting aside the fact that Howe's patent drawing showed diagonals spanning over two panels, did significant differences exist between Howe's design and the St. Andrew's cross? An important distinction lay in the use of wooden blocks, or bearings, that were keyed in the chords as shown in figure 5.30. The keying allowed the transfer of any unbalanced horizontal force components from the diagonals into the chords, which was necessary to achieve truss action. Neither the

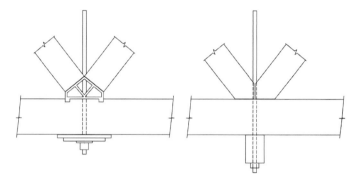

Figure 5.30 In the Howe truss node **Left:** (example 5.30a, based on the Moose Brook Bridge nodal casting), the iron casting was keyed into the chord, allowing unequal horizontal components of the forces in the diagonals to be transferred into the chord. Without this casting, the St. Andrews cross node **Right:** (example 5.30b) had only limited truss action and a high probability of becoming loose through time.

European drawings from the 1820s nor those in Ellet's 1840 pamphlet show keying of the diagonals into the chords.[49] Without keying, there is only the friction at the interfaces between the diagonals and the chords to make a St. Andrew's cross behave as a true truss. Moreover, the extension of the bolt through the floor beam in the St. Andrew's cross form increased the probability that the diagonals would become loose due to wood viscosity and shrinkage. The wood node blocks in the Howe design also allowed the diagonals to have simple square ends, assuring axial stresses in the along-grain direction of the diagonals.

The Western Railroad and International Dissemination

William Howe had the foresight and good fortune to develop his truss in conjunction with the building of a critically important American railroad, the Western Railroad. In October 1836, the railroad hired West Point graduate and former topographical engineer George Washington Whistler, who became chief engineer for the railroad in 1840, serving until 1842. His engineering leadership resulted in the Western Railroad being labeled "Whistler's railroad." He can be credited with the incredibly rapid national and international adoption of the Howe truss because, following Howe's successful erection of a small bridge for the railroad, Whistler awarded Howe and Howe's brother-in-law, Amasa Stone, the prized contract for the Connecticut River Bridge at Springfield. Howe had been working with Stone since 1836, principally building churches and dwellings near Warren, Massachusetts.[50] They continued their collaboration by successfully completing the bridge, shown in partial elevation in figure 5.31, in the summer of 1841.

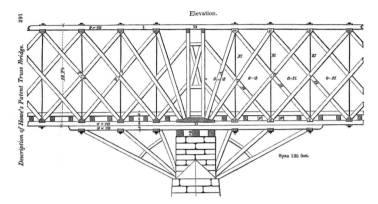

Figure 5.31 Partial elevation of the Western Railroad Connecticut River Bridge at Springfield. The "inferior arch braces" were soon recognized to be unnecessary and thus were not commonly used. From Lewis M. Prevost, "Description of Howe's Patent Truss Bridge," *Journal of the Franklin Institute* 3, no. 5 (May 1842): 291. Courtesy of George Peabody Library, The Sheridan Libraries, Johns Hopkins University.

The Western Railroad's 1842 annual report provided a detailed assessment of the bridges on the road.

> The railroad bridges east of the Connecticut River are constructed of truss frames, after the plan of Long's patent, and are made for two tracks. The Connecticut River Bridge, and those westward of it, on the Western road, are of truss frames, of Howe's more recent patent, and they are constructed for one track only. The truss frames of all are covered in on the sides and top, and thoroughly white-washed. The entire floor of the Connecticut River Bridge is covered with tin, painted of a dark color. This bridge is 1,264 feet long, of 7 spans, 180 feet each. The whole length of wooden superstructure of bridges is 6,092.5 feet or 1 mile, 812.5 feet and they are in number 48, both exclusive of road bridges over the railroad.[51]

The reports also indicated that the West Stockbridge and Albany Railroad had seventeen wooden Howe trusses, all covered and whitewashed, two of which had spans of 160 feet.[52]

Almost overnight, Howe's design had made Long's truss obsolete, leading to a frenzy of Howe-truss railroad-bridge construction in the fall of 1841 and throughout 1842. A biographer in 1869 indicated that much of this work fell to Stone. The winter of 1841 was "most trying and arduous. About a thousand lineal feet of bridging on the Western Railroad, in the Green Mountains [the Berkshires] had to be completed, and Mr. Stone and his men were called upon to carry the work through." No doubt convinced of the superiority of the Howe design, Stone formed a partnership with Azuriah Boody and, in 1842, purchased Howe's bridge-patent rights for the New England states, "including all improvements and renewals," for $40,000. Boody, Stone, and Company was among the early bridge companies devoted to the design, fabrication, and erection of bridges in the United States.[53]

Lewis M. Prevost's 1842 illustrated article on the Connecticut River Bridge emphasized that "the stress comes upon the end grain of the main and counterbraces, and is in the direction of their length—consequently there is not the same danger of the settling which occurs in lattice bridges, in consequence of the crushing of the pins and the splitting of the lattices at their ends—and there being a free circulation of air between the main and counterbraces, the bridge is not as liable to the speedy decay which occurs in lattice bridges, wherever the lattices come in contact." He concluded "that in bridges with spans equal to, or exceeding, those of the bridge at Springfield, the peculiar truss above described, will be found superior in strength, stiffness, and durability, to those of Town's double lattice plan." The editors of the *American Railroad Journal* agreed, insisting in 1844 that Howe's was "the best patented American bridge." Howe's design became the most widely used bridge form during the railroad building mania of the 1840s, 1850s, and 1860s.[54]

After Howe-truss bridges were in service for some time, however, a flaw in the design became apparent. Rod forces decreased due to viscous wood behavior, wood shrinkage, and crushing on the chords under the vertical rod plates, frequently resulting in a looseness in the counter diagonals and reductions in stiffness. Stone recognized the problem and anticipated the unacceptable possibility of failure. After a sleepless night in which he nearly exhausted his "inventive thoughts," an idea occurred to him for "a better combination of the Howe bridge, but would not in principle be improved upon. Sleep immediately came." The next day, using models to prove the ideas to his satisfaction, he adopted them as his standard design.[55] Stone's improvements probably included an iron nodal casting with a sleeve extending through the chord thickness. It was, however, Howe who in 1846 received a patent for such a design.[56] Howe either simply patented Stone's ideas, devised the improvements independently, or reached an agreement with Stone to file the patent in Howe's name,

since "all improvements and renewals" were part of Stone's purchase. The iron nodes and single-panel diagonals came to define the "classic" Howe form. The first use of these improvements is unknown. Richard Osborne designed all-iron Howe trusses with single-panel diagonals in 1845, and Frederick Harbach patented a similar all-iron Howe truss in 1846, making it likely that classic Howe trusses were in use before 1845. By 1877, Stone claimed to have constructed "from ten to fifteen miles in length of Howe bridges." He must have been the most prodigious builder of Howe bridges in history.[57]

Figure 5.32 Casting with sleeves that transferred rod tension forces directly into the casting without causing bearing stresses in the chords and possibly crushing them. Found on the Rexleigh Bridge, a Howe truss dating to 1874 in Washington County, New York. Dario Gasparini, photographer, 2011.

In addition to revolutionizing American bridge building, the Connecticut River Bridge became an international engineering sensation. After being personally recruited by two Russian engineering officers representing Czar Nicholas I, Whistler resigned from the Western Railroad in May 1842 to accept the post of consulting engineer for the St. Petersburg–Moscow (or Nikolaev) Railway. While en route to Russia, Whistler traveled through London and provided drawings of the Connecticut River Bridge to publisher John Weale, who included the drawings in his 1843 volume on stone, iron, timber, and wire bridges.[58] After arriving in Russia, Whistler made recommendations on the road's alignment, the gauge of the rails, rolling stock types, and bridge forms. His recommendation to employ wooden Howe-truss bridges was fully embraced, and about sixty were built along the nearly 400-mile Nikolaev Railway before 1851. The grandest were the Msta Bridge, shown in figure 5.33a, which had nine continuous 177-foot spans, and the very similar Verebia Bridge, designed in partnership with the brilliant Russian engineer D. I. Jouravsky (or Zhouravsky), with nine continuous 200-foot spans.

Figure 5.33 Examples of George Washington Whistler's Howe truss bridges on the St. Petersburg–Moscow (Nikolaev) Railway, ca. 1860. **Above top:** 5.33a) is the nine-span, 1,600-foot Msta Bridge; **Above:** 5.33b) is the three-span Tverca River Bridge. Courtesy of DeGolyer Library, Southern Methodist University, Dallas, Texas, Views of the Nikolaev Railway.

Jouravsky studied Howe bridges using physical models and developed mathematical methods of structural analysis. He considered continuity and post-tensioning forces from tightening the iron rods. He published his work in a book, won the Demidoff Medal in 1855, and later published in the *Annales des Ponts et Chaussees*.[59]

Engineer Carl Ritter von Ghega (or Carlo Ghega) also disseminated the Howe bridge form in Europe. Following an 1842 study tour of American bridges, he published a book of observations and analyses. He explicitly illustrated and discussed the Connecticut River Bridge and offered extensive comments on the Howe form; in fact, the phrase *"Howe'shchen Brücken"* ("Howe's bridges") is part of his book title.[60] Ghega's pioneering work likely influenced Carl Culmann's own paper on American wooden bridges; Culmann wrote, "this design is the best known and widely employed here in Europe, particularly in Austria," and felt no need to devote space to explaining the type.[61] Culmann did illustrate a Howe bridge over the Chicopee River in Connecticut which had diagonals spanning only one panel and carefully discussed the details of the iron node castings. Clearly, Howe's design was recognized as distinct from the St. Andrew's cross truss and was widely used in Europe in the 1840s. Two Howe bridges remain in Bavaria dating to the 1850s whose form is very similar to the Connecticut River Bridge, although they have iron nodes.[62]

Structural Behavior of Howe trusses

The classic Howe truss was a post-tensioned, statically indeterminate system. The post-tensioning eliminated the need to design tension connections for the diagonals. The design did not use treenails to transfer forces, and the member stresses were in the direction of the grain. Only minimal wood joinery was required, primarily in the bottom chord tension splices.

Because the Howe truss was statically indeterminate, nineteenth-century designs must have been based on simplified analyses using only equilibrium equations. The chords of Howe trusses were commonly designed using Navier's analogy of a truss as a beam, exactly as Long had done; the forces in the diagonals were generally understood to increase from midspan toward the ends. Therefore, the sizes of the diagonal members, as well as the sizes of the iron rods, increased from midspan to the supports. (The ability to use joint-by-joint equilibrium to determine forces in the diagonals of statically determinate forms became common only in the 1870s, when the Pratt truss became dominant for all-metal designs.) Counters were understood to be needed near midspan, where "reversals of the direction of shear forces" could occur under heavy moving live loads. Counter diagonals were also understood to contribute to stiffness and to be necessary if "tightening" or post-tensioning was to be done. Because it was not possible at this time to predict forces from post-tensioning, these forces were generally ignored.

Unfortunately, the construction techniques used to build classic, statically indeterminate Howe trusses are now largely forgotten. However, an 1853 document describing the construction of a 200-foot Howe railroad truss illuminates the methods used to achieve camber and to tighten the truss. The camber criterion was apparently based on modeling the top and bottom chords as arcs of circles with radii of curvature differing by the depth of the truss. With a prescribed camber, the difference between the chord arc lengths in one panel was computed. This difference was then used to define an upper-chord panel length that was slightly longer than the lower chord. This placed the iron rods in a radial rather than exactly vertical orientation. Rods were tightened using a wrench "with about a two feet leverage" beginning at the ends of the bridge and working toward midspan. Some retightening was likely required after a period of service. Ole Haldorson, a highway bridge builder who worked in Oregon during the 1930s and 1940s, indicated that adjusting the tension rods in Howe bridges "was something we did" a year or two after the completion of a bridge. "From then on, you could go out every ten to twelve years before retrussing [re-tensioning]."[63]

The effects of post-tensioning and the linear elastic behavior of classic Howe bridges under moving loads may now be easily estimated using computer-based structural analysis programs, as was done during the HAER documentation of the Pine Bluff Bridge in Indiana in 2002.[64] Wood is, however, a viscous, hygroscopic material whose behavior depends on moisture content and is a function of time. Therefore, linear elastic models are not sufficient for predicting the full range of structural behavior in a wood structure. Moreover, truss design based on linear elastic load effects and element design provides only a lower bound for the actual strength or capacity of a real truss.

The classic Howe truss had diagonals and counter diagonals and was pre-tensioned. But statically determinate versions of the Howe truss, without counters, were also commonly built. Such designs with wooden verticals were sometimes called multiple-kingpost trusses, but structural engineers do not use this terminology. Single-diagonal Howe trusses could not be post-tensioned. They also could not accommodate reversals in panel shear forces unless the main diagonals were detailed with end connections that could transfer tension.

In many ways, the Howe truss and wood were an ideal combination. Pre-tensioning eliminated most tension connections except in the chords, and, although the main diagonals acted in compression, the sizes of the wood members were such that the allowable compressive stresses were not limited by buckling. For the more slender members that resulted from steel construction, the Pratt truss was definitely a more suitable form.

The Pratt Truss

The truss patented by Thomas Willis Pratt and his father, Caleb, made Long's 1839 suspension truss practical because it utilized wrought-iron rods for the tension diagonals. Thomas Pratt was born in Boston in 1812 and studied architecture at the Rensselaer School in Troy, New York. His professional career was spent principally with several Massachusetts railroads.[65] As a New England railroad bridge designer, he would have known Long's 1830 and 1839 designs and Howe's 1840 improvement. He patented his truss in 1844 while working on the Norwich and Worcester Railroad (figure 5.34).

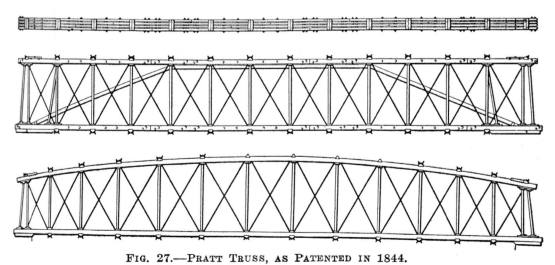

FIG. 27.—PRATT TRUSS, AS PATENTED IN 1844.

Figure 5.34 Thomas W. Pratt and Caleb Pratt, drawing for U.S. Patent No. 3,523, April 4, 1844.

Pratt's patent description demonstrated a thorough understanding of his invention's structural behavior. His statement that a "series of vertical posts . . . is elevated, the same resting upon shoes," implied that the verticals were not meant to be connected to the chords. Pratt correctly identified the members he labeled *D* on his patent drawing as "main braces" and those labeled *E* as "counter braces," exactly opposite to the roles of the same diagonals in a Howe truss. He also understood the effect of tightening the wrought-iron diagonals, stating that "they draw or confine the posts and stringers together." He relied on the compressive pre-load in the posts to keep them in position. The only differences between Pratt's design and Long's 1839 design were the elimination of wedges on the verticals, and the use of wrought-iron diagonals in place of wood.[66] The prestress conditions in Long's 1830 and 1839 patented trusses are compared with Howe's 1840 design and Pratt's 1844 design in figure 5.35.

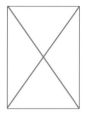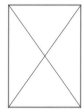

Figure 5.35 Left: 5.35a) Initial prestress forces in Long's 1830 patent truss and in a Howe truss; **Right:** 5.35b) initial prestress forces in Long's 1839 patent truss (no. 1,397) and in a Pratt truss. Red = compression, blue = tension

A comparison of the Howe and Pratt trusses from a variety of engineering viewpoints is both interesting and informative. The Pratt truss used twice as many diagonal rods as the Howe, and required them to be of wrought iron, the more expensive material in the mid-nineteenth century. The Pratt truss also required tensioning more diagonals. Increasing the size of the wrought-iron vertical components in a Howe truss could be done more easily than putting larger iron diagonals in a Pratt truss. It is likely a variable-depth truss could be more readily constructed in a Pratt form, as shown in the patent drawing. As indicated in figure 5.35, prestressing a Howe truss increased the gravity load tension in the bottom chord and decreased the gravity load compression in the top chord, while just the opposite was true in a Pratt truss. A Pratt truss's compression verticals were shorter than the compression diagonals of a Howe truss, but member buckling did not commonly determine the dimensions of a Howe's wooden diagonals. Bearing stresses were perpendicular to the grain of the chords in both designs, but the use of cast-iron nodal sleeves could minimize them in a Howe. Transferring unbalanced horizontal components of force into the chords at each truss node required notching the chords in both designs. A less evident difference was the "out-of-plane" stability of each truss panel during prestressing. The Howe-truss panel had no tendency to warp during prestressing and was, therefore, more stable. When a Pratt panel was prestressed, it was unstable out-of-plane. As a result, in wood-iron combinations the Howe truss was the more suitable form, as demonstrated by the dominance of the Howe truss for early railroad bridges. The relative advantages of the two forms were reversed for subsequent all-iron or all-steel bridges, where member stability was a governing design criterion.[67]

Bridge designers in the second half of the nineteenth century faced a choice of truss forms and had to consider how particular forms led to distinctly different structural behaviors. In brief, a designer could decide to use a form with *no counter diagonals,* a form with *non-prestressed counter diagonals,* or a form with *prestressed counter diagonals.*

> ***Forms with no counters***—If no counters were used, the basic Howe and Pratt trusses were statically determinate and could not be prestressed. In general, the main diagonals were sized

and connected to take both tension and compression. Tension-only or compression-only members could not be used except where the dead-load forces in the diagonals were dominant and not reversed by a moving live load. Force equilibrium was sufficient to determine the

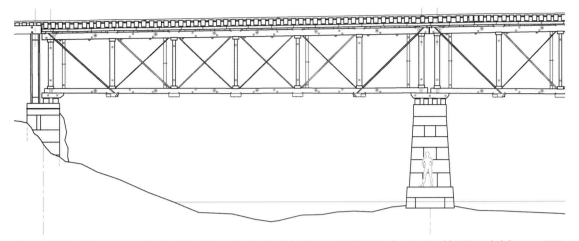

Figure 5.36 Partial elevation of the Sulphite Railroad Bridge Pratt deck truss. HAER NH-36, sheet 3, Arnold M. Kreisel, delineator 2003.

member forces for all live-load conditions.

Forms with counters, but not prestressed—This design choice allowed use of tension-only or compression-only members along an entire span. Only one diagonal was active in any one panel, and the truss remained statically determinate. The loose diagonals did not contribute to the stiffness of a truss. When a moving live load traversed a span, vibration noises might occur as the diagonals were stressed.

Forms with prestressed counters—Appropriate prestressing made all diagonals active for the dead load and for all positions of a live load. The system became statically indeterminate, and some assumptions had to be made before member forces could be determined by using equilibrium. All diagonals contributed to the stiffness of a truss, and some wood dimensional changes could occur without a loss of stiffness. If the members were ductile, the prestressing forces did not decrease the maximum live load a truss could carry.

The increased use of wrought iron and developments in structural analysis through the second half of the nineteenth century influenced designers' choices of truss forms. In general, stiffness and strength criteria

Figure 5.37 A 128-foot-long Pratt truss can be found in the center span of the Honey Run Bridge (ca. 1886), Butte County, California. HAER CA-312-5, Jet Lowe, photographer, 2004.

could easily be satisfied with all-metal, statically determinate forms. By the end of the 1870s, structural analysis and the design of statically determinate forms became basic engineering skills, codified in books and taught at all engineering schools. Since manual statically indeterminate analysis was still not practical, assumptions had to be made to determine member forces in statically indeterminate trusses. Many engineers saw these assumptions as undesirable, creating "ambiguities in stresses." Moreover, the understanding of structural behavior and structural analysis had not developed to the point that prestressing forces could be predicted and controlled by design engineers. Engineers were suspicious of contractor-controlled prestressing operations. For these reasons, designers increasingly chose statically determinate forms. However, since buckling was not a problem in tension-only diagonals, it was most efficient to use this type in all-metal trusses. Consequently, until the early twentieth century, designs using non-prestressed, tension-only main and counter diagonals remained in wide use in panels near the center of a span where a moving live load could cause a force reversal. The counters in the Sulphite Railroad Bridge, built in 1896 and studied by HAER in 2002, exemplify this view (figure 5.36).[68]

The Smith Truss

Robert Smith patented a timber truss in 1867 and started a company to build covered bridges using it. In 1869, he obtained a second patent, this time for bridge lateral-bracing systems. That year he built seventy-five bridges and moved the Smith Bridge Company from Miami County to Toledo, Ohio, a Great Lakes port and railroad hub. There he built a factory for the industrial manufacture of covered bridges. During the next two decades, the Smith Bridge Company prefabricated hundreds of bridges annually for shipment to locations throughout Ohio, Indiana, and Pennsylvania, where they were erected by the company's own crews or by others.[69]

Some of the company's success was due to the efficiency of Smith's truss design, both in the amount

Figure 5.38 The factory of the Smith Bridge Company in Toledo, Ohio, where workers prefabricated hundreds of timber bridges annually for shipment to sites across Ohio, Indiana, and Pennsylvania from 1869 to the 1880s. Courtesy of Miriam Wood Collection.

of materials it required and the amount of labor needed to fabricate it. Smith's trusses were essentially multiple-kingpost trusses whose web tension members (the vertical posts) had been tilted. Tilting the tension diagonals roughly doubled the panel length, so Smith's trusses required only about half as many panels as a multiple-kingpost bridge of the same length. The net effect was a reduction in the amount of timber used in the truss web. Smith trusses also required fewer notches (and thus less fabrication labor) than multiple-kingpost trusses. This was partly because there were fewer panels (although not true for Smith "double" or "triple" trusses, described below). Moreover, the posts on a vertical-kingpost truss had to be notched to create bearing surfaces for the compression diagonals, but on a Smith truss, where the tension and compression diagonals met at nearly a right angle, the latter could simply be butted against the former. This eliminated two notches per panel.

Smith introduced industrial techniques to reduce his labor costs. He planed his timbers to precise dimensions, which simplified making web-member joints and chord splices. This also allowed him to standardize the dimensions of some truss elements (such as fish plates, shear blocks, and metal castings) and mass produce them. His trusses were simple to lay out on a factory floor with few measurements. The use of scribed marks made the precise cutting of timber joints easy, even though truss diagonals were typically at odd angles. (At the Cataract Bridge in Indiana, for example, tension diagonals are at 56.4 degrees to the chords, and the compression diagonals are mostly at 50.8 degrees.) In short, Smith's designs incorporated characteristics of nineteenth-century industrialization: efficient use of materials, increased labor productivity, and mass production techniques that reduced the skill required of that labor.[70]

The company's success was also partly due to the industrial machinery Smith invented and installed in his factory, including "a gaining-machine [to cut notches in timbers] which does the work of 15 men," "a process for making a steel eye-bar [for which he received a patent in 1886]," and "a rotary saw, for making the joints of bridge-chords; and a multiple punch, by which six pieces of iron can be punched at one operation."[71]

The company not only built Smith trusses, it also built covered bridges using Howe and other truss types when its customers wanted them. Smith developed a composite truss, much like his patented all-timber truss but with iron rods for the tension diagonals, for use in railroad bridges. As early as 1870, the company began building all-metal bridges, and it became known for swing and draw bridges, too. By 1890, when Smith sold the company, it had stopped making wooden bridges altogether.[72] Renamed the Toledo Bridge Company, the firm continued in business until J. P. Morgan purchased it in 1901. Morgan combined it with twenty-four other bridge companies to create the American Bridge Company, which survives today.

The Smith truss was made entirely of wood, with all its web members, except the vertical posts at the ends, arranged diagonally. Tension timbers, which splayed outwards towards the ends of the bridge, alternated with compression timbers that tilted inwards. This arrangement made the Smith truss similar to the Warren truss, a design patented for use in iron bridges. In a Warren truss, however, adjacent diagonals met at the truss's chord, where both were joined to the chord with an iron pin. Such a three-piece joint could not be built with heavy timbers. In a Smith truss, only web tension members were joined to the chords; web compression timbers were butted into

Figure 5.39 "R.W. Smith's Patent Truss Bridge, Tippecanoe City, Miami Co., Ohio," by Strobridge and Company lithographers, Cincinnati, ca. 1868. Courtesy of Library of Congress, Prints and Photographs Division, Washington, D.C.

the tension ones just inside the chords.

An important facet of Smith's 1867 patent was that it allowed for two, three, or more sets of web members in the truss, "depending on the strength required."[73] In what the patent called a "single" truss, all the web members lay in a single vertical plane, with the tension members sandwiched between and notched into paired chord timbers, as in a multiple-kingpost or Burr-arch truss. Smith's patent, however, allowed for the addition of a third piece to the chords to sandwich a second set of web members (a "double truss") or four-piece chords to sandwich three sets of web members (a "triple truss"), and so on. An advertising lithograph for Smith's bridges from about 1868 clearly illustrates this idea. It shows three bridges: a short, single truss lightly loaded by a horse and rider, a longer double truss carrying a horse-drawn wagon, and a triple truss carrying a train (figure 5.39). The concept of using multiple planes of web members resembles, and was perhaps inspired by, Ithiel Town's second (1835) patent.

A Smith single truss looked like a series of inverted V's between the chords, with ends like a multiple-kingpost truss (where a compression diagonal met a vertical end post at the lower chord). Most of the weight of the bridge and the traffic on it was carried by the diagonal into the abutment below. The end post carried little vertical load, but it absorbed the diagonals' outward thrust and transferred it into the lower chord through the notched joint between them.

Three Smith single-truss bridges are known to survive. The Feedwire Road Bridge, a 42-foot span built in 1870 and the Jasper Road or "Mud Lick" Bridge, a 71-foot span from 1877, were both moved from their original Greene County, Ohio, locations and are now in Montgomery County. Both also have timber arches bolted to the trusses like on a Burr-arch truss, although these arches are thought not to be original. A third structure, the Salt Creek Bridge, an 83-foot span built in 1876 in Muskingum County, Ohio (figure 5.40), has no documented direct connection with Smith and lacks Smith's typical inclined end compression brace.

Figure 5.40 The 83-foot-long Salt Creek Bridge (1876) uses a single-web Smith truss with all inclined posts and braces in a single plane. HAER OH-127-9, Jet Lowe, photographer, 2004.

A Smith double truss had a second set of web members, offset lengthwise from the first. The two sets thus formed a series of X's along the length of the truss (figure 5.41). Offsetting the two sets had structural advantages but presented a problem at the ends of the bridge. There, the second set terminated, not with a compression diagonal carrying loads into the abutment, but with a tension diagonal notched to the upper chord. Smith added additional, steeply inclined compression timbers to meet these tension members and carry their vertical loads to the abutment (figure 5.41). Due to their acute angle of intersection, both the "extra" brace and the tension

Figure 5.42 Cataract Bridge (1876) is a 140-foot Smith "double-truss" (Wilson type 3). The truss, the portal bracing, and the lateral bracing between the upper chords were all patented by Robert Smith. Note how both tension and compression diagonals are notched into the chords at midspan. HAER IN-104-6, James Rosenthal, photographer, 2004.

Figure 5.41 Kidd's Mill Bridge (1868) is a 122-foot-long Smith "double truss" (Wilson type 2). Note the steeply inclined extra brace at the end panel, with a lightning bolt shaped notch. HAER PA-622-5, Jet Lowe, photographer, 2006.

diagonal were notched to provide an end bearing surface for their butt joint. This extra compression member, and the lightning-bolt shape of the notch at its end, were distinctive features of Smith trusses. About a dozen Smith double trusses survive, with spans between about 50 and 150 feet.

For longer spans Smith used triple trusses with three sets of web members and four-piece chords. The early Smith Bridge Company advertisement in figure 5.39 shows a triple truss where each of the three webs is offset from the others, and each diagonal therefore crosses two others. If any bridges

Figure 5.43 The Powder Works Bridge, built in 1872 by the Pacific Bridge Company, is a 180-foot Smith "triple truss" (Wilson type 4). One set of diagonals is sandwiched between and offset from two other sets of web members, connecting to four-piece chords. The image also shows the extra, inclined compression brace on the end panel, common to most Smith trusses (a block of wood obscures the notched joint). Note Smith-type castings fitted over notched joints in upper lateral braces. HAER CA-313-8, Jet Lowe, photographer, 2004.

were built this way, none remain. In all eight surviving Smith "triples," which span between 146 and 180 feet, the third set of web members is a duplicate of the first, with the second, middle, set offset as in a double truss (figure 5.43). Consequently, an elevation view of a Smith triple truss appears as a series of X's, just as a Smith double does.

Robert Smith's covered bridges were also distinguished by the use of the bracing elements contained in his 1869 patent, although other builders using Smith's truss did not always employ them. Smith's knee braces were used to keep the main trusses from leaning to either side. Conventional wooden knees at the time extended diagonally from a truss post to a cross beam between the upper chords. They were typically used in pairs, one on each side of the bridge, at intervals throughout its length. Smith's knee braces extended beyond the cross beam until they met just under the roof peak, and were joined to each other as well as to the cross beam and end posts. This was stronger than conventional knees would have been, but Smith never seems to have devised a means of attaching his knees to diagonal truss members, so his bracing was found only on the vertical posts at each end of the bridge. An example can be seen at the far end of the bridge in figure 5.42.

Smith's 1869 patent also covered his lateral bracing between lower chords under the bridge's floor and between upper chords under the bridge's roof. The system commonly used in Smith's time included iron rods in tension between the chords at intervals along the length of the bridge and, between adjacent rods, timbers crossed in an X, similar to a Howe truss in a horizontal plane. The timber ends in adjacent X's met, but did not cross, at the chords; they could work in compression but not tension. In Smith's system, the ends of these timbers crossed just before they reached the chords and were notched together, as seen in figures 5.42 and 5.43. Then, by means of an iron casting that fit over the notched joint, the timbers were bolted to the chord.

This connection enabled the timbers to resist tension as well as compression, eliminating the need for iron rods between the chords.

Over time, Smith altered the way he arranged the timbers near midspan on his trusses, although he never patented the changes. His first patent drawings in 1867 show a double truss in which, near midspan, each web set has a vertical tension member, with compression diagonals butting into notches on both sides of it below the upper chord. This vertical is just like the midspan post on a multiple-kingpost truss (figure 5.44a). No extant bridges use this arrangement.

Soon Smith eliminated the tension post and compression braces at midspan. His 1869 patent drawings show, instead, two tension diagonals (part of the middle web set of a triple truss) extending

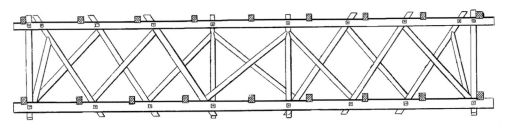

Figure 5.44a: Smith truss, from his 1867 patent (Wilson type 1)

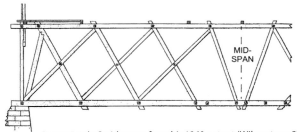

Figure 5.44b: Smith truss, from his 1869 patent (Wilson type 2)

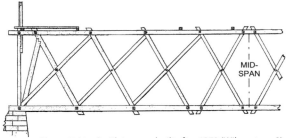

Figure 5.44c: Smith truss as built after 1870 (Wilson type 3)

Figure 5.44 Development of Smith's midspan web member arrangement, drawn by Matthew Reckard.

from midspan on the lower chord outwards in each direction to the upper chord (figure 5.44b). There are no corresponding midspan compression diagonals in the other web sets. Only the two oldest remaining Smith-truss bridges were built like this: the 1868 Kidd's Mill Bridge in Mercer County, Pennsylvania, and the 1870 Brushy Fork Bridge in Jackson County, Ohio. Similar arrangements are shown on all three bridges in his ca. 1868 advertisement (figure 5.39).

In the early 1870s, Smith began to include compression diagonals at midspan in the second and, if present, third web sets. Under some loading conditions these midspan truss diagonals could experience "stress reversal," i.e. be subjected to tension rather than compression. Smith therefore notched them into the chords rather than butt-jointing them to adjoining diagonals (figure 5.44c).

Raymond Wilson, in a paper published in 1967, classified Smith trusses into four types.[74] His type 1 had the midspan web-member arrangement shown in the first patent drawing; his type 2 had the one shown in the 1869 patent. Wilson's type 3 is the Smith double truss in the post-1870 style. Wilson's type 4 truss was not a chronological development, but rather a Smith triple truss in the post-1870 style. It is not clear if Wilson's type 2 included double trusses, triples, or both, and Smith single trusses were not included in his classification system. Despite these limitations, Wilson's taxonomy has commonly been used ever since its publication.

Structural Behavior of Smith Trusses

The Smith truss proved to be a robust and efficient form of timber truss, but, within a couple of decades of its introduction, it, like all timber bridge forms, was largely superseded by metal truss types.

As Smith's career ended and his company began building large steel movable bridges, he would have been using the period's most advanced structural analysis methods. What design method he used for bridge trusses earlier in his career (during the late 1860s and 1870s) is unknown. Analytic methods for indeterminate structures like the Smith truss were not available. Smith could have approximated his truss and analyzed it as a determinate structure, as a Warren truss.

A 2012 study for the Historic American Engineering Record examined two Smith truss bridges: Kidd's Mill Bridge, built in 1868 in Mercer County, Pennsylvania, and Rinard Bridge, built in 1876 in Washington County, Ohio.[75] The study, by Professor Stephen Buonopane and students at Bucknell University, used computerized finite element model (FEM) analysis for both bridges' trusses as originally built. (Post-construction damage and deterioration were not part of the study.) The study considered dead load and two live load cases for each bridge. The live load that produced higher forces in nearly all members was a linear load of about 550 pounds per foot along the length of each truss lower chord, corresponding to a uniform 65 pounds per square foot load on the deck. The study results indicated that the Kidd's Mill trusses, built following Smith's early form without compression diagonals in their central panels, developed substantial bending stresses in the lower chords near midspan, while the later Rinard Bridge trusses did not. It seems likely that Smith noted this weakness in his early designs and added compression diagonals to correct it.

The study further indicated that under combined dead and live loads, the lower chords of the Kidd's Mill trusses were stressed to almost 100 percent of their calculated allowable capacity, while the upper chords, and all the chords on Rinard Bridge, were stressed to considerably less than their capacities. The study, however, overestimated the chords' capacities. The lower chords' capacity was calculated based on the timbers' full size (gross cross-sectional area) rather than the reduced size at their notches (net section), while the allowable compressive stress for the upper chords was not reduced to account for buckling considerations. It appeared that, if such adjustments were made, the combined loads would stress the upper chords of both bridges, along with the lower chord of the Rinard Bridge, to between 90 and 100 percent of capacity, while the lower chord of Kidd's Mill Bridge would be overstressed. This result, that the allowable live load on the bridge chords was approximately 550 pounds per foot, suggests that Smith may have been designing his trusses for a live load of 1,000 pounds per foot (500 per truss), a typical design value for the period.

The forces in the notched joint between a tension diagonal and the lower chord at one location on the Kidd's Mill trusses were also considered in detail in the study. Several possible failure modes were examined, with the critical one found to be shearing of the tension diagonal's "shoulders" beyond the notch. The study indicated the shear force here under dead load alone (6 kips) exceeded its calculated allowable capacity (5.76 kips) and that under combined dead and live load, the shear force was almost four times the member's allowable capacity. It appeared, however, that these shearing forces may have been greatly overestimated due to methodological issues in the analysis. Nevertheless, the conclusion that notched tension joints were one of the weaker details in Smith trusses was correct. Buonopane found that the ends of several tension diagonals at Kidd's Mill had either failed in shear and been repaired or had been preemptively strengthened. The 2004–2005 rehabilitation of Cataract Bridge, an 1876 Smith double truss in Owen County, Indiana, required repair of shear failures in the ends of two tension diagonals and in twelve lower chord splices (either in the chord timbers or the connecting fish plates). It should be noted, however, that problems with timber tension joints were not unique to Smith's design but were endemic to timber trusses in general.

Observations

The concept of "trussing," or connecting members in triangulated networks to form a structure, is ancient. But it can be fairly said that the American contribution to the practice of using trusses as bridges is of international cultural importance. American truss bridges were widely admired and copied in Europe in the nineteenth century. Only the most important forms are described here; there are many others, representing variations among regions and builders. The variety of truss bridges testifies to great ingenuity and construction and engineering skill. Not only were truss bridges functional, but the best examples also had great aesthetic appeal.

Material technology affected truss designs. At the beginning of the nineteenth century, wood was the only widely available, economic material. Wood is a versatile, strong material, but it shrinks and swells as its moisture content changes and it has time-dependent strain responses to applied stress. It is difficult to design efficient connections that can transfer tension forces between wood members, and traditional wood joinery was often unsuitable for the force demands of truss bridges. The success of Town's lattice design was largely a consequence of its simple joinery. Simplified joinery was also a key feature of Long's truss designs, which utilized counters and prestressing to minimize tension connections. The prestressing process was simplified in the 1840s, when wrought-iron rods were introduced in truss bridges by Howe and Pratt. Cast iron was widely known to be relatively weak in tension and was used principally for nodal castings until the 1870s when riveted connections were introduced.

The need for reliable truss bridges spurred the development of structural engineering science, which in turn led to improved understanding of truss behavior and improved engineering design methods. Based on the theoretical developments of Navier, engineering analysis was first applied to the design of truss bridges in the 1830s by engineer S. H. Long. By the 1870s, engineers had an essentially complete understanding of the structural behavior of statically determinate trusses. Because of this, statically determinate forms of the Howe and Pratt trusses became dominant, and more complex forms, such as the Burr arch-truss and prestressed forms, fell into disuse.

Truss forms developed in response to changing transportation needs. There is a direct lineage between the small wooden trusses first built to carry people, wagons, and livestock over modest spans and the massive all-steel trusses built in the late nineteenth century to carry extremely heavy trains over great spans. As the origin of this lineage, American covered wooden truss bridges have a special significance in our cultural history.

Endnotes

1 Theodore Cooper, "American Railroad Bridges," *Transactions of the American Society of Civil Engineers* 21 (July–December 1889): 1–52; Robert Fletcher and J. P. Snow, "A History of the Development of Wooden Bridges," Paper No. 1864, *Transactions of the American Society of Civil Engineers* 99 (1934): 314–54; Richard Sanders Allen, "America's Covered Bridges," *Consulting Engineer* (April 1957): 92–100. Quote from Richard Sanders Allen, *Covered Bridges of the Northeast* (Brattleboro, Vt.: Stephen Greene Press, 1957), 12.

2 Dennis Hart Mahan, *An Elementary Course of Civil Engineering for the Use of the Cadets of the United States Military Academy* (New York: Wiley and Halsted, 1857), 175; Fletcher and Snow, "History of the Development of Wooden Bridges," 325; Andrea Palladio, *Four Books of Architecture* (reprint, New York: Dover Publications, Inc., 1965), third book, chapter 9.

3 Allen, "America's Covered Bridges," 11; Lola Bennett, "From Craft to Science: American Timber Bridges, 1790–1840," *APT Bulletin* 35, no. 4 (2004): 13–19; Squire Whipple, *A Work on Bridge Building Consisting of Two Essays, the One Elementary and General, the Other Giving Original Plans and Details for Iron and Wooden Bridges* (Utica, N.Y.: H. H. Curtiss, Printer, 1847), 6.

4 Mahan, *Elementary Course of Civil Engineering*, 241–42.

5 Cooper, "American Railroad Bridges," 8–9; "Old Highway Bridge at Waterford New York," *Engineering News* (June 1, 1889), 496–97; Fletcher and Snow, "History of the Development of Wooden Bridges," 331; Llewellyn Edwards, *A Record of History and Evolution of Early American Bridges* (Orono, Maine: University Press, 1959), 49–52; Thomas Pope, *A Treatise on Bridge Architecture* (New York: A. Niven, 1811), 129–39; Herman Haupt, *The General Theory of Bridge Construction* (New York: D. Appleton and Co., 1851), 242–43.

6 Hubertis M. Cummings, "Theodore Burr and His Bridges across the Susquehanna," *Pennsylvania History* 23, no. 4 (October 1956): 476–86.

7 Haupt, *General Theory of Bridge Construction*, 175.

8 Emory L. Kemp and J. Hall, "Case Study of Burr Truss Covered Bridge," *Engineering Issues: Journal of Professional Activities* 101, no. 3 (1975): 391–412; Rachel Sangree, "Gilpin's Falls Covered Bridge," HAER No. MD-174, 2012.

9 Edwards, *Record of History and Evolution of Early American Bridges*, 51. The existing patent consists of a drawing only.

10 Haupt, *General Theory of Bridge Construction*, 174.

11 "Jackson Covered Bridge," HAER No. IN-48; "Kennedy Bridge," HABS No. IN-24; "Forsythe Bridge," HAER No. IN-106; George E. Gould, *Indiana Covered Bridges Thru the Years* (Indianapolis: Indiana Covered Bridge Society, 1977), 11–16.

12 Theodore Burr to Reuben Field, February 26, 1815, quoted in "Some Early County Bridges," *Historical Papers and Addresses of the Lancaster County Historical Society* 11, no. 4 (April 5, 1907), 133.

13 David Billington, *Robert Maillart's Bridges: The Art of Engineering* (Princeton, N.J.: Princeton University, 1979), 93.

14 Roger H. Newton, *Town & Davis, Architects: Pioneers in American Revivalist Architecture, 1812–1870* (New York: Columbia University Press, 1942), 44, 73.

Endnotes

[15] Ithiel Town, *A Description of Ithiel Town's Improvement in the Principle, Construction and Practical Execution of Bridges* (New York, 1839), 6.

[16] John L. Sanders, "Biography of Ithiel Town," 2009, *North Carolina Architects & Builders: A Biographical Dictionary*, http://ncarchitects.lib.ncsu.edu/people/P000032.

[17] Ithiel Town, "Bridge," U.S. Patent No. 3,169X, January 28, 1820.

[18] Edwards, *Record of History and Evolution of Early American Bridges*, 56–59; Dylan Lamar and Ben Schafer, "Structural Analysis of Historic Covered Wooden Bridges," *Journal of Bridge Engineering* 9, no. 6 (December 2004): 623–33; Lewis M. Prevost, "Description of Howe's Patent Truss Bridge," *Journal of the Franklin Institute* 3, no. 5 (May 1842): 289–92.

[19] Carl Culmann, "Der Bau der hölzernen Brücken in den Vereingten Staaten von Nordamerika," *Allgemeine Bauzeitung* 16 (1851): 69–129.

[20] Cooper, "American Railroad Bridges," 11.

[21] Fletcher and Snow, "History of the Development of Wooden Bridges," 333; J. P. Snow, "Wooden Bridge Construction on the Boston and Maine Railroad," *Journal of the Association of Engineering Societies* (July 1895), 500–506.

[22] Town, *Description of Ithiel Town's Improvement*, 4.

[23] Snow, "Wooden Bridge Construction," 500–506; David Stevenson, *Sketch of the Civil Engineering of North America* (London: J. Weale, 1838), 234.

[24] Haupt, *General Theory of Bridge Construction*, 151.

[25] Lamar and Schafer, "Structural Analysis of Historic Covered Wooden Bridges," 632.

[26] Allen, *Covered Bridges of the Northeast*, 15; Edwards, *Record of History and Evolution of Early American Bridges*, 56; "Bunker Hill Bridge," HAER No. NC-46; Dick Roy, "Old Pompy," http://www. vermontbridges.com/cbmail.bag2.htm; "Cornish-Windsor Bridge," HAER No. NH-8; R. T. Dana, *The Bridge at Windsor, Vt.. and Its Economic Implications* (New York: Condex Book Co., 1926), 33–61; David Fischetti, *Structural Investigation of Historic Buildings* (New Jersey: John Wiley & Sons, Inc., 2009), 214–18.

[27] George Smart's bridge is referred to as an "iron bridge" in G. Drysdale Dempsey, *Tubular and Other Iron Girder Bridges* (London: John Weale, 1850), 33; a "mathematical chain bridge" in Olinthus Gregory, *Mathematics for Practical Men* (London: Baldwin, Cradock, & Joy, 1825), 233; and a "chain bridge" in David Guise, "Development of the American Metal Lattice Truss Bridge and the Hilton Truss," *Structure Magazine* (August 2011), 24–26.

[28] "Sir John McNeill," *A Dictionary of Contemporary Biography* (London & Glasgow: Richard Griffon and Company, 1861), 262; Dempsey, *Tubular and Other Iron Girder Bridges*, 36; Sir John Rennie, *Address of Sir John Rennie, President, to the Annual General Meeting, January 20, 1846* (London: Institution of Civil Engineers, 1846), 18. Quote from R. W. Liscombe, "A 'New Era in My Life': Ithiel Town Abroad," *Journal of the Society of Architectural Historians* 50, no. 1 (March 1999): 5.

[29] Olinthus Gregory, *Mathematics for Practical Men* (London: Baldwin, Cradock, & Joy, 1825), 239; Town, *Description of Ithiel Town's Improvement*, 4, 11.

[30] Whipple, *Work on Bridge Building*, 11–31.

Endnotes

31 The weight of half of the bridge span is 187,500 pounds, and the total brace force considers the fact that there are four truss frames.

32 William Humber, *Practical Treatise on Cast and Wrought Iron Bridges and Girders* (London: E. and F. N. Spon, 1857), 14, 92–100.

33 Stephen H. Long, *Rail Road Manual, or, a Brief Exposition of Principles and Deductions Applicable in Tracing the Route of a Rail Road* (Baltimore: William Wooddy, 1829). Long's patents include no. 5,862X, March 6, 1830; no. 7,351X, December 28, 1832; no. 7,372X, January 17, 1833; no. 7,570X, January 17, 1833; no. 9,340X, January 23, 1836; and nos. 1,397 and 1,398, both November 7, 1839.

34 The specifications for Long's 1830 patent appear in *Journal of the Franklin Institute* 5, no 4 (April 1830): 234. A Long truss built in 1831 at Mattawamkeag, Maine, by Capt. Charles Thomas on the Aroostook Military Road apparently used the upper arch braces, as suggested by an exterior photograph showing an odd cross gable roof.

35 Stephen H. Long, *Description of the Jackson Bridge, Together with Directions to Builders of Wooden or Frame Bridges* (Baltimore: Sands & Neilson, 1830), 7.

36 Stephen H. Long, "Remarks on the Jackson Bridge," *Journal of the Franklin Institute* 4, no. 2 (August 1830): 110, 112.

37 Allen, *Covered Bridges of the Northeast*; Richard Sanders Allen, *Covered Bridges of the Middle Atlantic States* (Brattleboro, Vt.: Stephen Greene Press, 1959); Stephen H. Long, *Description of Col. Long's Bridges Together with a Series of Directions to Bridge Builders* (Concord, N.H.: John F. Brown, Printer, 1836), 43–47.

38 Stephen H. Long, "Truss Bridge," U.S. Patent No. 9,340X, January 23, 1836.

39 Long, *Description of Col. Long's Bridges*, 25.

40 Culmann, "Der Bau der hölzernen Brücken," 69–129; D. Gasparini and C. Provost, "Contribution of Stephen Harriman Long to the Design of Trusses," *Proceedings of the CSCE Centennial Conference, Montreal, Canada, May 19–22, 1987*, 804–11; D. Gasparini and C. Provost, "Early Nineteenth Century Developments in Truss Design," *Construction History* 5 (1989): 21–33.

41 Stephen H. Long, U.S. Patent Nos. 1,397 and 1,398, November 7, 1839; idem, "Specification of a patent for a suspension bridge" and "Specifications of a patent for an improved bridge, denominated a brace bridge," *Journal of the Franklin Institute* 24, no. 5 (November 1839): 325–33; idem, "Colonel Long's Bridges," *Journal of the Franklin Institute*, third series, vol. 2, no. 3 (September 1841): 175.

42 Culmann, "Der Bau der hölzernen Brücken," 73–74. Dario Gasparini gratefully acknowledges the assistance of Dr. Frank Rausche of Cleveland, Ohio, who translated Culmann's remarks on Long from the German.

43 Dario Gasparini and David Simmons, "American Truss Bridge Connections in the Nineteenth Century. I: 1829–1850," *Journal of Performance of Constructed Facilities* 11, no. 3 (August 1997): 119–29; Fletcher and Snow, "History of the Development of Wooden Bridges"; Allen, *Covered Bridges of the Northeast*, 17–18; J. G. James, "The Evolution of Wooden Bridge Trusses to 1850 [part 2]," *Journal of the Institute of Wood Science* 9, no. 4 (December 1982): 176–77.

44 Marc Seguin, *Des Ponts en Fil de Fer*, 2nd ed. (Paris: Chez Bachelier, Libraire, 1826); Tom F. Peters, *Transitions in Engineering: Guillaume Henri Dufour and the Early 19th Century Cable Suspension Bridges* (Basel, Switzerland: Birkhäuser Verlag, 1987); M. Cotte, "The Tournon-Train Suspension Bridge: A Case Study in Technology Transfer and Innovation, 1821–1825," *Proceedings*

Endnotes

of an International Conference on Historic Bridges to Celebrate the 150th Anniversary of the Wheeling Suspension Bridge, Wheeling, W.Va., October 21–23, 1999, 47–58.

[45] "Description of the Freyburg Suspension Bridge," *Journal of the Franklin Institute* 16, no. 3 (September 1853), 202.

[46] A. Kahlow, "Johann August Roebling (1806–1869): Early Projects in Context," *Proceedings of the John A. Roebling Symposium organized by the New Jersey and Metropolitan Sections of the ASCE*, Brooklyn, New York, October 27, 2006; C. F. W. Berg, *Der Bau der Hängebrücken aus Eisendraht* (Leipzig, 1824); Emory Kemp, "Charles Ellet and the Wheeling Suspension Bridge," *Proceedings of an International Conference on Historic Bridges to Celebrate the 150th Anniversary of the Wheeling Suspension Bridge*, Wheeling, W.Va., October 21–23, 1999, 15–31; Charles Ellet, *A Popular Notice of Wire Suspension Bridges* (Richmond, Va.: P. D. Bernard, 1839); Charles Ellet, *Report and Plan for a Wire Suspension Bridge, Proposed to be Constructed Across the Mississippi River at Saint Louis* (Philadelphia: W. Stavely & Co. Printers, 1840); Charles Ellet, *A Popular Notice of Suspension Bridges, with a Brief Description of the Wire Bridge across the Schuylkill at Fairmount* (Philadelphia: J. Clark, 1843), 7, 30; D. Sayenga, "Fairmount Suspension Bridge," in *Baltimore Civil Engineering History,* ed. Bernard G. Dennis Jr. and Matthew C. Fenton IV (Reston, Va.: American Society of Civil Engineers, 2005), 265–309.

[47] William Howe, "Truss Frame for Bridges," U.S. Patent No. 1,685, July 10, 1840.

[48] William Howe, "Truss Bridge," U.S. Patent No. 1,711, August 3, 1840. A recent study of the Howe patent files suggests that the patent examiner recommended separating what had initially been a single application from Howe into two separate applications; Dario Gasparini, personal communication with D. Sayenga, 2006.

[49] Berg, *Bau der Hängebrücken aus Eisendraht*, table II, fig. 10; Seguin, *Des Ponts en Fil de Fer*, fig. 10; Ellet, *Report and Plan for a Wire Suspension Bridge*, plate 1, fig. 5.

[50] Albert Parry, *Whistler's Father* (Indianapolis: Bobbs-Merrill Company, 1937); C. E. Fisher, "Whistler's Railroad: The Western Railroad of Massachusetts," *Railway and Locomotive Historical Society Bulletin*, 69 (1947); Allen, *Covered Bridges of the Northeast*, 66; M. Joblin, *Cleveland, Past and Present* (Cleveland, Ohio: Fairbanks, Benedict, 1869), 301.

[51] *Annual Report of the Directors of the Western Railroad Corporation to the Stockholders* (Boston: S. N. Dickinson, 1840), 14.

[52] *Annual Report of the Directors of the Western Railroad Corporation to the Stockholders*, 14.

[53] Joblin, *Cleveland, Past and Present*, 302; Victor C. Darnell, *A Directory of American Bridge-Building Companies, 1840–1900* (Washington, D.C.: Society for Industrial Archaeology, 1984).

[54] Prevost, "Description of Howe's Patent Truss Bridge," 292; "Notes on Practical Engineering No. 5. Bridges," *American Railroad Journal and Mechanics' Magazine* 17 (January 1844): 42–43. The chord sizes given on the drawing published in the *Journal of the Franklin Institute* in 1842 do not agree with the chords illustrated on plate 122 of J. Weale's *Theory, Practice, and Architecture of Bridges* (London: John Weale Architectural Library, 1843). Since G. W. Whistler provided the drawings to Weale, we must assume that the sizes provided by the Franklin Institute are incorrect.

[55] Joblin, *Cleveland, Past and Present,* 300.

[56] William Howe, U.S. Patent No. 4,726, August 28, 1846.

[57] Joblin, *Cleveland, Past and Present*, 303; E. L. Kemp and R. K. Anderson, "The Reading-Halls Station Bridge," *IA* 13, no. 1 (1987): 17–40; Gasparini and Simmons, "American Truss Bridge Connections," 123; Ohio General Assembly, Joint Committee Concerning the Ashtabula Bridge Disaster, *Report of the*

Endnotes

Joint Committee Concerning the Ashtabula Bridge Disaster (Columbus: Nevins & Myers, 1877), 82.

58 James, "Evolution of Wooden Bridge Trusses to 1850 [part 2]," 192; John Weale, *The Theory, Practice, and Architecture of Bridges of Stone, Iron, Timber and Wire* (London: 1843), plate 122.

59 S. Timoshenko, "D. J. Jourawsky and His Contributions to Theory of Structures," in *Federhofer-Girkmann-Festschrift* (Vienna: F. Deuticke, 1950), 115–23; idem, *History of Strength of Materials* (New York: McGraw-Hill, 1953), 141, 186–89; D. Jouravsky, *About Bridges of the Howe System* (St. Petersburg: D. Kesneville, Typographers, 1855–56).

60 Carl Ghega, *Über Nordamerikanischen Brückenbau und berechnung des tragungsvermögens der Howe'shchen Brücken* (Vienna: Kaulfuss Witwe, Prandel and Compaigne, 1845).

61 Culmann, "Der Bau der hölzernen Brücken," 74.

62 Culmann, "Der Bau der hölzernen Brücken," plate 390; Philip S. C. Caston, *Germany's Remaining Historic Wooden Bridges* (Neubrandenburg, Germany: Hochschule Neubrandenburg, Fachbereich Landschaftsarchitektur, Geoinformatik, Geodäsie und Bauingenieurwesen, 2010), 144–45; Stefan M. Holzer, *Die König-Ludwig-Brücke Kempten*, Historische Wahrzeichen der Ingenieurbaukunst in Deutschland 11 (Berlin: Bundesingenieurkammer, 2012).

63 "Description of Howe's Bridge, 1853," *Covered Bridge Topics* 68 (Winter 2010): 3–7; "Ole Haldorson, Oregon Bridge Builder: An Interview," *Covered Bridge Topics* 71 (Winter 2013): 3–10.

64 Francesca da Porto, "Pine Bluff Bridge," HAER No. IN-103, 2002.

65 "Thomas Willis Pratt," *Annals of the Massachusetts Charitable Mechanics Association 1795–1892* (Boston: Press of Rockwell and Churchill, 1892), 211–12.

66 Caleb Pratt and Thomas W. Pratt, "Truss Bridge," U.S. Patent No. 3,523, April 4, 1844; Gasparini and Simmons, "American Truss Bridge Connections," 126.

67 Dario Gasparini, J. Bruckner, and Francesca da Porto, "Time-Dependent Behavior of Posttensioned Wood Howe Bridges," *Journal of Structural Engineering* 132, no. 3 (2006): 418–29.

68 Megan Reese, "Sulphite Railroad Bridge," HAER No. NH-36.

69 Clark Waggoner, ed., *History of the City of Toledo and Lucas County* (New York: Munsell & Co., 1888), 786–87; Eldon M. Neff, "Highlights in the Life of Robert W. Smith," *Connecticut River Valley Covered Bridge Society* 11, no. 4 (Spring 1963); S. Buonopane, S. Ebright, and A. Smith, "The Timber Trusses of R. W. Smith, History, Design and Behavior," *Proceedings of the Fourth International Congress on Construction History*, Paris, July 3–7, 2012, 599–606.

70 Matthew Reckard, "Smith Trusses: Bringing Covered Bridges into the Industrial Age," *Covered Bridge Preservation National Best Practices Conference*, University of Vermont, June 2003, www.uvm.edu/coveredbridges/papers/reckard.html.

71 Waggoner, *History of the City of Toledo*, 786.

72 Waggoner, *History of the City of Toledo*, 786; Neff, "Highlights in the Life of Robert W. Smith."

73 Robert W. Smith, U.S. Patent No. 66,900, July 16, 1867.

74 Raymond E. Wilson, "The Story of the Smith Truss," *Covered Bridge Topics* 25 (April 1967): 3–5.

75 Stephen Buonopane, Sarah Ebright and Alex Smith, "Structural Study of Smith Trusses," HAER No. PA-645, 2012.

Chapter 6

Builders and Practices

by Joseph D. Conwill

T he covered bridge builder comes down to us in folklore as a legendary figure akin to Paul Bunyan.[1] In reality the builders were a varied group of people. Despite the fact that some were self-educated and few had formal engineering training, they did not build their bridges by guesswork. Instead, covered bridge builders understood complicated structural principles through experience gained on the job and by observation. J. P. Snow, bridge engineer with the Boston and Maine Railroad, noted that "when an intelligent master-carpenter has had the care for a term of years of a line of wooden bridges covering any given style of truss, he gradually brings their parts, when building new ones, to almost the exact size called for by scientific

Figure 6.1 The Norris Ford Bridge, Rush County, Indiana, was constructed in 1916. White-bearded builder Emmett L. Kennedy (1848–1938) is second from the front. Courtesy of National Society for the Preservation of Covered Bridges.

analysis when actual loads are used in calculation."[2] This experiential knowledge was essential because building timber bridges is not, as is often stated, like building houses or barns. Some of the joinery skills may be similar, but the challenge of using timber to span a hundred feet or more of open space is quite different from building on a foundation. Although many covered bridge builders did other types of construction, particularly where their specialized knowledge of how to span open spaces was useful, it is, ultimately, for their covered bridges that these builders are remembered today.[3]

The term "builder" may be used in different ways. In the broadest sense, a builder uses tools to make something. In terms of covered bridges, the builder was really a contractor with the ultimate legal responsibility for completing a large construction job. Some builders, such as Theodore Burr or Lewis Wernwag, also provided original designs for their bridges—in other words, they functioned as engineer/architects. Others used patented designs that they adapted as needed. Builders usually

Figure 6.2 **Top:** 6.2a) Pine Grove Bridge (1884) once illustrated the general pattern of X-braced floor framing found in covered bridges in Lancaster County, Pennsylvania. Since the decking and stone abutments have been replaced by steel beams and concrete, these floor details no longer exist. HAER PA-586-2, Jet Lowe, photographer, 2002. **Above:** 6.2b) On the other hand, Dreibelbis Station Bridge (1869) retains the three-panel-long latticed style floor framing typical of covered bridges erected in Berks County, Pennsylvania. HAER PA-587-7, Jet Lowe, photographer, 2002.

had extensive hands-on experience in construction and closely supervised the layout even if their crews did most of the physical labor, but there were exceptions even to this. Lewis Wernwag was very skillful at construction, but for some of his later bridges it appears that he only provided plans and perhaps never even visited the sites in person. On the other hand, William Henry Gorrill of the Pacific Bridge Company is listed as builder for several significant California structures, but it is unlikely that he handled tools himself. He was a lawyer by training, and the actual construction of his bridges was done by subcontractors or hired crews whose names are largely forgotten.[4]

Builders worked for a variety of entities, since covered bridges were financed in a number of ways. The large, early covered bridges were generally built for toll-bridge companies, since governments typically did not have enough capital for large-scale construction projects in the early nineteenth century. Notable exceptions were the bridges on the National Road, whose construction was federally funded. Later in the nineteenth century, government entities contracted with builders to erect covered bridges on smaller crossings on local roads; tolls were not generally charged on these crossings. In New England and in New York, town governments were responsible for most of the public works within their boundaries. From Pennsylvania on south and west, public works were usually a county responsibility, and the elected county commissioners would award bridge contracts directly. (Naturally, the commissioners had their trusted favorites.) By the twentieth century, the county engineer typically made the maintenance decisions. While private contractors built Oregon's early covered bridges, county bridge crews erected those built into the mid-twentieth century. The state provided suggested plans, but county engineers modified them as they saw fit and designed the housings.[5]

The structure of the local government, therefore, influenced the design of covered bridges. Examining Pennsylvania's Burr-arch truss covered bridges illustrates the impact of having county commissioners award bridge contracts, as there are marked differences between counties. Covered bridges in Lancaster County exhibit classically framed Burr-arch trusses, including floor beams placed at the panel points and lower lateral bracing in the form of an X. Berks County Burr-arch trusses have floor beams placed throughout the panel and an unusual latticed style of lower laterals. (It is just such local framing details that are lost when floors are replaced with steel beams during repairs, or when engineers reconfigure covered bridges to generic designs.) Burr-arch trusses in Perry County sometimes use just a single treenail to fix the post at the top-chord joint instead of the usual two. Further west, the Burr-arch trusses of Somerset County usually have braces mitered into the post-chord joints instead of being placed on the shoulders of the posts.[6] In Oregon, Howe trusses are typically used, but they vary between counties, since county engineers had the authority to modify the basic plans. In Linn County, many of the Howe trusses have open sides and are painted white. Lane County also uses Howe trusses, but the sides are boarded nearly to the top.[7] Lincoln County's covered bridges have flared sides and are painted red, although most of them have been lost. County styles are less distinct in places like Ohio, where individual builders competed against larger companies, such as the Smith Bridge Company or the Hocking Valley Bridge Works, which built across a wide area. Uniformity in New England counties is non-existent since there were no big bridge companies involved in the region and town governments were responsible for transportation structures.

Figure 6.3 Top: 6.3a) The sides of the Howe trusses in Linn County, Oregon, as in Short Bridge (1945), were left open. HAER OR-120-6, Jet Lowe, photographer, 2004. **Above:** 6.3b) Covered bridges in Lane County, Oregon, like Horse Creek Bridge (1930, moved 1990), were covered nearly to the top chord. HAER OR-15-2, James Norman, photographer, 1987.

Figure 6.4 Sunday River Bridge (1872) in Oxford County, Maine, is a good example of the Paddleford truss, which became the dominant regional truss in parts of New Hampshire, Maine, and Vermont in the late-nineteenth century. HAER ME-69-11, Jet Lowe, photographer, 2003.

Existing bridges were another major design influence on newer bridges. While the written record rarely contains the reasons why bridge committees or county commissioners chose one kind of bridge construction over another, the built environment offers some clues. For example, Col. Stephen H. Long had just patented his bridge truss when the Aroostook Military Road (now U.S. Highway 2) was constructed through northeastern Maine. Capt. Charles Thomas used the Long truss for his 1831 bridge at Mattawamkeag in Penobscot County on this road. The Long truss then became, because of its familiarity, a dominant building type in central and eastern Maine, but it was not common elsewhere in the state.[8] Theodore Burr built many bridges in Pennsylvania, where the Burr-arch truss is still a dominant form today. However, Solon Chapin used the Town lattice truss for an 1835 bridge over the Delaware River at Lumberville, and in adjacent Bucks County this became the prevalent type instead of the Burr. Peter Paddleford of Littleton, New Hampshire, designed his own bridge truss and set a precedent by using it for several important crossings in the central part of his state. Even after Paddleford's death in 1859, other builders kept using his design, and it became a dominant form over a large portion of northern New England from Orleans County, Vermont, through Oxford County, Maine.[9]

Still more intriguing is the interplay between the Burr and the Wernwag trusses. Both forms involved an arch combined with a multiple-kingpost truss, and both had several framing variants. In general, the Burr-arch truss used posts which were vertical or nearly so, and it had a single truss sandwiched between a pair of arches. The Wernwag truss usually did the opposite and used a single heavy arch built up of several ribs sandwiched between a pair of trusses using flared posts; that is, the posts inclined outwards at the top, more so toward the ends of the bridge, being about perpendicular to the arch as they intersected it. There was interplay between the Burr and Wernwag forms. No purely Wernwag trusses exist today, but there are Burr-arch trusses which use the flared posts. Although the distribution of this framing variant is not regular, it is found especially along the southern border of Pennsylvania where Wernwag himself was once active. His building partners worked further west across southern Ohio and Indiana, and Burr-arch trusses with apparent Wernwag influence are found in this region and as far afield as northeastern Missouri.

Figure 6.5 Huffman Mills Bridge (1864) in Perry and Spencer counties, Indiana, is a Burr-arch truss with the flared-post style used in the Wernwag tradition. Joseph D. Conwill, photographer, 2003.

The cost of erecting a covered bridge varied not only because of the size of the structure, but also because of where and when it was built. The cost of stonework for the abutments could constitute half or more of the total expense, but sometimes the abutments from a prior bridge could be used. The Schuylkill Permanent Bridge at Philadelphia, the first known covered bridge in the United States, cost over $275,000 in 1801–1805, which was a fabulous sum of money at the time. The bridge was 550 feet long, a total of 1,300 feet with the stonework approaches, and it sat in the midst of some of this country's prime real estate. The total cost included the massive foundations and $40,000 for the land. As the technology became more common and covered bridges were built in more remote locations where land prices were not so expensive, the cost of construction decreased, as shown in the accompanying graph. Some very small bridges even went up for $500 or less. It is difficult to attribute these modest prices to a single cause, but one explanation may be the competition from iron-bridge builders. Another may be the deflationary trend of the late-nineteenth-century economy in general. Surprisingly low costs continued into the twentieth century in Oregon even as inflation rose, probably because first-class timber was abundant and inexpensive there.[10]

Comparison of Bridge Construction Costs

Name of bridge	Location	Date of construction	Length	Cost	Notes
Bath-Haverhill Bridge	New Hampshire	1829	256'	$2,400	
Eldean Bridge	Ohio	1860	219'	$4,080.83	Cost included foundations
Dreibelbis Bridge	Pennsylvania	1869	172'	$6,000	Cost included foundations
Johnson's Mill Bridge	Ohio	1876	83'	$1,302.22	Cost included foundations
Brown Bridge	Vermont	1880	112'	$1,078.37	Cost included foundations
Forsythe Bridge	Indiana	1888	186'	$3,800	
Ritner Creek Bridge	Oregon	1927	75'	$6,693.78	

The history of timber-bridge design is also characterized by an effort to reduce the use of custom joinery. Trusses such as the Burr, Long, and Paddleford required traditional woodworking skills. The Town lattice was the first attempt to use standardized pieces of timber, yet it should not be assumed that any carpenter was capable of building such a bridge. A high degree of skill was still required to lay out a Town lattice truss, especially given the camber that was required. Building

Figure 6.6 Arnold Graton erected a replacement for the Hall Bridge across Saxtons River in Windham County, Vermont, in 1982. Using traditional techniques, Graton Associates developed rough specifications from the original 1867 bridge and then framed it in a nearby field using traditional joinery and treenails. A team of oxen hauled the completed structure out across the river, and the bridge opened to traffic on September 6, 1982. Jack Peters, photographer, 1982. (See "Hall Bridge," HAER VT-40 for additional information.)

a Howe truss might seem to require less expertise if the pieces were precut elsewhere, but it, too, required special knowledge of such details as the correct spacing of the lower chord joints and the sequence of tightening the rods.[11] Bridge building was always a skilled job, no matter what truss type was used. The only clearly documented cases of covered bridges being built by truly untrained labor were the Town lattices of the 1890–1955 period designed by the Department of Colonization in Quebec for construction by settlers in new regions.[12] These bridges used spikes instead of wooden treenails at the lattice joints and required no custom cutting.[13]

Building a Typical Bridge

When residents of a New England town decided a new bridge was needed in their neighborhood, they brought the subject up at the annual town meeting. If voters approved the project, a bridge committee would be appointed and authorized to deal with a builder. A bridge request might be postponed for a year or more depending on finances, since bridge construction was one of a town's most expensive responsibilities. In other parts of the country, residents would petition the county commissioners, or a court with executive authority, that would appoint a committee of impartial viewers. If the ruling body judged the project worthy, the commissioners would then publish a call for bids. The same builder might submit several bids for bridges with different truss types or with varying degrees of finish.[14]

The builder might arrange for construction of the abutments, but these were often the subject of a separate contract. Bridge abutments used a wide variety of materials. New England bridges often used dry-laid split stone, sometimes in regular courses but usually in carefully chinked random courses.[15] Since stone was expensive to transport, local stone was typically used. A few covered bridges in Rutland County, Vermont, sat on marble abutments, for example, because the marble industry was centered there. Bridge abutments in southeastern Pennsylvania almost always used random-coursed, mortared masonry. Ohio and Indiana builders preferred regular courses of cut and dressed stone, although concrete was used for a few later bridges. The abutments of covered bridges in the South used a variety of materials, including brick in northeastern Mississippi. Oregon's twentieth-century covered bridges typically had concrete abutments. Those in Canada often used timber cribs.

In order to construct the bridge superstructure, the builder had to procure the timber, although in New England some towns made this purchase. Early in the nineteenth century, the timber might be cut on or near the site, such as was done at the 1836 Taftsville, Vermont, bridge. This practice extended into the twentieth century in timber-rich Oregon. When timber was cut near the site, there was inadequate time for seasoning. Designers such as Lewis Wernwag, Stephen Long, and William Howe, consequently, made allowances in their designs for timber shrinkage. When Ephraim Ballard built the Kennebec Bridge at Augusta, Maine, in 1827, it was reportedly completed and in service just seventy-four days after the timber had been cut. By the latter half of the nineteenth century, though, much of the good local timber in the East had been cut, so timber often had to be brought in from elsewhere. A few builders such as James Tasker of Sullivan County, New Hampshire, and John Davidson of Sullivan County, New York, owned woodlots and sawmills, but more often builders obtained timber through market distribution channels. Many timber species were used, the choice depending on a bridge's location, and different varieties could even be used within a single bridge if called for in the bridge specifications. For example, spruce was commonly used for lattice trusses in

New England. Midwestern covered bridges used pine or poplar for truss posts and braces. Indiana builder J. J. Daniels liked using white oak for his bottom chord sticks and various hardwoods for floor planks. Builders in New Brunswick used hackmatack (a regional term referring to tamarack or larch) for Howe-truss bearing blocks.[16] At the end of the nineteenth century, southern longleaf pine was widely used, due to the depletion of other species and its ready availability by rail shipment.[17]

Milled lumber was used for most later bridges, but the length of individual members was limited by the size of sawmill carriages.[18] The Town lattice used shorter lengths, and other trusses often used chords built up of short lengths. In those bridges where long, single sticks were desired, they were occasionally still hand-hewn even if the remainder of the bridge used milled lumber.[19] The layout and cutting of the timbers was done in advance at the bridge site, although a few builders such as the Kennedys of Indiana or Jacob Brandt of Ohio did this work in central work yards near their homes.[20] Smith-truss parts were nearly always prefabricated at the factory, as were some Howe trusses, especially those for railroad use. Once the stonework for the abutments was done, the truss framing could take as little as a few weeks to erect for a short bridge or up to several months for a long one.

The tools used to build a covered bridge varied with the type of truss. Traditionally framed designs such as the Paddleford, the Burr, or even the Howe as built in back-country Oregon required "axes, adzes, shovels, picks, hand saws, splitting froes, sledges, splitting mauls, dollies . . . augers, jacks, peavies, hammers, nails, ropes, hand winches, [and] drift pins" according to a 1902 account from Oregon.[21] Town-lattice construction required a hand-cranked boring machine to ensure that the holes were precisely perpendicular to the planks.[22] After the timbers were cut, the falsework (scaffolding) was placed

Figure 6.7 Falsework is in place for the construction of Hendricks Bridge over McKenzie River, Lane County, Oregon, in 1907. Courtesy of Bill Cockrell Collection.

Figure 6.8 Construction of the Hendricks Bridge in 1907 began by laying out the bottom chords on the falsework. Courtesy of Bill Cockrell Collection.

Figure 6.9 With its Howe trusses fully erected, the Hendricks Bridge was nearing completion when this photograph was taken in 1907. Courtesy of Bill Cockrell Collection.

in the river, and the truss was assembled piece by piece atop the falsework. It was not uncommon to open a bridge to traffic before the roofing and siding had been completed. The work was subject to final inspection by the bridge committee or the commissioners, and, if they found deficiencies in construction, they could reduce the builder's pay accordingly. Sometimes builders performed a follow-up visit a few years later to make adjustments for shrinkage of the timber.[23]

In contrast, covered railroad-bridge construction involved the mobilization of vast resources over an extended territory and, consequently, was handled in a more centralized manner. Some railroads had their own engineers for design, and others even used their own building departments, resulting in similarly designed bridges across the railroad. The vast expanses to be traveled by railroads in the Midwest and West required a high degree of organization, and large outside contracting firms specializing in railroad work were generally hired to do the building. Stone and Boomer of Chicago was one of the largest and best-known railroad-bridge contractors, working with many lines throughout the Midwest. Since partner Andros B. Stone was brother to the wife of truss-inventor William Howe, and his older brother, Amasa Stone Jr., had been involved in the actual development of the Howe truss, their bridges primarily utilized the Howe truss. In Oregon, the firm of Hoffman and Bates handled a great deal of railroad construction and pioneered a radical housing style with rakish back-slanted portals and a hip roof; unfortunately, no examples of this survive.[24] Because of the rapid increase in size and weight of rolling stock throughout the nineteenth and early twentieth centuries, railroad bridges usually had short service lives, sometimes as little as fifteen years. If a main-line bridge was still sound when replaced, it was not uncommon to move it elsewhere on a branch line where service demands were lower.[25]

Covered Bridge Builders

The names and stories of many covered bridge builders have been lost. Most used the designs of others, such as Theodore Burr, Ithiel Town, William Howe, and Robert W. Smith, sometimes adding their own distinctive variations. A comprehensive listing of known covered bridge builders would require a book in itself, but some of the best known are included here to illustrate their widely differing backgrounds and the various ways in which covered bridge construction took place.

Lemuel Chenoweth was born in 1811 near Beverly, Virginia (now West Virginia). The mellifluous family name is of Cornish origin. Although Chenoweth was listed in census records as "bridge builder," he also undertook many other construction projects, including building houses, a church, wagons, and furniture. Chenoweth was also an inventor, working on sawmill equipment and a machine to lay the Atlantic telegraph cable, although the

Figure 6.10 Barrackville Covered Bridge (1853), a Burr-arch truss built by Lemuel Chenoweth on the Fairmont and Wheeling Turnpike in Marion County, West Virginia. HAER WV-8-25, Jet Lowe, photographer, 2002.

latter was never put to use. Two of his covered bridges survive; both are in West Virginia, one in Philippi and the other in Barrackville. Because these bridges saw heavy use, they have been the subject of major restoration work. Steel beams have carried the live loads at Philippi since the 1930s, and the bridge was damaged by a serious fire in 1989. Chenoweth preferred the Burr-arch truss, and he placed the tie beams on the post tops high over his two-part top chords.[26] His fame rests on his personal versatility as an inventor and on the fact that his covered bridge at Philippi is the last in service on a U.S. numbered highway.[27]

Joseph John Daniels (commonly known as J. J. Daniels) was one of the most skillful and prolific covered bridge builders in western Indiana. Born in 1826 in Marietta, Ohio, he was the son of Stephen Daniels, an agent for the Stephen H. Long bridge interests. J. J. Daniels is said to have had limited exposure to formal education, but he was apparently educated at home by his parents, read very widely on a variety of subjects, and knew ancient Greek and Latin. Before the age of twenty-one, he was building bridges and moved his practice to western Indiana in the 1850s. Bridge construction was apparently his primary activity, and he built over fifty of them, both for highway and for railroad use. Daniels built his last covered bridge in 1904 around the age of seventy-eight; he lived to ninety. J. A. Britton and his sons built bridges until 1920 that are somewhat similar in detail to Daniels's bridges, and both Daniels and Britton account for the majority of covered bridges in Parke County, Indiana, which is a great center of covered bridges.[28]

Daniels used a variety of trusses, but he preferred the Burr, to which he introduced some distinctive modifications. In most Burr-arch trusses, the arches are notched into the trusses. In Daniels's bridges, they splay outwards and pass outside of the bottom chords of the truss instead of being notched in. He did not tighten the bolts connecting the arches to the truss until after the falsework had been removed, indicating that he intended the arches mainly to carry the live load on the bridge.[29]

Figure 6.11 A view underneath West Union Bridge (1876) in Parke County, Indiana, shows how J. J. Daniels splayed his arches around the bottom chords of the trusses. HAER IN-105-9, James Rosenthal, photographer, 2004.

In some of his multi-span bridges, he built continuous top chords over the piers. This increased load capacity of the bridge overall and was a sophisticated engineering feature. His bridges are also characterized by the use of iron rods rather than wooden tie beams in the upper lateral systems, which is unusual in Burr-arch trusses.[30]

Figure 6.12 Powder Works Bridge (1872) in Santa Cruz Couty, California, is an excellent example of the early work of the Pacific Bridge Company and of the Smith type 4 triple-web truss. HAER CA-313-10, Jet Lowe, photographer, 2004.

William Henry Gorrill, born in Ohio in 1841, was trained as a lawyer, and his firm was retained by the Smith Bridge Company. Moving to San Francisco in 1869 in the hope of finding a climate that might improve his tuberculosis, he became a Smith Bridge agent. After founding the Pacific Bridge Company in 1870 at Vallejo, Gorrill secured a major contract for a bridge at Oroville in 1871, and thereafter built a number of important covered bridges, of which the Powder Works Bridge still survives in Santa Cruz, California. The company soon moved to Oakland but also owned a mill yard in San Francisco that it used for precutting truss timbers, just as Smith Bridge Company itself was doing back in Ohio. After several years, Pacific Bridge built fewer timber Smith trusses and more iron bridges. Gorrill was not a builder in the usual sense, although he probably had a hand in preparing bridge plans. Through his contracting, the Smith truss became established as an important bridge form in California, and another prominent builder, A. S. Miller, brought it to Oregon. Gorrill died in 1874 of typhoid fever, although Pacific Bridge Company and its corporate successors remained an important player in the construction field into the 1960s, long after the Smith truss had been forgotten.[31]

Figure 6.13 Emmett L. Kennedy was photographed around 1935 holding a model he built in 1872 to help his family secure bridge contracts. Courtesy of National Society for the Preservation of Covered Bridges.

Three generations of the Kennedy family of Rushville, Indiana, built nearly sixty covered bridges, mostly in the eastern part of the state. Archibald M. Kennedy, born in 1818 in North Carolina, moved with his family to Indiana in 1825 and began working as a general carpenter in the 1840s. His first major bridge job was at Dunlapsville, Indiana, in 1870, with his twenty-two-year-old son Emmett assisting. Archibald retired in the mid-1880s to continue a long-standing interest in state politics. Meanwhile, another son, Charles F., had become involved in the bridge-building business, and Emmett's own sons, Karl and Charles R., later joined the family business. At first the Kennedys used local timber but later purchased Michigan white pine. They preferred to prefabricate the truss parts at their work yard in Rushville. While many Indiana counties began favoring iron bridges after 1890, the Kennedys were called into service again to build covered bridges after the destructive flood of 1913 wiped out bridges in the region. They built their last covered bridge in 1918.

The Kennedys almost always used the Burr-arch truss, and their bridges are notable for the perfect form of the arches. Their trusses used a two-part top chord with the posts notched through the space in between, instead of the usual one-piece top chord with the posts mortised into the bottom face.[32] The posts, therefore, had relish on the ends—referring to the extension of a timber to prevent shear from undoing a joint—and this allowed the braces to be dapped with confidence into the posts fairly near the panel point, resulting in an efficient transmission of stress with minimal bending moments. Their brace-post daps used double tables for maximal efficiency with minimal section loss. The wide area on top of their chords also allowed the Kennedys to do away with sway bracing in the upper corners of the roadway, relying instead on the large bearing area of the tie beams to serve as wind bracing. To the casual observer, however, the most distinctive feature of a Kennedy-built bridge is its finish. The portals have graceful arches and are ornamented with roof brackets and scroll-sawn millwork. The sides are neatly clapboarded, and the exteriors are painted white. While the Kennedy's last few bridges lacked decorative millwork, they still retained the arched portals, clapboards, and white paint. Kennedy bridges are widely recognized as among the most beautiful covered bridges ever built.[33]

Figure 6.14 Forsythe Bridge (1888) in Rush County, Indiana, is typical of Kennedy family framing and exhibits the beautiful portal that is a hallmark of Kennedy construction. **Top:** 6.14a) HAER IN-106-12 and **Above:** 6.14b) HAER IN-106-9, James Rosenthal, photographer, 2004.

Horace King of Georgia was born a slave in South Carolina in 1807 and showed aptitude for carpentry and heavy construction at a young age. John Godwin, a prominent building contractor, purchased King at the age of twenty-three, and they eventually moved to Girard (now Phenix City), Alabama. In 1832–33, King and Godwin built a three-span, 600-foot Town lattice truss high over the Chattahoochee River at Columbus, Georgia, and this spectacular bridge secured King's reputation as a master craftsman. He went on to build major bridges and handled other types of heavy construction, too. In choosing the Town lattice, King may have followed an example set by Ithiel Town himself, who built some well-known early prototypes in the Carolinas. King used the Town lattice as far afield as northeastern Mississippi during an association with contractor Robert Jemison Jr. of Tuscaloosa, Alabama.

Figure 6.15 Horace King (ca. 1850) was able to successfully pursue an independent bridge building career after being freed from slavery in 1846. Daguerreotype ca. 1855 from the collection of the Columbus Museum, Columbus, Georgia; Museum purchase.

King was freed in 1846, which allowed him to pursue a career as an independent contractor.[34] The Civil War wreaked havoc on the South's road system, and Horace King was involved in the rebuilding effort. Since many of his bridges were on major traffic arteries, none of them survive today. His son, Washington W. King, also became a builder, and at least two of his covered bridges still exist. It is hard to evaluate Horace King's structural contributions with no surviving bridges to inspect. His legacy, instead, is as an example of a former slave who was able to contribute significantly to the built environment and economy of the South at a time when African Americans were often restricted from such opportunities.[35]

Elias McMellen, born in Lancaster County, Pennsylvania, in 1839, had built his first bridge by the age of twenty-one. After service in the Civil War, during which he rose to the rank of captain, he returned to bridge building in Lancaster. He built over thirty bridges in his career but also constructed other types of structures and owned a hotel. Although he used stone and iron for several bridges, McMellen is best known for his immaculately framed Burr-arch truss covered bridges. Eleven of these remain and most still carry traffic.[36] Captain McMellen died in 1916, but he is well remembered for his many contributions to the built heritage of southeastern Pennsylvania, a region rich in covered bridges.

The perfection of the arches is the most obvious feature of McMellen's bridges. Many builders found the arches of a Burr-arch truss difficult to lay out, so close inspection often reveals slight irregularities. There are no such problems in McMellen's bridges, which stand as some of the finest examples of Burr-arch truss framing.

Figure 6.16 Elias McMellen's bridges, like the Kauffman's Distillery Bridge (1874) in Lancaster County, Pennsylvania, are known for their perfectly formed arches. Joseph Conwill, photographer, 1980.

Nichols M. Powers was one of Vermont's best-known builders, with at least fifteen covered highway bridges to his credit. Four of these remain.[37] He also did railroad work, which may have involved bridges, but apart from his work in Maryland little evidence of this facet of his career remains. Born in 1817 in a section of Pittsford, Vermont, that later became part of Proctor, he spent most of his life in Clarendon until his death in 1897.

In 1837, while still a minor, Powers built his first bridge, a Town lattice truss in Pittsford Mills. He tried other trusses but favored the Town lattice for most of his work. In 1855, he bridged Schoharie Creek at North Blenheim, New York, with a 210-foot single span using the Long truss plus arch.[38] Until its loss to Hurricane Irene in 2011, this bridge had the longest clear span of any covered bridge in America.[39] Powers traveled to Maryland in 1866 where he superintended construction of a railroad bridge being built over the mouth of the Susquehanna River at Havre de Grace. After this lengthy sojourn away from home, he returned to Vermont for good but remained active as a bridge builder through 1880. His youngest son, Charles F. Powers, born in 1850, entered the bridge-building field, too, assisting his father at Havre de Grace while still a teenager.[40]

Figure 6.17 Clarendon, Vermont, resident Nichols M. Powers was among the state's most prominent bridge builders. Courtesy of National Society for the Preservation of Covered Bridges.

The Town lattice truss is more standardized than other designs, and the bridges of any given builder are only rarely so distinctive as to be identifiable on sight, as is sometimes the case in other building traditions. However, a close look shows that Powers brought sophisticated thought to his bridges. The 1880 Brown Bridge at Shrewsbury, Vermont, for example, has chord planks of variable sizes. The typical standard for early Town lattices was nominal 3 x 10 inches everywhere. In Brown Bridge, the lattice planks and the top chords (both primary and secondary) are the usual 3 x 10 inches, but the bottom primary chord measures net 3 x 11-1/2 inches and the bottom secondary chord is 3 x 11 inches. These member dimensions help compensate for section loss due to splices, since the bottom chords are in tension. Powers also took care to use long chord sticks, which added overall strength to the bridge.

The wooden trusses erected by the Smith Bridge Company, established in 1867, were competitive against iron-bridge manufacturers into the late nineteenth century because of Robert W. Smith's efficient use of wood in his trusses. Not only was Smith's truss innovative, but his methods of manufacture were, too. While the Howe truss was sometimes prefabricated, especially for use on railroads, the Smith truss made almost exclusive use of the nation's new large-scale industrial organization. Smith trusses found east of the Mississippi were mostly prefabricated at the company yards in Ohio. In California, Smith licensee William Henry Gorrill prefabricated the trusses at his San Francisco yard. It was possible for a builder to obtain Smith patent rights and cut the timbers himself, but more often the pieces were cut at the plant even if a local contractor did the construction.[41]

Figure 6.18 The Smith Bridge Company of Toledo, Ohio, shipped the parts for a patented Smith truss to local communities for other contractors to erect. Local contractor W. T. Washer built the Wheeling Bridge in Gibson County, Indiana, in 1877. Joseph D. Conwill, photographer, 2003.

With the Smith Bridge Company the distinction between fabricator and erector, which is so important in metal-bridge history, is encountered in timber. The Smith Bridge Company competed directly against local builders. It was not the only large-scale company building timber highway bridges, but it was almost certainly the biggest, even though there were no known Smith Bridge Company bridges in New England or New York. The company's work was centered in Ohio and Indiana, where it was a major player. The Smith Bridge Company also began offering iron bridges at an early date and switched to iron exclusively toward the end of the nineteenth century. Under a new name, the Toledo Bridge Company, it lasted until 1901, when it was swallowed up by the newly formed American Bridge Company.[42]

Jonathan Parker Snow was bridge engineer for the Boston and Maine Railroad (B&M) and was responsible for the continued construction of covered railroad bridges into the first decade of the twentieth century when most other roads had turned to steel.[43] Born in Concord, New Hampshire, in 1848, he received formal training at the Thayer School of Civil Engineering, from which he graduated in 1875. After trying several different branches of engineering, he turned to bridges in 1880 and began working for the B&M in 1888. This line served a region rich in spruce construction timber, and Snow was convinced that timber bridges were still economical. Indeed, in 1895, the B&M still had over a thousand timber bridges of every kind: trestles, stringers, pony trusses, through trusses, and deck trusses.

Snow was a tireless advocate for wood, even in the face of his profession's nearly complete acceptance of steel, and continued to design new covered railroad bridges almost until his retirement in 1911. He used the double Town lattice truss, patented by Ithiel Town in 1835, as further developed by David Hazelton for the Boston and Lowell Railroad, a B&M predecessor. For a few bridges, however, he cleverly included a large laminated arch within the two lattice webs to carry the live load. The extra care he devoted to proportioning timber sizes to loads is an interesting facet of his work; the planks in his lattices increase in width toward the ends of his bridges. Snow continued to practice engineering as a consultant until his death in 1933.[44]

Figure 6.19 Wright's Bridge (1906) over Sugar River near Newport, New Hampshire, combined a heavy laminated arch for the live load with a stiffening Town lattice truss for the dead load. It is a fine example of the careful design work of J. P. Snow for the Boston and Maine Railroad. HAER NH-35-5, Jet Lowe, photographer, 2003.

Arthur Clayton "Art" Striker was bridge superintendent for Lane County, Oregon, and oversaw the construction of dozens of covered bridges. Born in 1885 at Brighton, Ontario, he moved with his family to Oregon at the age of six. His father, Aaron Noble Striker, was a noted builder of covered

bridges and other public works, and A. C. Striker worked with him on some of his projects. He joined the Lane County highway department in the early 1920s just as the county was becoming firmly committed to the idea of building bridges with its own labor instead of using outside contractors. At this time the covered bridge was still the standard solution to Oregon's rural-road needs.

Striker soon became the county's bridge superintendent and worked with the county engineer and various trusted on-site supervisors, especially Miller Sorensen.[45] Striker preferred using Howe trusses, often with one-piece hewn chords that were sometimes of gigantic proportions. The bottom chords of the existing Pengra Bridge, for example, measure 16 inches x 18 inches x 126 feet. Most of the bridges had beautifully proportioned portals with classic, elliptically arched entries, were clad in board-and-batten siding, and were neatly painted white.[46] A. C. Striker retired in 1950 just as the covered bridge era was drawing to a close, and he died in 1962.[47]

Figure 6.20 Pengra Bridge (1938) is typical of the many bridges built in the 1930s in Lane County, Oregon, under the supervision of A. C. Striker. HAER OR-119-4, Jet Lowe, photographer, 2004.

Figure 6.21 Milton Graton repaired the Whittier Bridge (1871) in Carroll County, New Hampshire, using traditional techniques. The cables form part of a temporary suspension system used to support the bridge during the work. Joseph Conwill, photographer, 1983.

Milton S. Graton was a pivotal figure in the twentieth-century covered bridge preservation movement. Born in 1908, he spent the early part of his life at a variety of jobs, including timber hauling and rigging. After being

called upon to help dismantle a covered bridge in New Hampshire in the 1930s and marveling at the high quality of workmanship he saw in the structure, he became interested in covered bridge construction. In the late 1950s, Graton began moving and repairing covered bridges, dedicating himself to using traditional techniques. He then built an all-new covered bridge at Woodstock, Vermont, in 1968–69 and several others afterwards in other areas. Graton built his bridges entirely

Figure 6.22 Top: 6.22a) The work done by Tim Andrews during the rehabilitation of Gilpin's Falls Covered Bridge in Cecil County, Maryland, carefully ensured the preservation of historic details. **Above:** 6.22b) Traditional timber-framing tools used in carving out the step in a vertical post on the Gilpin's Falls project include (left to right): a framing chisel, a corner chisel, a ca. 1930 line bevel, and a urethane carver's mallet. Will Truax, photographer, 2009

on land and often moved them into place over their rivers using oxen and a capstan. There is so far no evidence that this method was used in the past, but it generated much public interest.

Many covered bridges owe their continued existence to his timely repairs, often performed under very tight budgetary constraints. Before Graton, it was accepted practice to add steel to covered bridges or to modify the trusses because there were few people working with bridges in the mid-twentieth century who were knowledgeable about traditional woodworking. Destructive repair practices are still common, but Graton showed that in most cases it is possible to restore covered bridges using techniques that the original builders would have recognized. He inspired a new generation of timber framers dedicated to traditional covered bridge work. Milton Graton died in 1994, but his son Arnold M. Graton was closely involved in his projects and continues the family business.[48]

Timothy Andrews is among the foremost skilled timber framers working with covered bridges today. Born in 1959 in Littleton, New Hampshire, he is descended from a long line of woodworkers from Nova Scotia who were involved with sawmilling, ship and church building, and other major projects. Andrews grew up familiar with covered bridges because his grandparents lived next to one in Lancaster, New

Hampshire. He became a carpenter as soon as he was out of high school, specializing at first in high-quality interior finish work. His parents happened to buy property adjacent to Milton Graton's land in 1979, and Graton became aware of Andrews's talents. He asked Tim to build him a timber-truss frame for a water-tower tank and was so impressed with the quality of the work that he hired him for a variety of other projects, including covered bridge construction, rigging work, and masonry dam repair.

As of 2011, Andrews has built, repaired, or salvaged fifteen covered bridges, either on his own or with others. He built a new covered bridge at Ashland, New Hampshire, completed while working for Arnold Graton, and executed major repairs to the Cilleyville and the Ashuelot Upper Village bridges in New Hampshire, the Bennett Bridge in Maine, and Hall's Bridge in Vermont. Andrews is careful to save as much original historic timber as possible and to restore bridges to their as-built conditions, without introducing modern materials. He has worked on a variety of other timber-framing projects, too, such as repairs to roof trusses for an old theatre in Boston's Back Bay and the construction of a large sugar house deep in the woods of Andover, New Hampshire, where there was no road access.

The covered bridge builders discussed in this chapter were among the best known, but there were hundreds of others in America. Their ability to build so many useful, graceful, and long-lasting structures of wood had a significant impact on the American landscape.

Endnotes

[1] A widespread and picturesque piece of folklore has builders winning a contract by presenting a well-built model and standing on it. See, for example, Richard Sanders Allen, *Covered Bridges of the Middle Atlantic States* (Brattleboro, Vt.: Stephen Greene Press, 1959), 89, and Allen's same comments on James F. Tasker in *Rare Old Covered Bridges of Windsor County* (Brattleboro, Vt.: The Book Cellar, 1962), 32–33.

[2] J. Parker Snow, "Wooden Bridge Construction on the Boston and Maine Railroad," *Journal of the Association of Engineering Societies* 15, no. 1 (July 1895): 39.

[3] For example, Canadian builder Albert E. Smye was based in the fishing port of Alma, New Brunswick, where he specialized in wharfs and warehouses as well as bridges. Nichols Powers, a famous Vermont builder, also did rigging, quarrying, and railroad work and owned a cheese factory. Stephen Gillis and John Gillis, *No Faster Than a Walk: The Covered Bridges of New Brunswick* (Fredericton, New Brunswick: Goose Lane Editions, 1988), 17–18. On Nichols Powers, see "Brown Bridge," HAER No. VT-28.

[4] On Lewis Wernwag, see Richard Sanders Allen, *Covered Bridges of the Middle Atlantic States* (Brattleboro, Vt.: Stephen Greene Press, 1959), 14–16, and F. E. Griggs Jr., "Colossus Bridge Designer Lewis Wernwag," *Structure Magazine* (October 2004), 34–36. On William Henry Gorrill, see Lola Bennett, "William Henry Gorrill and the Pacific Bridge Company," *Covered Bridge Topics* (Fall 2010), 5–6.

[5] Many details are provided in Lee H. Nelson's excellent book, *A Century of Oregon Covered Bridges 1851-1952* (Portland, Oreg.: Oregon Historical Society, 1960).

[6] Observations of building styles are from visits made by the author, who saw every covered bridge in North American over a ten-year period from 1966–77. For an example of a typical Lancaster County Burr-arch truss, see "Pine Grove Bridge," HAER No. PA-586. For a representative Berks County Burr-arch truss, see "Dreibelbis Covered Bridge," HAER No. PA-587. In regard to Somerset County's Burr-arch trusses, Theodore Burr described the practice of mitering the brace-post joints in his 1817 patent text, but he seems not to have followed this method himself, so the origin of the Somerset style is unclear.

[7] For an example of a Linn County Howe truss, see "Larwood Bridge," HAER No. OR-124, while "Pengra Bridge," HAER No. OR-119, is a typical Lane County Howe truss.

[8] For examples of the Long truss in central and eastern Maine, see Joseph D. Conwill, *Maine's Covered Bridges* (Charleston, S.C.: Arcadia, 2003), 58–63, 93–95, 108, 111, 113–14, and 122. The name "Long's plan" was known as far west as Franklin County, but it is uncertain if the term referred there to the true Long patent.

[9] It was once thought that Paddleford designed his truss in the early 1840s, but it now appears that he built one as early as 1834 over the Connecticut River between Monroe, New Hampshire, and McIndoe Falls, Vermont.

[10] The cited construction cost of Bath-Haverhill Bridge comes from Rev. David Sutherland, *Address Delivered to the Inhabitants of Bath With an Historical Appendix by Rev. Thomas Boutelle* (Boston: Geo. C. Rand & Avery, 1855), 73. Town records are incomplete, so it is unclear whether the stonework for the foundations was included. For additional information see: "Bath-Haverhill Bridge," HAER No. NH-33; "Eldean Bridge," HAER No. OH-122; "Dreibelbis Covered Bridge," HAER No. PA-587; "Forsythe Covered Bridge," HAER No. IN-106; "Johnson's Mill Bridge," HAER No. OH-127; and "Brown Bridge," HAER No. VT-28. See also Nelson, *Century of Oregon Covered Bridges*, 168, 200.

[11] For a description of the mischief a truly unskilled builder could do with a Howe truss, see the letter by C. H. Wright in *Engineering News* 30 (November 9, 1893), 376–77, reproduced in *Covered Bridge Topics* (Summer 2008), 11.

Endnotes

12 A 1962 date is sometimes cited erroneously for the Émery-Sicard Bridge of St-Maurice-de-Dalquier, but this represents the date of major repairs; the construction date was actually 1946. On the Quebec colonization bridges, see Gérald Arbour, et al., *Les Ponts Couverts au Québec* (Quebec: Les Publications du Quebec, 2005). For background on the colonization movement itself, which required the construction of special bridges, see Joseph D. Conwill, "Return to the Land: Quebec's Colonisation Movement," *History Today* (April 1984), 16–21.

13 Quebec's "colonization bridges" have held up surprisingly well over the years. Sixty-nine still exist, and the majority still carry traffic. They tend to sag slightly because the bearing surface of spikes is much less than that of treenails so the spikes cut into the wood. Even constructing these bridges required a body of specialized knowledge, such as clinching some of the spikes to prevent the lattice planks from separating. Untrained Civilian Conservation Corps labor also built a few bridges in the western United States, but the crews appear to have had some experienced help.

14 Terry E. Miller has recorded extensive details of bids received by one Ohio county in *The Covered Bridges of Coshocton County, Ohio: A History* (Kent, Ohio: by the author, 2009).

15 Techniques for splitting stone changed around 1830, as James L. Garvin has documented. Previously, stonecutters chiseled a line of small square holes into the stone, into which they inserted wedges. Later, stone cutters adopted the plug drill, which created round holes. Stone split by the earlier method may be observed in the abutments and pier of the Bath-Haverhill Bridge (1829) at Woodsville, New Hampshire. See James L. Garvin, "Appendix A: Notes on Materials and Construction Techniques of Bath-Haverhill Covered Bridge," in "Bath-Haverhill Bridge," HAER No. NH-33, 2002, and also his book, *A Building History of Northern New England* (Hanover, N.H.: University Press of New England, 2001), 42–47.

16 Hackmatack (alternatively hacmatac or hack) is a regional term used in the Maritimes and New England for this versatile species. The butt area of the trunk with major roots attached was favored for producing ships' knees. The name hackmatack is thought to derive from a Native American word meaning "snowshoe wood."

17 For the history of Kennebec Bridge, see "Maine's Covered Bridge Past," *Covered Bridge Topics* (Winter 2001), 6–7. On the use of green lumber, see J. W. Buchanan's recollections quoted in Richard Sanders Allen, *Covered Bridges of the Middle West* (Brattleboro, Vt.: Stephen Greene Press, 1970), 27–28. See also "Taftsville Bridge," HAER No. VT-30.

18 Milled lumber was readily available after about 1830, at least for shorter lengths, but sometimes hand-hewn lumber continued in use in remote, rural areas. For example, some hand-hewn lumber was used by Jerome Moot as late as the first decade of the twentieth century for bridges in the Dry Brook Valley of Ulster County, New York, although it may have been reused from previous structures.

19 This is the case at Taftsville Bridge, in Windsor County, Vermont. A number of Oregon covered bridges have single-hewn chord sticks with sawn braces and counters.

20 Historians of timber framing note a change in work practice shortly before 1830. In the older scribe-rule method, every piece was custom cut to the place it was to occupy. In the square-rule method, standard pieces were cut to a reference line and were interchangeable. It might seem from this procedure that the scribe-rule method of layout continued to be used even in a late period. This must have been the case for those bridges using traditional joinery that also had features such as timber sizes proportioned to the load or varying panel lengths. See Jan Lewandoski's remarks on Blenheim Bridge in *Timber Framing* 102 (December 2011), 23–24. Very little is known about the actual techniques in the work yard. It is surprising, for instance, that covered bridges only rarely show marriage marks. Illinois builder Jacob Allaman used standard templates for his Burr-arch truss posts, which strongly suggests that he used square-rule framing. See Thelma Eaton, *The Covered Bridges of Illinois* (Ann Arbor, Mich.: Edwards Brothers, 1968), 21. James L. Garvin notes clear structural evidence for square-

Endnotes

rule layout in the tie beams, wind braces, and rafters of Bath-Haverhill Bridge in Woodsville, New Hampshire; see Garvin, "Appendix A." Curiously, evidence for scribe-rule framing can be found in the non-covered Howe trusses of New Brunswick, which sometimes show marriage marks. They date from the first half of the twentieth century, a hundred years after square-rule framing was introduced, and they use a truss form that would easily have allowed standardization.

21 Builders also commonly carried rifles, shotguns, and fishing equipment to the work site; see Nelson, *Century of Oregon Covered Bridges*, 139. The question of whether bridge timber was usually finished with an adze or a broadaxe has been much discussed by timber framers in recent years, although tool marks seem to indicate that the adze was frequently used.

22 For a photograph of such a machine in use, see Richard Sanders Allen, *Covered Bridges of the Northeast* (Brattleboro, Vt.: Stephen Greene Press, 1957), 26.

23 Contemporary descriptions of covered bridge construction are rare. One of the best comes from Oregon bridge builder Ole Haldorson, interviewed by Bill Cockrell in 2006; see "Ole Haldorson, Oregon Bridge Builder: An Interview," *Covered Bridge Topics* (Winter 2013), 3–10. See also David Stephenson's 1830s account as quoted in Herbert Wheaton Congdon, *The Covered Bridge* (Middlebury, Vt.: Vermont Books, 1959), 83; Theodore Burr's letter describing the construction of McCall's Ferry Bridge in 1815 in "Theodore Burr on the Challenges of Building McCall's Ferry Bridge," *Covered Bridge Topics* (Winter 2009), 9–11; J. W. Buchanan's recollections quoted in Allen, *Covered Bridges of the Middle West*, 27–28; various photographs from the Archives Nationales du Québec shown in "Did They Build the Covered Bridges on Land First, or Over the Water?" *Covered Bridge Topics* (Summer 2011), 16 (although the bridge shown may not have been housed); and several descriptions quoted in Nelson, *Century of Oregon Covered Bridges*. George E. Gould provides useful construction notes that were probably based on information from interviews with builder Karl Kennedy in *Indiana Covered Bridges Thru the Years* (Indianapolis: Indiana Covered Bridge Society, 1977). See also the 1905 photograph of construction of a covered railroad bridge in Vermont in Claire Dunne Johnson, *St. Johnsbury* (Charleston, S.C.: Arcadia, 1996), 61; note especially the stack of pre-bored lattice planks waiting to be installed.

24 Allen's *Covered Bridges of the Middle West* is excellent on Stone and Boomer and other railroad contractors; see especially pages 114–20. See also Kramer A. Adams, *Covered Bridges of the West* (Berkeley: Howell-North, 1963), 43.

25 This practice complicates research on covered railroad bridges. For example, the uncertainty about the building date of the Shoreham Railroad Bridge in Addison County, Vermont, is due to the fact that it was moved to its current site from places unknown, although the housing style resembles that of several former railroad bridges in Connecticut and Rhode Island. "Shoreham Railroad Bridge," HAER No. VT-32.

26 This is a regional practice sometimes found from the upper South through Ohio. The two-part top chords also allowed Chenoweth to place the brace-post joint directly at the panel point, but this advantage is partly lost by the fact that the brace-chord joint at the bottom is offset from the panel point by the thickness of the floor beam. The building record on Chenoweth, however, is incomplete because there are only two surviving bridges.

27 Biographical information from Randy Allan, *Lemuel Chenoweth, 1811–1887: Bridging the Gaps* (Parsons, W.Va.: McClain, 2006). See also "Barrackville Bridge," HAER No. WV-8, and Emory L. Kemp and J. Hall, "Case Study of Burr Truss Covered Bridge," *Engineering Issues: Journal of Professional Activities* 101, no. 3 (1975): 391–412. A case study of the restoration of the Philippi Bridge appears in Emory L. Kemp, "Restoration Techniques for American Covered Bridges," *Proceedings of the International Historic Bridges Conference*, Columbus, Ohio, August 27–29, 1992, 318–31. The existing covered bridge at Carrollton is also sometimes credited to Chenoweth, but Allen states it was not built by him. A brother, Eli, worked with Lemuel on many bridges but is much less well known.

Endnotes

28 Dann Chamberlin, "Joseph J. Daniels and His Indiana Covered Bridges," paper presented at North Central College, Naperville, Ill., January 1958, 20.

29 Gould, *Indiana Covered Bridges*, 14–17. Daniels refers to this practice in his specifications for a wooden-truss bridge in Morgan County, Indiana, written in 1900, preserved in the Indiana Historical Society, Indianapolis; a typescript copy is in the National Society for the Preservation of Covered Bridges Archives, Concord, N.H., "Builders and Patents" drawer, "J. J. Daniels" file.

30 It has been widely reported that the tie rods pass through the post-chord tenon and serve to replace treenails, but close examination proves this to be untrue. The joints are treenailed in the usual way, although the treenails are not visible from inside the bridge because they are covered by the bearing plate for the upper lateral bracing.

31 On Gorrill, see "Powder Works Bridge," HAER No. CA-313, and Bennett, "William Henry Gorrill and the Pacific Bridge Company." For more on A. S. Miller, see Lee H. Nelson, *A Century of Oregon Covered Bridges, 1851–1952* (Portland: Oregon Historical Society, 1960).

32 Some Ohio builders also used a two-part top chord, but the one-piece chord was much more common in Burr-arch trusses. For more on the Kennedys and on the Burr-arch truss in general, see Joseph D. Conwill, "Burr Truss Framing," *Timber Framing* 78 (December 2005), 4–11.

33 See "Forsythe Covered Bridge," HAER No. IN-106, and Gould, *Indiana Covered Bridges*, 11–14. Gould provides a useful chronological table of Kennedy bridges divided according to which family members worked on them. See also Allen, *Covered Bridges of the Middle West*, 64–69.

34 While 1848 is often given as the date of his emancipation, that date is based on King's recollection in his later years when his memory may have been faulty. Contemporary documentation shows that the date was 1846. On King generally, see John S. Lupold and Thomas L. French Jr., *Bridging Deep South Rivers: The Life and Legend of Horace King* (Athens, Ga.: University of Georgia Press, 2004).

35 Local tradition credits Horace King with the construction of the existing Red Oak Creek Bridge in Meriwether County, Georgia, but there is no written documentation supporting this attribution. See "Red Oak Creek Bridge," HAER No. GA-138.

36 This figure does not include the Pool Forge Bridge; although sometimes credited to McMellen, it shows structural evidence of having been built by someone else. Unfortunately, one of the most beautiful of the surviving bridges, the Pine Grove Bridge, has been compromised by the removal of the abutments and floor system and the addition of steel beams. It was extensively recorded in "Pine Grove Bridge," HAER No. PA-586.

37 His first name has been widely misunderstood as "Nicholas," but contemporary records, including his original signature, prove that it was "Nichols."

38 The use of an integral arch with the Long truss was very unusual, but otherwise the truss of Blenheim Bridge was close to the patent type. It had counterbrace wedges intended for prestressing, which were located at the tops of the counterbraces, although they were mounted transversely to the chords, not parallel with them as in the usual Long form.

39 The clear span had been shortened by repair and stabilization work. See "Blenheim Bridge," HAER NY-331. Bridgeport Bridge in Nevada County, California, was a near tie for the longest single-span record and is the undisputed champion now that Blenheim is gone. On this complicated question, see "Blenheim versus Bridgeport Revisited," *Covered Bridge Topics* (Winter 2009), 16, and "Bridgeport Covered Bridge," HAER No. CA-41.

40 Charles F. Powers later did railroad bridge work in Maine, apparently using the Howe truss, but he died at the age of thirty and is not well known today. See "Charles F. Powers, Bridge Builder," *Covered Bridge Topics* (Spring 2003), 3.

41 Jackson County, Ohio, builders followed this practice of obtaining Smith patent rights but cutting the timber themselves. See Miriam Wood, *The Covered Bridges of Ohio* (Columbus, Ohio: by the author, 1993), 34. Locust Creek Bridge in Pocahontas County, West Virginia, is probably another example, as it is far afield and displays minor differences in framing from the usual highly standardized Smith type. A practice developed in Kentucky of referring vaguely to trusses of the Warren type as "Smith," but these trusses were not connected with the Smith Bridge Company and differ so widely from the patent type that they are not really part of the tradition.

42 Another company that successfully made the transition from timber to metal bridges was Kellogg and Maurice of Athens, Pennsylvania, builder of the famous covered bridge over the Delaware River between Columbia, New Jersey, and Portland, Pennsylvania, which was lost to high water in 1955. The Champion Bridge Company of Wilmington, Ohio, is another example. It remains in business, and one of its covered bridges still survives.

43 Boston and Maine was not, however, the last railroad to build covered wooden bridges. The Chicago, Milwaukee, St. Paul, and Pacific ("the Milwaukee Road") was still building them as late as 1938.

44 On Snow's career, see "Wright's Bridge," HAER No. NH-35. The designation "Town-Pratt" found in some books to describe the double Town-lattice form is erroneous, because T. Willis Pratt had no involvement with the development of this design.

45 Striker's bridges are sometimes credited to his on-site supervisors; for example, Miller Sorensen is often cited as the builder of Mapleton and other bridges for which he had direct charge. See the interesting interview with Sorensen in *The Bridge Tender* (Summer 1980), 3–5.

46 The portal style is thought to have been derived from bridges built by Lord Nelson Roney. See Nelson, *Century of Oregon Covered Bridges*, 192.

47 Few details of Striker's life have been found considering how recently he lived. See "Pengra Bridge," HAER No. OR-119; "Striker Services Held Wednesday," *Siuslaw News* (Florence, Oreg.) August 30, 1962, 4. Bill Cockrell also provided information, including his 2006 interview with Ole Haldorson, and Bill Morgan, Lane County Engineer, kindly tracked down some leads.

48 A comprehensive biography of Milton Graton remains to be written. Graton's own book, *The Last of the Covered Bridge Builders* (Plymouth, N.H.: Clifford-Nicol, 1978), gives details of many of his construction and repair projects.

Chapter 7

The Preservation and Future of Covered Bridges in the United States

by Justine Christianson and Christopher H. Marston

Figure 7.1 "Many a bashful swain has found his tongue in the darkness of a covered bridge!" reads the caption on the back of this photograph. Constructed in 1853 in Tompkins County, New York, the Newfield Bridge was rebuilt in 1972. John L. Warner, photographer. Courtesy of Richard Sanders Allen Collection, National Society for the Preservation of Covered Bridges.

During the tumultuous first half of the twentieth century, when increasing immigration, the Great Depression, and worldwide events like World Wars I and II changed both the American landscape and the American way of life, local communities hailed their covered bridges as symbols of a bygone, simpler era. As one unnamed writer for *The Christian Science Monitor* proposed,

> It may be that covered bridges recall more peaceful times for many. They may bring memories of carefree days when boys dove from the bridges' abutments into cool water below. Too, there's many a man today who remembers how the hollow caverns of the bridges' interiors made wonderful places to hear the echo of their voices. They'd laugh, hoot, and holler 'til three boys sounded like 30.[1]

Covered bridges evoked both pleasure (the title "kissing bridges" was bestowed on them because of the private moments they afforded young lovers) and fear (the experience of passing through a dark, shadowy tunnel). For many, they were also tangible reminders of home, of life in rural and small-town America. Burrell Burke, a reporter, explained,

> To me the covered bridge means the way to home. Home, with a loving, gray-haired mother bustling about in preparation of the evening meal, and father with his newspaper, reading by the light of the kerosene lamp . . . . It brings back memories of carefree childhood days when this bridge, so unattractive to me now, was a marvel, a mystery, and was approached with a feeling of awe and peril . . . . The old bridge was then a link with the future; now it remains a symbol of the past.[2]

As a powerful symbol and reminder of the American past, the covered bridge became an object worthy of preservation through both private and government efforts well before formal federal preservation laws, such as the 1966 National Historic Preservation Act, were enacted.

The number of standing covered bridges has steadily decreased from the type's heyday in the mid-nineteenth century. According to preeminent covered bridge historian Joseph Conwill (perhaps the only person to have visited all the surviving covered bridges in the United States), there are currently 672 historic covered bridges remaining in the country, of which approximately half have been heavily modified.[3] In contrast, Richard Sanders Allen reported 1,617 extant covered bridges in 1954, far fewer than the approximately 2,000 purportedly standing only five years earlier. Between 1959 and 1965, another 188 were lost.[4]

Figure 7.2 Built in 1859, the ten-span Conowingo Bridge crossed the Susquehanna River in Maryland. This photograph from ca. 1925 shows the new steel trusses being constructed in the background while the original wooden Burr-arch trusses are being dismantled. Courtesy of Richard Sanders Allen Collection, National Society for the Preservation of Covered Bridges.

The rapid rate of loss can be attributed to a number of factors. Periodic large-scale flooding has destroyed many covered bridges. Spring flooding in Vermont in 1927 and 1928, for example, resulted in the loss of wooden spans, the majority of which were replaced by steel-and-concrete bridges as the state decided to modernize its transportation infrastructure. The *Christian Science Monitor* reported the modernization was a "systematic program of replacement to supplant wood with steel and concrete," an effort that was not unnoticed by local historical societies and covered bridge enthusiasts. Yet, there were compelling reasons not to replace covered bridges in kind. Steel bridges were an economical choice that could accommodate the heavier loads of automobile traffic. Concerns about sparks from locomotives setting fire to railroad covered bridges and heavy winds knocking down bridges, as well as the declining availability of wood in some regions, were other motivating factors for not building new covered bridges in place of the old.[5]

Figure 7.3 Historically, flooding frequently resulted in covered bridges being washed downstream. The North Enosburg Covered Bridge spanning the Missisquoi River in Franklin County, Vermont, floated downstream during a 1927 flood. Courtesy of Richard Sanders Allen Collection, National Society for the Preservation of Covered Bridges.

More recently, a number of New England covered bridges were destroyed or seriously damaged by flooding caused by hurricanes Irene and Lee in 2011. As many as forty bridges in five states were damaged. Two significant losses were the Blenheim Bridge in New York, a National Historic Landmark, and the Bartonsville Covered Bridge in Vermont. The Blenheim Bridge, built by Nichols Powers in 1855, had one of the longest clear spans of any surviving covered bridge in the world and was one of only six surviving double-barrel covered bridges in the United States, but the structure could not withstand the violent flood waters of the Schoharie River. A video of the destruction of the Bartonsville Bridge was captured by a local resident and went viral on social media following the storm, becoming a symbol of Mother Nature's destruction. Unlike Blenheim, Bartonsville was insured by the town of Rockingham and has since been replaced with a modern covered bridge. However, these storms reveal the vulnerability of historic bridges set in low-lying flood zones and highlight the need for securing bridges to their abutments.[6]

The modernization of the U.S. highway system and changing requirements for transportation structures impacted the survival of covered bridges. The advent of increasingly heavy vehicles along with the rising overall numbers of vehicles in use resulted in the establishment of rigorous standards governing the design and construction of transportation structures. By the mid-twentieth century, lightly traveled local roads were increasingly being replaced by wider ones capable of moving greater numbers of automobiles at higher speeds, and bridges had to be able to accommodate the greater demands. In the early 1950s, the Ohio State Highway Department undertook a concerted effort to remove the forty remaining state-owned covered bridges, citing safety concerns. E. M. Bollerer, assistant bridge inventory engineer, stated in *The Christian Science Monitor*, "we're getting rid of them [covered bridges] as fast as possible." He went on to explain, "They are all past their age limit now. As one after another goes, we don't get very much complaining from sentimental people any more. Of course, anyone with any love of historical lore hates to see them go. But people now are more interested in highway safety. They want safer and newer bridges." Although many covered bridges were removed in the name of progress and to maintain safety standards, their place in the American collective memory ensured that preservation efforts started early in the twentieth century.[7]

Figure 7.4 Following road realignment in 1929, the Humpback Bridge in Alleghany County, Virginia, was bypassed and a new steel truss bridge was built, seen in the distance. HAER VA-1-11, Jack Boucher, photographer, 1971.

Studying Covered Bridges

As early as the 1890s, covered bridges were seen as "antiquities" worth being inventoried. Around the turn of the twentieth century, covered bridge "collecting" became popular. This often took the form of traveling to as many covered bridges as possible and photographing them or amassing covered bridge postcards. By the mid-twentieth century, concerns about the attitude of government and transportation officials toward covered bridges, as well as the rapid rate of loss, led to increasing preservation efforts. As Leo Litwin, who in 1948, two years before serving as the first president of the National Society for the Preservation of Covered Bridges, warned, "the day is fast approaching when this interesting bit of Americana will be no more." Thus, throughout the twentieth century, systematic studies and inventories of covered bridges were undertaken as a way to create a lasting record of extant covered bridges.[8]

Rosalie Wells's *Covered Bridges in America*, published in 1931, is one early inventory. While Wells waxed poetic about the solidity of the covered bridges built by her pioneer forebears, she also systematically listed notable extant covered bridges state by state. She presented the location and basic dimensions of each bridge along with any stories or legends associated with the structure and ample photographs. Other early books, like Clara E. Wagemann's 1931 *Covered Bridges of New England* and Adelbert Jakeman's 1935 *Old Covered Bridges*, focused on examining the role of covered bridges in American history and listing extant bridges in particular regions, although both neglected to include builder or designer information. Conspicuously lacking from this early scholarship was any identification of truss types and analysis of the structures. That shortcoming was remedied by the work of Richard Sanders Allen (1917–2008), who systematically studied covered bridge truss types and organized covered bridges in his writings by truss type rather than solely by location. Allen's development of more rigorous methods influenced other scholars and can be seen in Herbert Wheaton Congdon's *The Covered Bridge: An American Landmark Whose Romance, Stability, and Craftsmanship are Typified by the Structures Remaining in Vermont* (1941).[9]

Figure 7.5 Richard Sanders Allen is justifiably known as the "father of covered bridge history." Courtesy of National Society for the Preservation of Covered Bridges.

Allen became interested in covered bridges around the age of twenty and educated himself by reading widely, researching patents, and engaging in voluminous correspondence with local residents, historical societies, and other knowledgeable persons. In the 1940s, he began inventorying covered bridges and studying the trusses, initially publishing a census of extant structures in 1946 in *Covered Bridge Topics*, a mimeographed sheet with information about covered bridges that he produced six times a year beginning in 1943. Allen started *Topics* as a way to disseminate information on covered bridges after his correspondence became so great that he could no longer respond to individual letters personally. He went on to publish a number of books on covered bridges, including *Covered Bridges of the Northeast* (1957), *Covered Bridges of the Middle Atlantic States* (1959), *Covered Bridges of the South* (1970), and *Covered Bridges of the Middle West* (1970), which are still standard texts in the field. While following the general historiographical trend of looking at bridges by region, Allen also introduced discussions of truss type in these works. By studying and focusing on truss types, scholars elevated the covered bridge from mere nostalgic artifact to significant engineering structure.[10]

The work of Philip and Betsy Clough paralleled that of Allen. The Cloughs proposed compiling an exhaustive list of all covered bridges still standing in the United States and assigning each bridge a unique identifying number. This list was eventually released in 1956 as the *Guide to Covered Bridges of the United States*. Three years later, the National Society for the Preservation of Covered Bridges (NSPCB) published the *World Guide to Covered Bridges* based on the Cloughs' *Guide*. The publication included bridges in Canada, Europe (mainly Austria, Switzerland, and Germany), and Asia (mostly China). Regular updates to the guide have been made since the initial 1959 publication, the latest in 2009. Each bridge listed in the *World Guide* has been assigned a unique number, with additional information provided such as the location, truss type, basic dimensions, builder (if known), and any other available historical information. Bridges that have been removed or lost due to weather, arson, or dismantling are deleted from the database. While "lost" bridges are removed from the *World Guide*, information about them is being maintained through the efforts

Figure 7.6 HABS architects measured the Howe truss bridge spanning the Salt Fork River in Champaign County, Illinois, only days before its collapse. HABS photographer Chauncey Buck captured the remains of the bridge on April 13, 1934. "It makes my hair stand on end when I think of how we galloped across that bridge, stamping vigorously to keep warm," said team member Ralph Varney. "It must have come very close to being our 'Bridge of San Luis Rey.'" HABS IL-25-19, Chauncey Buck, photographer, 1934.

of Bill Caswell and Trish Kane and their "Covered Spans of Yesteryear" Web site.[11]

Another early documentation effort was that by the Historic American Buildings Survey (HABS), a federal program established in 1933 to document the nation's built environment through large-format photographs, hand-measured drawings, and written reports. As part of its early efforts, HABS recorded forty-six covered bridges, twenty-one of which are no longer extant. While the documentation was sometimes cursory and typically did not include information about the trusses, it provided an early record of bridges that were disappearing from the American landscape.[12]

The Covered Bridge Preservation Movement

Organizations devoted to preserving covered bridges exist on both the national and local levels. The National Society for the Preservation of Covered Bridges, as the name suggests, has dedicated itself to the plight of covered bridges across the country. Organized in early 1950 by a group of covered bridge enthusiasts in Boston, Massachusetts, the society was incorporated in 1954 with Leo Litwin (1909–87) as the first president. A Russian immigrant and pianist with the Boston Pops Orchestra, Litwin had some influence with Boston's elite. The group started with around one hundred members but now numbers five hundred across North America. Due to the geographic location of the president and organizing members, the membership has been concentrated in New England, but the society's scope has always been national in focus. In addition to collecting information about covered bridges, which has become the basis of the group's archives as well as the Cloughs' work and the *World Guide*, the society has worked to preserve the covered bridges that continue to disappear from the American landscape. This has taken the form of raising awareness by holding covered bridge festivals and meetings at covered bridges. In 1966, for example, the society organized the first New England Covered Bridge Festival, spanning three days over an early August weekend near Keene, New Hampshire. The festival included automobile tours of the area's six covered bridges, a lantern-slide presentation, and a lecture on covered bridges.[13]

The NSPCB's preservation philosophy, as articulated by David Wright, its late president, is that as "venerable antiques," the bridges "should be treated as such; that is to say, with great respect for the technology which produced them in the first place, and with equal respect for the superb craftsmanship which is often on display within them." Consequently, the organization is at "the forefront of those arguing for the use of traditional materials and procedures in Covered Bridge renovation projects." Preservation efforts undertaken by the organization include letter-writing campaigns and meetings at bridge sites in order to raise awareness and educate local government officials and citizens about the historic nature of the bridges as well as to exert political pressure.[14]

One early preservation battle in which the NSPCB became involved centered on the Tannery Bridge (also known as Goodhue) in the little town of Enfield, New Hampshire (population 1,600). The battle began after town officials developed a plan to improve the road on which the Tannery Bridge was located in order to bring it up to state transportation standards. New Hampshire regulations allowed municipalities to hand over roads and bridges that met state standards to the state for maintenance and control, thereby reducing the town's financial obligations, but the bridge did not meet the requirements. Noting that the bridge was excluded from transfer to the state, the town's women's club took their concerns about the removal of the covered bridge to the state Federation of Women's Clubs. That organization got Sen. Katharine Jackson to sponsor legislation authorizing the inclusion of covered bridges in existing provisions regarding the repair and maintenance of bridges and roads. The bill had a broad base of support and was passed, but not until after Enfield had decided the fate of its bridge. Residents voted to replace the bridge with a concrete and steel structure by a vote of ninety to forty-seven and also defeated a motion to put off the vote for a year until the state legislation could be passed. Undeterred, a group of citizens banded together to raise funds to dismantle the bridge and re-erect it elsewhere, forming a "Save-the-Bridge Fund" to which readers of the *Reporter-Advocate* (whose editor, Edward Bennett, served as coordinator of the preservation campaign) were urged to donate a dollar. Meanwhile, NSPCB members wrote to government officials, urging preservation. The preservation advocates decided not to use nostalgia to advance their cause, but instead resorted to economic reasoning, pointing out that it was cheaper

Figure 7.7 Goodhue/Tannery Bridge in Enfield, New Hampshire, was the object of an intense, multi-year preservation battle that ended with its removal. Richard Sanders Allen, photographer, August 11, 1941. Courtesy of Richard Sanders Allen Collection, National Society for the Preservation of Covered Bridges.

to repair the bridge than tear it down and build a new one. When the issue was brought before the town for a second vote, however, it was defeated, and the Tannery Bridge was removed in 1954.[15]

The preservation of the Cornish-Windsor Bridge represents a landmark case study in rehabilitation and a concerted preservation effort by the NSPCB, although the eventual solution was not the one preferred by the organization. A two-lane, two-span bridge built across the Connecticut River in 1866, the Cornish-Windsor Bridge is the only remaining notched Town-lattice truss as well as the longest historic covered bridge in the country at 450 feet.[16] In 1984, the New Hampshire Department of Transportation announced that it planned to correct the bridge's increasing sag and replace the deteriorated members with steel. In response, the NSPCB began lobbying for a sympathetic restoration of the bridge and commissioned engineer David C. Fischetti to provide a

Figure 7.8 The introduction of glulam lower chords and floor beams on the Cornish-Windsor Bridge, although opposed by many preservationists, helped achieve the positive camber required to keep the bridge in use. James Garvin, photographer, December 1988 and June 1989.

structural analysis. In 1986, Fischetti developed a proposal to replace the lower chords, floor beams, and bolster beams with glued laminated (glulam) timbers instead of traditional solid-sawn timbers. While purists, including the NSPCB, opposed the introduction of glulam, it was embraced by the New Hampshire and Vermont departments of transportation and State Historic Preservation Officers as the best solution to both strengthen the bridge and keep it open with a fifteen-ton weight limit. According to Fischetti, glulam's advantages were that it could be fabricated in longer lengths than available solid timber and, being an engineered product, could be manufactured and shipped more quickly. In addition, glulam was pressure treated, which controlled moisture content, minimized shrinkage, and extended the life of the structural members. The disadvantages were that glulam was not a true in-kind replacement for historic timber members (newly cut Douglas fir would have been closer to the original material), and that long glulam members were difficult to handle, requiring expert precision to integrate them into existing truss fabric. Timber framer Jan Lewandowski successfully accomplished the installation of the glulam timbers using a cable-stayed system with Dywidag bars during the construction phase. Fischetti's system allowed work to continue through snow and ice over the winter of 1988–89 and achieved the positive camber needed to keep the bridge in use. Although possibly not an optimal choice for other projects, the glulam solution here achieved the goal of strengthening and upgrading the bridge structure, maintaining its profile in a historic landscape, and preserving an important highway crossing.[17]

The NSPCB has had success in preserving other covered bridges and consulting on the most sensitive ways to restore them, such as the Contoocook Railroad Bridge in Contoocook, New Hampshire, which was in active service on the Concord and Claremont Railroad (later part of the Boston and Maine) until 1962. After a public effort to save it, the bridge ended up under the ownership of the New Hampshire Department of Resources and Economic Development (DRED) in 1989. The agency did not have funding for maintenance and repairs, but the NSPCB developed a preservation project with DRED (Jim Garvin, New Hampshire state architectural historian, served as point person), Barns and Bridges of New England (owned by Timothy Andrews), and D. C. F. Engineering (owned by David C. Fischetti), using funds from the society's Eastman-Thomas Fund for Covered Bridge Preservation, which was established in the mid-1950s.[18]

Garvin and DRED applied for federal Transportation Enhancement (TE) grant monies for fire retardant and dry-pipe sprinkler systems for the Contoocook Railroad Bridge. In order to receive the TE funds, an engineering study needed to be done to demonstrate that the railroad bridge was safe for pedestrian use and in

Figure 7.9 The two-span, double-web Town lattice truss Contoocook Railroad Bridge was originally located on the Boston and Maine Railroad. It is one of only eight surviving covered railroad bridges in the United States and remains standing thanks to the multi-year efforts of preservationists working in partnership with the state from 1989 to 2007. HAER NH-38-5, Jet Lowe, photographer, 2003.

Figure 7.10 The replacement bed timbers installed on Contoocook used a bolted coupling splice inspired by a technique developed for similar structures by Snow and Fletcher in the 1930s. Note the granite pedestal supporting the corbel. Will Truax, photographer, 2007.

good repair. David Fischetti completed the study and analysis for a fraction of his regular fee. The rehabilitation work was completed over a period of several years, with the NSPCB providing $110,000 and Barns and Bridges donating services totaling approximately $50,000. The project involved cleaning out a significant amount of debris that had accumulated in the four corners of the bridge, including a tree that had taken root. Once the bridge was cleaned out, it became apparent that the bed timbers and corbels were deteriorated and required replacement. In addition, in the area where the tree had taken root, the bottom chord was rotting. In order to replace the necessary components, each corner of the bridge had to be lifted and shored, using I-beams lent by the New Hampshire Department of Transportation. The rotten chord was spliced using a technique described by J. P. Snow and Robert Fletcher in 1932.[19] Short granite pedestals were installed to replace thin cross blocks that had been crushed under each bed-timber assembly. The corbels (bolster beams) were replaced in-kind, using old growth, long-leaf southern pine. Once the engineering and repair work were complete, the TE grant of $129,000 funded the application of fire retardant and the installation of a sprinkler system, work carried out by a contractor. The NSPCB provided matching funds of $29,800 to complete the project, which was undertaken over a two-year period from 2005 to 2007.[20]

In addition to the National Society for the Preservation of Covered Bridges, there are regionally-focused groups that work to preserve and maintain the covered bridges within their areas. These groups, in general, promote interest in covered bridges and raise awareness about their significance. The activities of regional preservation groups can be broadly classified as collecting information about the covered bridges under their purview, publishing newsletters or magazines to educate both their membership and the general public about covered bridges, holding covered bridge safaris and other social events, and advocating for their covered bridges.

Regionally-focused preservation groups have augmented the collection of information on covered bridges started by the large-scale efforts of the Cloughs and Richard Sanders Allen. The executive committee of the Indiana Historical Society, for example, established a committee to research, document, and promote the preservation of the state's covered bridges in March 1931. The resulting Covered Timber Bridge Committee solicited donations of materials about covered bridges and also asked each county for information on extant covered bridges. The materials it collected are still available to researchers in the William Henry Smith Library at the Indiana Historical Society. In 1937, Robert B. Yule, the group's first chairman, published *Covered Bridges of Indiana*, a pamphlet detailing the location of existing covered bridges, in collaboration with Richard C. Smith of the William Henry Smith Library.[21]

The New Hampshire Covered Bridge Association was established in 1957. One of its first tasks was to survey the sixty-one covered bridges then extant in the state. The resulting 1961 publication was produced in cooperation with the New Hampshire Department of Public Works and Highways and the New Hampshire Council of Regional Associations and consisted of a folder with a map showing the locations of covered bridges and brief descriptions. Signs were also erected at each bridge site. The covered bridge association, according to one newspaper article, had "vigilante committees" keeping "watch over each of the 55 [covered bridges] still left standing" in the state.[22]

In today's Internet age, Web sites can serve as clearinghouses of information, such as "Maryland Covered Bridges" at www. mdcoveredbridges.com, which was established in August 2008 by James B. Smedley. While doing research on covered bridges in the state, Smedley found that as many as 125 had once existed, and his website provides information on both the historic as well as the six extant covered bridges in the state.[23]

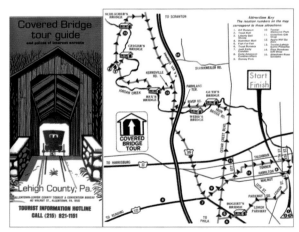

Figure 7.11 The Allentown-Lehigh County Tourist and Convention Bureau of Allentown, Pennsylvania, published a "Covered Bridge tour guide" for use in local heritage tourism. The pamphlet included a driving map showing the location of the county's covered bridges. The tour was promised to offer "each person, young or old, male or female, an opportunity to blend the truth and the imagination." Pamphlet, date unknown, in HAER office files.

Visiting covered bridges was a popular recreational activity in the first half of the twentieth century, and covered bridge preservation groups held "covered bridge safaris" after 1950 that highlighted a region's collection of covered bridges and thereby raised awareness of the importance of the structures. It was not just preservation groups that used covered bridge safaris to raise awareness, however, as local communities and chambers of commerce soon realized that their covered bridges could be used in heritage tourism to boost the local economy. To guide visitors to the bridges, pamphlets and brochures were developed with maps showing bridge locations and providing some historical information. For example, the Theodore Burr Covered Bridge Society of Pennsylvania, incorporated in 1959, holds an annual covered bridge safari to a county or particular region in the state.[24]

Figure 7.12 The Theodore Burr Covered Bridge Society of Pennsylvania visited Jonathan Speakman's Mill No. 1 Bridge (1881) in Chester County as part of its 1974 annual safari. Courtesy of Theodore Burr Covered Bridge Society of Pennsylvania.

Parke County, Indiana, is known as the "Covered Bridge Capital of the World" because of its thirty-one extant covered bridges, and it hosts one of the largest and longest-running covered bridge festivals. The festival was established by volunteers in 1957 as a way to showcase the county's numerous covered bridges after two were lost to flooding and a third faced demolition. The first three-day festival attracted twenty-five hundred attendees. These initial efforts expanded when Judy Snowden and W. B. Hargrave established the nonprofit Parke County Incorporated in 1961. The Covered Bridge Festival Committee was part of the nonprofit and was charged with planning the festival, which focused not only on covered bridges but also the county's agricultural heritage. The festival included both bus tours of the county's covered bridges and such characteristically American activities as a barbecue and a pancake breakfast. Parke County Incorporated continues to provide information on covered bridges to the public and oversees and organizes the Covered Bridge Festival, while also working with government officials on the preservation of covered bridges and occasionally donating funds to maintain, preserve, and rebuild them.[25]

Covered bridge preservation groups do not simply celebrate the past and distribute information; they also work to physically preserve their local bridges. On March 31, 1960, a group of amateur photographers began meeting monthly at the Zanesville, Ohio, home of Anita Knight and soon they realized they had a common interest in covered bridges. From this, the Southern Ohio Covered Bridge Association was formed (so named because there was already a northern association); it became the Ohio Historic Bridge Association in 1996 and broadened its scope to the preservation of all types of historic bridges, becoming the first such organization in the nation. One of the association's major projects, and a part of its articles of incorporation, was the purchase of the Salt Creek Covered Bridge in Muskingum County. The bridge had been bypassed by a welded-steel one and was no longer needed. Muskingum County transferred ownership to a farmer, but when the possibility arose that the farmer might demolish the bridge, the association acted to save it. Ownership of the bridge was returned to the county, and the association used Federal Highway

Figure 7.13 Thanks to the efforts of the Ohio Historic Bridge Association dating back to 1960, the Salt Creek Bridge continues to survive as a historic landmark in Muskingum County, Ohio. Preservationists across the country have volunteered their time to preserve covered bridges like this one. **Left:** 7.13a) David Simmons, photographer, 1998; **Above:** 7.13b) HAER OH-127-1, Jet Lowe, photographer, 2004.

Administration funds to do extensive repairs in the 1990s.[26]

The Government and Covered Bridge Preservation

There have been successful state and federal government initiatives to promote covered bridge preservation. As early as the 1950s, the state of Massachusetts attempted to institute a policy of replacing covered bridges with new covered ones instead of building steel and concrete spans. Massachusetts Department of Public Works commissioner William F. Callahan (1891–1964) became an advocate for the construction of new covered bridges as the state worked to preserve its few remaining ones. Reportedly influenced by a poem written by selectmen of the town of Charlemont about the original 1833 Bissell Bridge, Callahan approved the bridge's replacement with a new covered span despite initial plans for a modern concrete and steel bridge. In Callahan's view,

> The covered bridge is a New England symbol of romance and the rich, romantic past. To tear one down without rebuilding a duplicate would be equal to desecrating 'Old Ironsides' or destroying Bunker Hill Monument. Furthermore, we can build replicas of covered wooden bridges that are more efficient than the 19th century originals, will last just as long as steel bridges, and also carry the loads.[27]

By 1951, the new, larger, covered bridge at Charlemont had been erected, and another was built in Sheffield in 1952, but the efforts died out by the mid-1950s.[28]

In 1959, the state of Maine became the first state to enact preservation legislation protecting its ten remaining covered bridges. The state also instituted a maintenance and rehabilitation program under the State Highway Department and appropriated $50,000 for covered bridge renovation.[29] Other states have also developed bridge preservation plans that include covered bridges. In 1998, the state of Vermont established the Vermont Historic Bridge Program through a programmatic agreement among numerous state and federal agencies. Managed by the Vermont Agency of Transportation

(VTrans), the program seeks to preserve the state's historic covered, metal-truss, and masonry- and concrete-arch bridges and to recognize their economic, aesthetic, and educational value.[30] One way it does this is though cooperative agreements between towns, VTrans, and the Vermont Division of Historic Preservation. By enrolling bridges in the program, towns agree to convey a preservation easement to VTrans, preserve the structure, and undertake specified maintenance while VTrans pays for rehabilitation and restoration. Historic bridges owned by the state are automatically part of the program. In addition, the program assigns VTrans the responsibility of scheduling and undertaking regular maintenance, rehabilitation, and restoration. If bridges in the program can no longer be used on highways, they are relocated and used for alternative transportation.

The Historic Covered Bridge Committee, whose mission is to "insure that the historic integrity of Vermont's covered bridges is preserved to the greatest extent possible," oversees Vermont's Historic Covered Bridge Preservation Plan. The committee is tasked with reviewing the condition of all covered bridges and making specific recommendations for their preservation. The plan establishes a priority-of-uses list for covered bridges (the highest priority being maintaining a bridge in use on roads with maximum preservation of structural members) and a priority-of-treatments list (the optimal treatment being retention of all historic materials).[31] One of the members of the Historic Covered Bridge Committee is from the Vermont Covered Bridge Society.[32]

Twenty-three covered bridges have been rehabilitated in Vermont as part of this program from 2003 to 2013, assisted by funding from the National Historic Covered Bridge Preservation (NHCBP) Program. Several of these bridges remain in service. For example, the Cooley Covered Bridge in Pittsford, a Town-lattice truss, was rehabilitated in 2003. The rehabilitation involved installation of timber decking and siding and glulam floor beams, replacement of selected chord and lattice members, and repairs to the slate roof. While the use of glulam remains controversial in covered bridge circles, that treatment is consistent with the state's priority of treatments.[33]

In recent years, other states such as Ohio, Indiana, and Oregon have also developed programs to evaluate, save, and preserve their covered bridges, making them a priority in statewide historic-

Figure 7.14 In 2002, the HAER documentation team found the original lower chord, lateral bracing, and stone abutments of Pine Grove Bridge in Lancaster County, Pennsylvania, as constructed by Elias McMellen in 1884, still intact. While the Pennsylvania Department of Transportation saved the Burr-arch trusses in 2008, they unfortunately replaced the lower timbers with steel I-beam and removed all of the stonework, constructing new concrete abutments with a form liner surface treatment. **Top:** 7.14a) HAER field photo, 2002; **Above:** 7.14b) Tom Vitanza, photographer, 2009.

bridge management plans.[34] The commonwealth of Pennsylvania, however, has resorted to the use of steel I-beams in several of its replacement floor systems. While this methodology has kept several historic covered bridges in service with ten- to twenty-ton weight limits and original truss timber, it is an unfortunate trend. The use of steel compromises the integrity of the historic covered bridge, particularly because skilled engineers and timber framers are still able to use properly treated Douglas fir timbers as a sensitive engineering solution.

As Sheila Rimal Duwadi explains in chapter 2, the National Historic Covered Bridge Preservation program was created at the federal level in 1998. Preservation, research, and dissemination of information are the primary goals of the NHCBP program, which it has achieved by allocating funds in two areas from 2000 to 2012. First, the program has provided funds to states to repair, rehabilitate, restore, and otherwise preserve covered bridges that are listed in or eligible for listing in the National Register of Historic Places. Second, the program has granted monies for education and research on restoration and protection methods. In addition, the NHCBP program has funded the Historic American Engineering Record's initiative to document covered bridges, known as the National Covered Bridges Recording Project. HAER teams have documented more than eighty covered bridges, and that documentation has formed the basis for additional work, such as the completion of a National Historic Landmark (NHL) Theme Study, multiple NHL nominations, and a traveling exhibition on covered bridges produced in conjunction with the Smithsonian Institution. In addition, a deeper understanding of covered bridge truss technology has become possible through the use of new technologies, such as laser scanning the bridges during documentation, state-of-the-art load- and environmental-testing, and the development of partnerships with such universities as Case Western Reserve, Johns Hopkins, and Bucknell.[35]

Studies funded by the NHCBP program have tackled some of the key issues faced by those preserving covered bridges, such as decay and fire. Slowing the decay of the timbers used in covered bridges is a significant challenge. Preservative treatments can be costly, however, and the chemicals used can leach over time, creating long-term environmental effects. In addition to natural factors, arson and vandalism threaten covered bridges. Fire retardant treatments have thus been developed to spray on covered bridges. These treatments form a layer of char when heated, protecting the wood underneath. While the treatments do not fire-*proof* the wood and do not extinguish a fire, they can make it more difficult for a would-be arsonist to set a structure on fire. Heat- or smoke-activated alarm systems and sprinkler systems for wood bridges have also been developed.[36]

Preservation of covered bridges remains difficult, however. The complexity and inflexibility of government contracting and project-management systems discourages the hiring of the best independent craftsmen and hinders nimble preservation action in emergency situations. Furthermore, there are few specialized engineers and even fewer master carpenters capable of planning and executing the type of sensitive, in-kind repairs preferred by the preservation community, a deficit compounded by a lack of instruction in America's engineering schools in traditional building techniques.[37] As engineer Jim Barker succinctly states,

> It is important for an engineer who works in preservation to deeply respect the builders who created these structures, and to preserve their original vision as closely as possible. A designer who is concerned about our history, and who has taken the time to learn about Theodore

Burr, Louis Wernwag, Stephen Long, Hardy Cross, and etc., will probably do a better job on a historic restoration than one who views the project as one more "profit center."[38]

The late David Fischetti, an engineer on several covered bridge preservation and rehabilitation projects, added these words on cooperation amongst professionals.

Structural engineers with timber design experience must become actively involved in historic preservation in order to save our remaining historic covered bridges. Highway department engineers must seek out consultants with timber design experience. By working together, we can save an important part of our civil engineering heritage.[39]

The forthcoming publication *Guidelines for Rehabilitating Historic Covered Bridges*, being produced jointly by the National Park Service and the Federal Highway Administration, will provide case studies of best practices in the preservation of covered bridges. As Tim Andrews stated in the opening plenary talk at the Second National Covered Bridge Conference in 2013, "What would the original builder/designer do if presented with the same problems? Finding solutions which best meet the goals and aspirations of both pragmatist and preservationist needs to be accomplished."[40]

Future

The loss of the National Historic Landmark Blenheim Bridge to flooding in 2011 and the persistent threat of arson to other bridges stand as poignant reminders of the fragility of covered bridges. What is the future of these historic resources, which have such a hold on the American imagination? Thanks to the efforts of individuals and covered bridge preservation societies, the development of best practices and rehabilitation guidelines, and the increasing historical awareness of transportation officials and engineers, these structures, with their attendant cultural meanings, may long remain standing in the American landscape.

Endnotes

1. "Covered Bridges Draw Visitors to Massachusetts," *Christian Science Monitor*, April 19, 1955, 11.

2. Burrell Burke, "Reflections on a Covered Bridge," *Christian Science Monitor*, February 16, 1955, 17.

3. Joseph Conwill defines a historic covered bridge as one built before 1930 in New England, before 1945 in other parts of the country east of the Rocky Mountains, and before 1960 in the West and Canada. See Joseph Conwill, "Covered Bridge Truss Types," *Timber Framing* 102 (December 2011): 14–21.

4. David Wright, correspondence with the authors, February 2012; "2000 Covered Bridges Still Remain in Use," *Los Angeles Times*, November 30, 1949, 21; "Land of Covered Bridges," *Chicago Daily Tribune*, October 8, 1961, B10.

5. "Covered Bridge Leaving Main Vermont Roads," *Christian Science Monitor*, February 18, 1932, 3; W. Clifford Harvey, "Saving of Covered Bridges Possible," *Christian Science Monitor*, October 22, 1938, 9; Miriam F. Wood and David A. Simmons, "Introduction," in *Covered Bridges: Ohio, Kentucky, West Virginia* (Wooster, Ohio: Wooster Book Company, 2007), 2–16.

6. A complete list of the covered bridges damaged in hurricanes Irene and Lee can be found at http://www.coveredbridgesociety.org/news.html; "Lower Bartonsville Covered Bridge Collapses into the Williams River in Vermont," http://www.youtube.com/watch?v=WyO18one8fU.

7. E. M. Bollerer quoted in Helen Waterhouse, "Ohio Dooms Covered Bridge," *Christian Science Monitor*, November 23, 1953, 14. For a discussion of road construction, see Albert C. Rose, *Historic American Roads: From Frontier Trails to Superhighways* (New York: Crown Publishers, 1976).

8. "Old Bridge Cult Gains," *Baltimore Sun*, October 17, 1948, A16; quote from Leo Litwin, "Romance of the Covered Bridge," *Christian Science Monitor*, June 12, 1948, WM8.

9. Rosalie Wells, *Covered Bridges in America* (New York: William Edwin Rudge, 1931); Clara Wagemann, *Covered Bridges of New England* (Rutland, Vt.: Tuttle Co., 1931); Adelbert Jakeman, *Old Covered Bridges: The Story of Covered Bridges in General, with a Description of the Remaining Bridges in Massachusetts and Connecticut* (Brattleboro, Vt.: Stephen Daye Press, 1935); Herbert Wheaton Congdon, *The Covered Bridge: An Old American Landmark Whose Romance, Stability, and Craftsmanship are Typified by the Structures Remaining in Vermont* (Brattleboro, Vt.: Stephen Daye Press, 1941); Joseph Conwill and David Wright, telephone conversation with the authors, February 13, 2012.

10. Telephone conversation with Conwill and Wright; Wright, correspondence with authors, February 2012.

11. Telephone conversation with Conwill and Wright; David Wright, ed., *World Guide to Covered Bridges*, 7th ed. ([Hillsboro, N.H.]: National Society for the Preservation of Covered Bridges, Inc., 2009). The National Park Service produced a geo-referenced version of the *World Guide* in 2009–11, available online through the National Center for Wood Transportation Structures, http://www.woodcenter.org/CoveredBridges/. "Covered Spans of Yesteryear" can be found at www.lostbridges.org.

12. For more on the early years of HABS, see *American Place: The Historic American Buildings Survey at Seventy-five Years* (Washington, D.C.: U.S. Department of the Interior, National Park Service, 2008), 17. The work done during the original HABS surveys occasionally led to subsequent confusion. Two covered bridges once stood in Newton Falls in Trumbull County, Ohio, but only one—a Howe truss no longer standing–was recorded by HABS. Researchers seeking photographs of the still extant Newton Falls Covered Bridge, a Town lattice, have often become confused as a result.

13. Michael Strauss, "A Roof Above, River Below: A Weekend of Homage to Covered Bridges in New Hampshire," *New York Times*, July 24, 1966, 292; Jean Erickson, "Save a Covered Bridge," *Boston Globe*, July 24, 1966, A34.

Endnotes

[14] Wright, correspondence with authors, February 2012.

[15] "Outsiders Are Helping in Save-Bridge Drive," *Hartford Courant*, April 14, 1953, 8C; Edward Lathem, "Battle in Enfield, N.H., to Save Covered Bridge," *Daily Boston Globe*, March 7, 1954, C69.

[16] The 450-foot measurement represents the length at the deck. The four-span Smolen-Gulf Bridge (World Guide no. 35-04-64) in Ashtabula County, Ohio, built in 2008 by John Smolen, is the longest non-historic covered bridge at 613 feet.

[17] A detailed description of the Cornish-Windsor Bridge rehabilitation is found in David C. Fischetti, *Structural Investigation of Historic Buildings: A Case Study Guide to Preservation Technology for Buildings, Bridges, Towers, and Mills* (Hoboken, N.J.: John Wiley and Sons, Inc., 2009), 227–39. See also "Cornish-Windsor Covered Bridge," HAER No. NH-8, and Laura S. Black, "Cornish-Windsor Covered Bridge," in *Guidelines for the Rehabilitation of Historic Covered Bridges*, ed. Thomas Vitanza (Washington, D.C.: Government Printing Office, forthcoming).

[18] Wright, correspondence with authors, February 2012.

[19] J. P. Snow and Robert Fletcher, "A History of the Development of Wooden Bridges," *Transactions of the American Society of Civil Engineers* 96 (1932): 351.

[20] Tim Andrews, email to Christopher Marston, October 24, 2012.

[21] The committee disbanded in 1960 and was replaced by the Indiana Covered Bridge Society, established on September 8, 1963, with 150 charter members. The society focuses on the preservation of the state's remaining covered bridges; John C. Murray, letter to the authors, March 29, 2012. See also Laurie Randall, Janet Schmidt, and Dorothy A. Nicholson, "Historical Sketch," in *Covered Timber Bridge Committee Collection*, 1930–1979 (archival finding aid, October 2009), Manuscript and Visual Collections Department, William Henry Smith Memorial Library, Indiana Historical Society, Indianapolis, Ind., available online at www.indianahistory.org/.

[22] "New Hampshire Group Aims to Protect Covered Bridges," *Christian Science Monitor*, September 24, 1957, 7; quote from Roger Greene, "Trend Grows to Retain Shed Covered Bridges," *Hartford Courant*, November 27, 1958, 17; "New Folder Lists New Hampshire's Covered Bridges," *Hartford Courant*, April 16, 1961, 5B; Earl Banner, "Country Diary: Covered Bridges at a Glance," *Boston Globe*, April 8, 1961, 22.

[23] James B. Smedley, correspondence with the authors, April 2012.

[24] Vera Wagner and Sylvester K. Stevens, the executive director of the Pennsylvania Historical and Museum Commission, organized the first meeting of the Theodore Burr Covered Bridge Society, held April 5, 1959. Stevens was concerned about the perception held by transportation officials that covered bridges were impediments that needed to be removed and believed that creating an advocacy group could slow the bridges' removal. "Covered Bridges Revealed," *Hartford Courant*, May 11, 1969, 4F; Joyce Soroka, letter to the authors, March 30, 2012; see also the Web site of the Theodore Burr Covered Bridge Society, of which Soroka is president, at www.tbcbspa.com.

[25] "Roofed Bridge Fans Tour 25 in Indiana Fete," *Chicago Daily Tribune*, October 21, 1957, 23; "Hoosiers Plan Bridge Festival," *Chicago Tribune*, October 7, 1963, B5; Michael Schafer, "Covered Bridge County," *Chicago Tribune*, October 10, 1965, I60; Cathy Harkrider, letter to the authors, March 28, 2012. Parke County Inc.'s Web site is www.coveredbridges.com.

[26] David A. Simmons, "Restoration of the Salt Creek Covered Bridge," booklet prepared by the Ohio Historic Bridge Association to commemorate the rededication of the Salt Creek Covered Bridge, September 10, 1998; David A. Simmons and Miriam Wood, letter to the authors, March 2, 2012. See also the Ohio Historic Bridge Association Web site, http://oldohiobridges.com/ohba.

Endnotes

27 Paul Kneeland, "Why Sheffield Is Going to Have a New Covered Bridge," *Daily Boston Globe*, March 11, 1951, A5.

28 The Charlemont Bridge was once again under consideration for replacement with a concrete and steel bridge in the mid-2000s, but it was instead rehabilitated with the addition of steel rods. The Lower Sheffield Bridge (World Guide no. MA/21-02-02#2X), spanning the Housatonic River, was a Pratt truss built in 1952 and removed in 1988. For information on Callahan and the movement to build new covered bridges, see "Poem Leads Bay State to Rebuild Covered Span," *New York Times*, May 11, 1950, 31; "Covered Bridges Draw Visitors to Massachusetts," *Christian Science Monitor*, April 19, 1955, 11; Bernard J. Malahan Jr., "Old Bridges Saved," *New York Times*, April 26, 1953, X17; Lucia Mouat, "National Society Boosts Antique Bridges," *Christian Science Monitor*, December 11, 1962, 3; Richard Sanders Allen, *Covered Bridges of the Northeast* (Brattleboro, Vt.: Stephen Greene Press, 1957), 69–72.

29 Joseph C. Ingraham, "Maine to Maintain its Covered Bridges," *New York Times*, March 27, 1960, XX13.

30 The Vermont Historic Bridge Program was established through a programmatic agreement between the Federal Highway Administration, the Advisory Council on Historic Preservation, the Vermont Agency of Transportation, the Vermont State Historic Preservation Office, and the Vermont Agency of Natural Resources. The agreement permits inclusion of bridge types beyond covered bridges once preservation plans for those bridge types have been established. The next plan will be for reinforced concrete slab, T-beam, and through-girder bridges, although only one in the last category survives. Robert McCullough, email to the authors, September 6, 2013.

31 See the Vermont Historic Bridge Program's program agreement (1998) and Historic Covered Bridge Preservation Plan (2003) at http://historicbridges.vermont.gov/.

32 William McKone, Joseph Nelson, and Edward Barna established the Vermont Covered Bridge Society in February 2000 after the Cambridge Junction Covered Bridge was threatened by its poor state of repair. The society has developed a bridge-watch program, dividing the state into bridge-watch areas to monitor the condition of Vermont's covered bridges. Joseph Nelson, letter to the authors, March 9, 2012.

33 Robert McCullough, email to the authors, September 28, 2012.

34 The Ohio Department of Transportation is creating an interactive map locating the state's historic bridges. For information on the state's historic bridges, see http://www.dot.state.oh.us/divisions/planning/environment/cultural_resources/historic_bridges. The Indiana Department of Transportation funded a context study and survey as part of a programmatic agreement governing historic covered bridges. See Mead and Hunt, *Indiana Bridges Historic Context Study*, 1830s–1965, Indiana Department of Transportation, 2007, available at http://www.in.gov/indot/files/INBridgesHistoricContextStudy1830s-1965.pdf. Oregon has also developed a best-selling guide to the state's covered bridges. See http://www.oregon.gov/ODOT/HWY/BRIDGE/pages/covered_bridges.aspx.

35 Sheila Rimal Duwadi and James P. Wacker, "Covered Bridges in the United States and the Preservation Program," *Proceedings of the 10th World Conference on Timber Engineering*, Miyazaki, Japan, June 2008, available at http://www.treesearch.fs.fed.us/pubs/34809; Philip C. Pierce, Robert L. Brungraber, Abba Lichtenstein, and Scott Sabol, *Covered Bridge Manual*, publication no. FHWA-HRT-04-098, U.S. Department of Transportation, Federal Highway Administration, April 2005.

Endnotes

36 Information provided by Jim Barker of J. A. Barker Engineering, Inc. One study funded by the NHCBP program is Stan Lebow, Grant Kirker, Robert White, Terry Amburgey, H. Michael Barnes, Michael Sanders, and Jeff Morrell, *Guide for In-Place Treatment of Wood in Historic Covered and Modern Bridges* (U.S. Department of Agriculture, Forest Service, Forest Products Laboratory, in cooperation with U.S. Department of Transportation, Federal Highway Administration, General Technical Report FPL-GTR-205, March 2012), also available online at http://www.fhwa.dot.gov/bridge/covered.cfm.

37 Telephone conversation with Wright and Conwill.

38 Jim Barker, "Restoration of a Covered Bridge over Troubled Waters and Underneath Calm Ones," *Structure Magazine* (October 2007), 22–25.

39 Fischetti, *Structural Investigation of Historic Buildings*, 210.

40 Timothy Andrews, "Rehabilitating 19th Century Bridges using 19th Century Solutions," *Second National Covered Bridge Conference*, Dayton, Ohio, June 2013, available at http://www.woodcenter.org/2013-national-covered-bridge-conference/papers.cfm.

Selected Bibliography

The following selection is only a portion of the available literature on covered bridges. Due to space constraints, this bibliography focuses on national and regional studies, generally omitting studies of individual bridges.

Books

Adams, Kramer A. *Covered Bridges of the West, A History and Illustrated Guide: Washington, Oregon, California*. Berkeley, Calif.: Howell-North, 1963.

Allen, Richard Sanders. *Covered Bridges of the Middle Atlantic States*. Brattleboro, Vt.: Stephen Greene Press, 1959.

_____ . *Covered Bridges of the Middle West*. Brattleboro, Vt.: Stephen Greene Press, 1970.

_____ . *Covered Bridges of the Northeast*. Rev. ed. Brattleboro, Vt.: Stephen Greene Press, 1974.

_____ . *Covered Bridges of the South*. Brattleboro, Vt.: Stephen Greene Press, 1970.

Auvil, Myrtle. *Covered Bridges of West Virginia, Past and Present*. 3rd ed. Parsons, W.Va.: McClain Print Co., 1977.

Baker, Jeanne. *An Undercover Story: Covered Bridges of California*. Chapel Hill, N.C.: Chapel Hill Press, 2000.

Barna, Ed. *Covered Bridges of Vermont*. Woodstock, Vt.: Countryman Press, 1996.

Brandenburg, Phyllis, and David Brandenburg. *Kentucky's Covered Bridges: Vanishing Kentucky Scenes*. Cincinnati, Ohio: Harvest Press, 1968.

Brydon, Norman F. *Of Time, Fire and the River: The Story of New Jersey's Covered Bridges*. New Vernon, N.J.: New Vernon Business Service, 1970.

Burk, John S. *Massachusetts Covered Bridges*. Charleston, S.C.: Arcadia Publishing, 2010.

Caswell, William S., Jr. *Connecticut and Rhode Island Covered Bridges*. Charleston, S.C.: Arcadia Publishing, 2011.

Cockrell, Bill. *Oregon's Covered Bridges*. Charleston, S.C: Arcadia Publishing, 2008.

Cockrell, Bill, and Nick Cockrell. *Roofs over Rivers: A Guide to Oregon's Covered Bridges*. Beaverton, Ore.: Touchstone Press, 1978.

Cohen, Stan. *West Virginia's Covered Bridges: A Pictorial Heritage*. Charleston, W.Va.: Pictorial Histories Publishing Co., 1992.

Congdon, Herbert Wheaton. *The Covered Bridge: An Old American Landmark Whose Romance, Stability, and Craftsmanship Are Typified by the Structures Remaining in Vermont*. Brattleboro, Vt.: Stephen Daye Press, 1941.

Conwill, Joseph D. *Covered Bridges*. Oxford: Shire Publications, 2014.

_____ . *Covered Bridge Across North America*. St. Paul, Minn.: MBI, 2004.

_____ . *Maine's Covered Bridges*. Charleston, S.C.: Arcadia Publishing, 2003.

_____ . *Vermont Covered Bridges*. Charleston, S.C.: Arcadia Publishing, 2004.

Eaton, Thelma. *The Covered Bridges of Illinois*. Ann Arbor, Mich.: Edwards Brothers, 1968.

Edwards, Llewellyn Nathaniel. *A Record of History and Evolution of Early American Bridges*. Berkeley, Calif.: University Press, 1959.

Evans, Benjamin D., and June R. Evans. *New England's Covered Bridges: A Complete Guide*. 2nd ed. Lebanon, N.H.: University Press of New England, 2004.

————. *Pennsylvania's Covered Bridges: A Complete Guide*. Pittsburgh, Pa.: University of Pittsburgh Press, 1993.

French, Thomas L., Jr., and Edward L. *Covered Bridges of Georgia*. Columbus, Ga.: Frenco Co., 1984.

Fischetti, David C. *Structural Investigation of Historic Buildings: A Case Study Guide to Preservation Technology for Buildings, Bridges, Towers, and Mills*. Hoboken, N.J.: John Wiley and Sons, 2009.

Fitzsimons, L. Neal, et al. *American Wooden Bridges*. ASCE Historical Publication No. 4. New York: American Society of Civil Engineers, 1976.

Gibbons, Faye. *Horace King: Bridges to Freedom*. Birmingham, Ala.: Crane Hill Publishers, 2002.

Gould, George E. *Indiana Covered Bridges Thru the Years*. Indianapolis: Indiana Covered Bridge Society, 1977.

Graton, Milton S. *The Last of the Covered Bridge Builders*. Plymouth, N.H.: Clifford-Nicol, 1990.

Guise, David. *Abstracts and Chronology of American Truss Bridge Patents, 1817–1900*. Houghton, Mich.: Society for Industrial Archeology, 2009.

Hagerman, Robert L. *Covered Bridges of Lamoille County, Vermont*. Morrisville, Vt.: by the author, 1972.

Haupt, Herman. *General Theory of Bridge Construction*. New York: D. Appleton and Co., 1851.

Hammer, Arthur F., ed. *Romantic Shelters: A Supplement to the World Guide to Covered Bridges*. Marlboro, Mass.: National Society for the Preservation of Covered Bridges, 1989.

Harvey, Max. *The Covered Bridges of Parke County, Indiana*. Montezuma, Ind.: Wabash Valley Printing Co., 1959.

Howard, Andrew R. *Covered Bridges of Bennington County, Vermont: A Guide*. Unionville, Conn.: Village Press, 1997.

————. *Covered Bridges of Connecticut: A Guide*. Unionville, Conn.: Village Press, 1985.

————. *Covered Bridges of Madison County, Iowa: A Guide*. Unionville, Conn.: Village Press, 1998.

————. *Covered Bridges of Maine: A Guide*. Unionville, Conn.: Village Press, 1982.

————. *Covered Bridges of Massachusetts: A Guide*. Unionville, Conn.: Village Press, 1978.

————. *Covered Bridges of Virginia: A Guide*. Unionville, Conn.: Village Press, 1999.

Jakeman, Adelbert M. *Old Covered Bridges: The Story of Covered Bridges in General*. Brattleboro, Vt.: Stephen Daye Press, 1935.

Kemp, Emory L. *American Bridge Patents: The First Century (1790–1890)*. Morgantown: West Virginia University Press, 2005.

————. *West Virginia's Historic Bridges*. Morgantown: West Virginia University Press, 1984.

Kenyon, Thedia Cox, and Stan Snow. *New Hampshire Covered Bridges*. Sanbornville, N.H.: Wake-Brook House, 1957.

Ketcham, Bryan E. *Covered Bridges on the Byways of Indiana*. Lockland, Ohio: by the author, 1949.

————. *Covered Bridges on the Byways of Ohio*. Cincinnati, Ohio: by the author, 1969.

Knoblock, Glenn A. *New Hampshire Covered Bridges*. Charleston, S.C.: Arcadia Publishing, 2002.

Krekeler, Brenda. *Covered Bridges Today*. Canton, Ohio: Daring Books, 1989.

Laughlin, Robert W. M., and Melissa C. Jurgensen. *Kentucky's Covered Bridges*. Charleston, S.C.: Arcadia Publishing, 2007.

Lewandoski, Jan, et al. *Historic American Roof Trusses*. Becket, Mass.: Timber Framers Guild, 2006.

Long, Stephen Harriman. *Description of Col. Long's Bridges, Together With a Series of Directions to Bridge Builders*. Concord, N.H.: John F. Brown Printers, 1836.

Lupold, John S., and Thomas L. French Jr. *Bridging Deep South Rivers: The Life and Legend of Horace King*. Athens: University of Georgia Press, 2004.

Marshall, Richard G. *New Hampshire Covered Bridges: A Link with Our Past*. Nashua, N.H.: TDS Printing, 1994.

McKee, Brian J. *Historic American Covered Bridges*. New York: American Society of Civil Engineers Press, 1997.

McCullough, Robert. *Crossings: A History of Vermont Bridges*. Barre, Vt.: Vermont Agency of Transportation and the Vermont Historical Society, 2005.

Miller, Terry E. and Ronald G. Knapp, photography by A. Chester Ong. *Covered Bridges: Practical Crossings—Nostalgic Icons*. Rutland, Vt.: Tuttle Publishing, 2014.

Moll, Fred J. *Covered Bridges of Berks County, Pennsylvania*. Reading, Pa.: Reading Eagle Press, 2001.

_____ . *Pennsylvania's Covered Bridges*. Charleston, S.C.: Arcadia Publishing, 2012.

Moore, Elma Lee. *Ohio's Covered Bridges*. Charleston, S.C.: Arcadia Publishing, 2010.

Morley, S. Griswold. *The Covered Bridges of California*. Berkeley: University of California Press, 1938.

Morse, Victor. *Windham County's Famous Covered Bridges*. Brattleboro, Vt.: The Book Cellar, 1960.

Nelson, Joseph C. *Spanning Time: Vermont's Covered Bridges*. Shelburne, Vt.: New England Press, 1997.

Nelson, Lee H. *A Century of Oregon Covered Bridges, 1851–1952*. Portland: Oregon Historical Society, 1960.

_____ . *The Colossus of 1812: An American Engineering Superlative*. New York: American Society of Civil Engineers, 1990.

O'Grady, Patrick. *Replicate: The Rebuilding of the Corbin Covered Bridge in Newport, New Hampshire*. Concord, N.H.: by the author, 1998.

Patton, L. K., and R. W. MacGregor Laughlin. *Kentucky's Timbered Tunnels: A Presentation of Kentucky's Thirteen Covered Bridges*. Fort Thomas, Ky.: Kentucky Covered Bridge Association, 1994.

Petersen, Herman. *The Covered Bridge*. New York: Thomas Crowell Co., 1950.

Petersen, Hegen. *Kissing Bridges*. Brattleboro, Vt.: Stephen Greene Press, 1965.

Pope, Thomas. *A Treatise on Bridge Architecture*. New York: Printed for the author by Alexander Niven, 1811

Pierce, Leola B. *Covered Bridges in Virginia*. Glen Rose, Tex.: Upstream Press, 2002.

Reed, Robert. *Indiana's Covered Bridges*. Charleston, S.C.: Arcadia Publishing, 2004.

Sangree, Rachel Herring. "Covered Wooden Bridges: An Experimental and Numerical Investigation of System and Component Behavior." Ph.D. diss., Johns Hopkins University, 2006.

Sangster, Tom and Dess L. *Alabama's Covered Bridges*. Montgomery, Ala.: Coffeetable Publications, 1980.

Schlotterbeck, Seth S. *Covered Bridges of Preble County, Ohio*. Eaton, Ohio: Preble County Historical Society, 1994.

Schneider, Norris F. *Muskingum River Covered Bridges*. Zanesville, Ohio: Southern Ohio Covered Bridge Association, 1971.

Sloane, Eric. *American Barns and Covered Bridges*. Mineola, N.Y.: Dover Publications, 2002.

Smith, Elmer L., and Mel Horst. *Covered Bridges of Pennsylvania Dutchland*. Lebanon, Pa.: Applied Arts Publishers, 1988.

Swanson, Leslie C. *Covered Bridges in Illinois, Iowa and Wisconsin*. Moline, Ill.: by the author, 1960.

Town, Ithiel. *A Description of Ithiel Town's Improvement in the Construction of Wood and Iron Bridges: Intended as a General System of Bridge-Building*. New Haven, Conn.: S. Converse, 1821.

Wagemann, Clara. *Covered Bridges of New England*. Rutland, Vt.: Tuttle Co., 1931.

Way, R. Bruce. *The Life and Careers of William Henry Gorrill 1841–1874*. Lanham, Md.: University Press of America, 1996.

Weber, Wayne M. *Covered Bridges in Indiana*. Midland, Mich.: Northwood Institute, 1977.

_____ . *The Covered Bridges of Parke County, Indiana*. Indianapolis: Indiana Covered Bridge Society, 1980.

Wells, Rosalie. *Covered Bridges in America*. New York: William Edwin Rudge, 1931.

White, W. Edward. *Covered Bridges of New Hampshire*. Littleton, N.H.: Courier Printing Co., 1942.

Whipple, Squire. *A Work on Bridge Building Consisting of Two Essays, the One Elementary and General, the Other Giving Original Plans and Details for Iron and Wooden Bridges*. Utica, N.Y.: H. H. Curtiss, Printer, 1847.

_____ . *An Elementary and Practical Treatise on Bridge Building. Enlarged and Improved Edition of the Author's Original Work*. 2nd. ed. New York: D. Van Nostrand, 1872.

White, Vernon. *Covered Bridges: Focus on Kentucky*. Berea, Ky.: Kentucky Imprints, 1985.

Wilson, Richard R. *New York State's Covered Bridges*. Charleston, S.C.: Arcadia Publishing, 2004.

Wood, Miriam F. *The Covered Bridges of Ohio: An Atlas and History*. Columbus, Ohio: Old Trail Printing Co., 1993.

Wood, Miriam F., and David A. Simmons. *Covered Bridges: Ohio, West Virginia, Kentucky*. Wooster, Ohio: Wooster Book Co., 2007.

Wright, David, ed. *World Guide to Covered Bridges*. 7th ed. National Society for the Preservation of Covered Bridges, 2009.

Zacher, Susan. *The Covered Bridges of Pennsylvania: A Guide*. Harrisburg: Pennsylvania Historical and Museum Commission, 1994.

Ziegler, Phil. *Sentinels of Time: Vermont's Covered Bridges*. Camden, Maine: Down East Books, 1983.

Articles and Journals

Allen, Richard Sanders. "America's Covered Bridges." *Consulting Engineer*, April 1957, 92–100.

_____ . "Crossings under Cover." *Trains*, June 1955, 45–50.

_____ . "Uncovering Covered Bridge Lore." *Profitable Hobbies*, October 1948, 26–29, 56.

Beach, Ursula Smith. "Tennessee's Covered Bridges, Past and Present." *Tennessee Historical Quarterly* 28, no. 1 (Spring 1969): 3–23.

Bennett, Lola. "From Craft to Science: American Timber Bridges, 1790–1840." *APT Bulletin* 35, no. 4 (2004): 13–19.

Bock, Eugene R. "The Covered Bridge and Indiana." *Indiana History Bulletin* 37, no. 5 (1960): 5–28.

Buonopane, S., S. Ebright, and A. Smith. "The Timber Trusses of R. W. Smith: History, Design and Behavior." *Proceedings of the Fourth International Congress on Construction History*, Paris, July 3–7, 2012, 599–606.

Caston, Philip S. C. "Doing It the American Way: Federal Historic Building Recording in the United States." *In Forschung und Praxis: Arbeitsberichte aus dem Fachbereich Bauingenieur- und Vermessungswesen der Fachhochschule Neubrandenburg und befreundeter Institutionen*. Neubrandenburg, Germany: Fachhochschule Neubrandenburg, 2005, 63–97.

Conwill, Joseph D. "Burr Truss Bridge Framing." *Timber Framing* 78 (December 2005): 4–100.

_____ . "Covered Bridge Truss Types." *Timber Framing* 102 (December 2011): 14–21.

_____ . "The Howe Truss Goes Low-Tech." *Timber Framing* 85 (September 2007): 20–25.

_____ . "Long Truss Bridge Framing." *Timber Framing* 87 (March 2008): 4–5.

_____ . "Oregon's Covered Bridges in Context." *The Bridge Tender* 4 (Winter 1983): 1–3.

_____ . "Paddleford Truss Framing." *Timber Framing* 75 (March 2005): 12–15.

Cooper, Theodore. "American Railroad Bridges." *Transactions of the American Society of Civil Engineers* 21 (July–December 1889): 1–52.

Covered Bridge Topics. A quarterly journal published by the National Society for the Preservation of Covered Bridges. 1943 to present.

Cummings, Hubertis M. "Theodore Burr and His Bridges across the Susquehanna." *Pennsylvania History* 23, no. 4 (October 1956): 476–86.

Diehl, John. "Bridges to the Past." *Timeline* 15, no. 3 (May–June 1998): 30–51.

Dreicer, Gregory K. "Building Bridges and Boundaries: The Lattice and the Tube, 1820–1860." *Technology and Culture* 51, no. 1 (2010): 126–63.

Fletcher, Robert, and J. P. Snow. "A History of the Development of Wooden Bridges." *Transactions of the American Society of Civil Engineers* 99 (1934): 314–408.

Garvin, James. "Wooden Bridges on the Boston & Maine Railroad." New Hampshire Division of Historical Resources, Publications, June 5, 2004. Available at http://www.nh.gov/nhdhr/publications/documents/wooden_bridges_on_bm.pdf.

Gasparini, Dario, and David Simmons. "American Truss Bridge Connections in the 19th Century. Part I: 1829–1850." *Journal of Performance of Constructed Facilities* 11, no. 3 (August 1997): 119–129.

_____. "American Truss Connections in the 19th Century. Part II: 1850–1900." *Journal of Performance of Constructed Facilities* 11, no. 3 (August 1997): 130–40.

Gasparini, Dario, J. Bruckner, and F. da Porto. "Time-Dependent Behavior of Posttensioned Wood Howe Bridges." *ASCE Journal of Structural Engineering* 132, no. 3 (March 2006): 418–29.

Gasparini, Dario, J. Bruckner, and C. Tardini. "G. W. Whistler and the Howe Bridges on the Nikolaev Railway, 1842-1851," *ASCE Journal of Performance of Constructed Facilities* (June 22, 2015).

Griggs, Francis E. "It's a Pratt! It's a Howe! It's a Long! No, It's a Whipple Truss!" *Civil Engineering Practice*, Spring/Summer 1995, 67–85.

_____. "Colossus Bridge Designer Lewis Wernwag." *Structure Magazine,* October 2004, 34-36.

Guise, David. "Abstracts & Chronology of American Truss Bridge Patents." *Society for Industrial Archeology Occasional Electronic Publication No. 1* (2009). Available at http://www.sia-web.org/occasionalpub/electronic/pub1/SIAOccElectPub1.pdf.

James, J. G. "The Evolution of Wooden Bridge Trusses to 1850." *Journal of the Institute of Wood Science* [London] 9, no. 3 (June 1982): 116–35, and 9, no. 4 (December 1982): 168–93.

Jones, Harvie P. "The Town Lattice Truss in Building Construction." *Bulletin of the Association for Preservation Technology* 15, no. 3 (1983): 39–41.

Kemp, Emory L. "Lemuel Chenoweth: Pioneer Bridge Builder." *Virginia Highway Bulletin* 40 (March 1974): 13–16.

_____. "Restoration Techniques for American Covered Bridges." *Proceedings of the International Historic Bridges Conference* (Columbus, Ohio), August 1992, 318–31.

Kemp, Emory L., and J. Hall. "Case Study of Burr Truss Covered Bridge." *Engineering Issues: Journal of Professional Activities* 101, no. 3 (1975): 391–412.

Kniffen, Fred. "The American Covered Bridge." *Geographical Review* 41, no. 1 (January 1951): 114–23.

Lamar, Dylan M., and Benjamin W. Schafer. "Structural Analyses of Two Historic Covered Wooden Bridges." *Journal of Bridge Engineering* 9, no. 6 (2004): 623–33.

Levin, Ed. "Covered Bridge Truss Engineering." *Timber Framing* 105 (September 2012): 10–15.

"Lewis Wernwag, The Bridge Builder," *Engineering News* 14 (August 15, 1885): 98-99.

Long, Stephen H. "Remarks on the Jackson Bridge." *Journal of the Franklin Institute* 4, no. 2 (August 1830): 110–12.

Machtemes, Allison. "Investigation of the Structural Behavior of Historical Covered Timber Bridges." Master of Science thesis, Iowa State University, 2011.

Marston, Christopher H. "Craftsmanship across the Cornfields: A Survey of Midwestern Covered Bridges." *Structures Congress 2006: Structural Engineering and Public Safety*, St. Louis (May 18–21, 2006).

_____. " 'Covered Bridges: Spanning the American Landscape' Traveling Exhibit Debuts in Harrisburg." *Society for Industrial Archeology Newsletter* 35, no. 2 (Spring 2006): 1–3.

Mill, Randall V. "The Covered Bridge in Oregon: A Continuing Tradition." *Western Folklore* 7, no. 2 (April 1948): 101–14.

Mitchell, Harry E., Jr. "The Covered Bridges of Berks County." *Historical Review of Berks County* 13, no. 1 (October 1947): 2–13.

Pease, George B. "Timothy Palmer, Bridge-Builder of the Eighteenth Century." *Essex Institute Historical Collections* 83, no. 2 (April 1947): 97–111.

Prevost, Lewis M. "Description of Howe's Patent Truss Bridge." *Journal of the Franklin Institute* 3 (May 1842): 289–92.

Robison, Jon. "Covered Bridges of Madison County." *Annals of Iowa* 38 (Fall 1966): 414–26.

Royce, Edmund Homer. "Covered Bridges of Vermont." *Vermont Life*, Spring 1947, 12–17, 40.

Sloane, Eric. "The First Covered Bridge in America." *Geographical Review* 49, no. 3 (1959): 315–21.

Snow, J. Parker. "Wooden Bridge Construction on the Boston & Maine Railroad." *Journal of the Association of Engineering Societies* 15 (July 1895): 31–43.

Wilson, Raymond E. "The Story of the Smith Truss." *Covered Bridge Topics* 25, no. 1 (April 1967): 3–5.

Government Publications

Avery, Floyd L. "Report of Covered Bridges in New Hampshire." Concord: New Hampshire Department of Public Works and Highways, 1965.

Bennett, Lola. "Covered Bridges NHL Context Study." U.S. Department of the Interior, National Park Service. 2012. Available at: http://www.nps.gov/nhl/learn/specialstudies/CoveredBridges.pdf.

_____. "Humpback Bridge" (National Historic Landmark Nomination). U.S. Department of the Interior, National Park Service. 2012. Available at: http://www.nps.gov/nhl/news/LC/spring2012/HumpbackBridge.pdf.

_____. "Knight's Ferry Bridge" (National Historic Landmark Nomination). U.S. Department of the Interior, National Park Service. 2012. Available at: http://www.nps.gov/nhl/news/LC/spring2012/KnightsFerry.pdf.

_____. "Brown Bridge" (National Historic Landmark Nomination). U.S. Department of the Interior, National Park Service. 2013. Draft available at: http://www.nps.gov/nhl/news/LC/fall2013/BrownBridge.pdf.

_____. "Duck Creek Aqueduct" (National Historic Landmark Nomination). U.S. Department of the Interior, National Park Service. 2013. Draft available at: http://www.nps.gov/nhl/news/LC/fall2013/DuckCreek.pdf.

_____. "California Powder Works Bridge" (National Historic Landmark Nomination). U.S. Department of the Interior, National Park Service. 2014. Draft available at: http://www.nps.gov/nhl/news/LC/spring2014/CAPowderWorksBridge.pdf.

Pierce, Phillip C., Robert L. Brungraber, Abba Lichtenstein, Scott Sabol, J. J. Morell, and S. T. Lebow. *Covered Bridge Manual*. U.S. Department of Transportation, Federal Highway Administration. Publication No. FHWA-HRT-04-098. April 2005.

Patents

Burr, Theodore. U.S. Patent No. 2,769X, April 3, 1817.

Childs, Horace. U.S. Patent No. 4,693, August 12, 1846.

Haupt, Herman. U.S. Patent No. 1,445, December 27, 1839.

Howe, William. U.S. Patent No. 1,711, August 3, 1840.

_____ . U.S. Patent No. 4,726, August 28, 1846.

Long, S. H. U.S. Patent No. 5,862X, March 6, 1830.

_____ . U.S. Patent No. 1,397, March 6, 1830.

_____ . U.S. Patent No. 1,398, November 7, 1839.

_____ . U.S. Patent No. 5,366, November 13, 1847.

Partridge, Reuben L. U.S. Patent No. 127,791, June 11, 1872.

Post, Andrew J. U.S. Patent No. 81,817, September 1, 1868.

Post, S. S. U.S. Patent No. 38,910, June 16, 1863.

Pratt, Caleb, and Thomas W. Pratt. U.S. Patent No. 3,523, April 4, 1844.

Sherman, Everett. U.S. Patent No. 191,522, June 5, 1877.

Smith, Robert W. U.S. Patent No. 66,900, July 16, 1867.

_____ . U.S. Patent No. 97,714, December 7, 1869.

Town, Ithiel. U.S. Patent No. 3,169X, January 28, 1820.

Wheeler, Isaac H. U.S. Patent No. 107,576, September 20, 1870.

Web Sites

"Covered Bridge Preservation: National Best Practices Conference," June 5–7, 2003. http://www.uvm.edu/coveredbridges/conference/2003.html.

Covered Spans of Yesteryear Project. http://www.lostbridges.org.

Historic American Buildings Survey / Historic American Engineering Record / Historic American Landscapes Survey, Prints and Photographs Division, Library of Congress. http://www.loc.gov/pictures/collection/hh/.

Federal Highway Administration, National Historic Covered Bridge Preservation Program. http://www.fhwa.dot.gov/bridge/covered.cfm.

"Second National Covered Bridge Conference," June 5–8, 2013. http://www.woodcenter.org /2013-national-covered-bridge-conference/papers.cfm.

World Guide to Covered Bridges database. http://www.woodcenter.org/CoveredBridges/.

Covered Bridge Societies

Bucks County Covered Bridge Society. http://www.buckscountycbs.org/.

Covered Bridge Society of Oregon. http://www.covered-bridges.org.

Indiana Covered Bridge Society. http://www.indianacrossings.org/.

National Society for the Preservation of Covered Bridges. http://www.coveredbridgesociety.org/.

New York State Covered Bridge Society. http://www.nycoveredbridges.org/.

Ohio Historic Bridge Association. http://oldohiobridges.com/ohba/.

The Theodore Burr Covered Bridge Society of Pennsylvania. http://www.tbcbspa.com/.

Vermont Covered Bridge Society. http://www.vermontbridges.com/index.htm.

Author Biographies

James Barker is president of J. A. Barker Engineering, Inc., a structural engineering firm that specializes in the rehabilitation of historic bridges. He and his firm have designed significant repairs and rehabilitations for about forty-five historic bridges and barns, with twenty of those projects being timber-truss bridges. He is a registered professional engineer in Indiana, Kentucky, and New Hampshire.

Lola Bennett is a bridge historian with a master's degree in historic preservation. She has conducted research on covered bridges across the United States since 2002. Her recent work with HAER's National Covered Bridges Recording Project has included writing a comprehensive National Historic Landmark Context Study and preparing National Historic Landmark nominations for selected covered bridges.

Justine Christianson has been a historian with the Historic American Engineering Record since 2001 and has worked on a variety of projects, including documentation of an oyster mill in Maryland and the Henry Hudson Parkway in New York City. In addition, she has prepared hundreds of projects for transmittal to the Library of Congress and authored the current HAER *Guidelines for Historical Reports*. She holds a master's degree in history with a concentration in historic preservation from the George Washington University.

Joseph Conwill, photographer and historian, has documented over twelve hundred covered bridges since 1966, many of which no longer exist. He is the author of five books and the editor of *Covered Bridge Topics*, the quarterly magazine of the National Society for the Preservation of Covered Bridges. His photography of religious architecture is in the collections of several museums. He is a graduate of Northwestern University, where he majored in American studies.

Sheila Rimal Duwadi is the Hazard Mitigation Team Leader at the Federal Highway Administration (FHWA). As such she is responsible for research and development of bridge technologies and methodologies for all extreme events. She also manages wood research and the National Historic Covered Bridge Preservation Research and Development Program. She represents the FHWA on a number of White House National Science and Technology Council subcommittees and is active within the engineering profession, currently the past chair of the Structural Engineering Institute's Technical Administrative Division Executive Committee. She is a registered professional engineer in Virginia.

Dario Gasparini is a professor of civil engineering at Case Western Reserve University. He has published on the history of structural engineering with a particular focus on prestressing technologies. He has authored and presented papers at several international conferences and has conducted numerous engineering studies for the Historic American Engineering Record since 1996. Chair of the History and Heritage Committee of the Cleveland Section of the American Society of Civil Engineers (ASCE), he is a corresponding member of the national ASCE History and Heritage Committee.

Michael R. Harrison is the Robyn and John Davis Chief Curator of the Nantucket Historical Association. He has held curatorial positions at the National Building Museum, the Smithsonian's National Museum of American History, and the Glasgow Museum of Transport, and is the author of nearly seventy historical reports for HABS, HAER, and HALS. He is a graduate of the University of Pennsylvania and holds a master's degree in museum studies from the George Washington University.

Christopher H. Marston has been an architect with the Historic American Engineering Record since 1989, serving as the project leader of the HAER National Covered Bridge Recording Project since 2002. He was co-editor of the award-winning *America's National Park Roads and Parkways: Drawings from the Historic American Engineering Record*. He has presented on HAER work at a variety of national conferences and is an active member of several preservation organizations, including the Society for Industrial Archeology, Preserving the Historic Road, Transportation Research Board ADC50 Committee, and Rustic Roads Advisory Committee in Montgomery County, Maryland. He has degrees in architecture from the University of Virginia and Carnegie-Mellon University.

Richard O'Connor is division chief of the National Park Service's Heritage Documentation Programs (HABS, HAER, and HALS) and acting chief of the Historic American Engineering Record. He earned his Ph.D. at the University of Pittsburgh and has taught at several colleges and universities. Prior to assuming his current positions at the NPS, he served as a historian for the HAER program, preparing historical studies on a wide variety of historic industrial sites, including glass manufacturing, brick making, iron-pipe founding, and waterworks. His current interests involve the history and restoration of historic wood- and metal-working machinery.

Matthew Reckard is a licensed engineer with an MS in historic preservation, working in the Anchorage, Alaska, area. He has performed historical research, condition evaluation, structural analysis, plan preparation, and project management for repair and rehabilitation of many covered bridges and other historic structures. His early career was spent in engineering research at Brookhaven National Laboratory and the Alaska Department of Transportation and Public Facilities. He now divides his time between consulting engineering, managing an Alaskan hot springs resort, and professional piano playing.

Rachel Herring Sangree is the director of undergraduate studies and a lecturer in the Department of Civil Engineering at the Johns Hopkins University. A professional engineer in Maryland, she has degrees in civil engineering from Bucknell University and the Johns Hopkins University, where she earned her Ph.D. In addition to historic structures, she is interested in improving the quality of undergraduate engineering education as well as exploring methods to attract and retain future generations of civil engineers. She was principal investigator for the HAER engineering study of the reconstruction of the Gilpin's Falls Covered Bridge in Cecil County, Maryland.

David A. Simmons is senior editor of *Timeline*, a popular history journal published by the Ohio Historical Society (now the Ohio History Connection). Previously, he directed the process for listing properties in the National Register of Historic Places in the Ohio State Historic Preservation Office. The recipient of several writing awards for excellence in industrial archaeology, he currently serves as president of the Ohio Historic Bridge Association. He holds undergraduate and graduate degrees from Miami University in Oxford, Ohio.

Appendix
Covered Bridges in the
HABS/HAER Collection

HABS/HAER Number	Name	Location	Truss Type	World Guide No.	Date
Alabama					
HAER AL-201	Swann Bridge (Joy Bridge)	Cleveland vicinity, Blount County	Town lattice	01-05-05	1933
HAER AL-203	Horton Mill Bridge	Oneonta vicinity, Blount County	Town lattice	01-05-07	1934
HABS AL-361	Cripple Deer Creek Covered Bridge	Allsboro vicinity, Colbert County	Town lattice	01-17-02x	ca. 1820 (HH); 1859 (WG)
HABS AL-361-A	Big Bear Creek Covered Bridge	Allsboro vicinity, Colbert County	Town lattice	01-17-03x	Unknown
HABS AL-361-B	Buzzard Roost Covered Bridge	Cherokee vicinity, Colbert County	Town lattice	01-17-01x	ca. 1866
HABS AL-445	Covered Bridge	Eastaboga, Talladega County	Town lattice, Kingpost	01-61-06x	pre-1861
Arkansas					
HAER AR-42	Fourteenth Street Bridge	North Little Rock, Pulaski County	Kingpost uncovered	01-17-01x	ca. 1925
California					
HABS CA-1401	[Bridgeport] Covered Bridge	Bridgeport, Nevada County	Howe	05-29-01	1862
HAER CA-41†	Bridgeport Covered Bridge	Bridgeport, Nevada County	Howe	05-29-01	1862
HABS CA-158	[Knight's Ferry] Covered Bridge	Knights Ferry, Stanislaus County	Howe	05-50-01	1863
HAER CA-314†	Knight's Ferry Bridge	Knights Ferry, Stanislaus County	Howe	05-50-01	1863
HAER CA-106†	Wawona Covered Bridge	Wawona, Mariposa County	Queenpost	05-22-01	1868; rebuilt 1956
HAER CA-312†	Honey Run Bridge (Carr Hill Bridge)	Paradise vicinity, Butte County	Pratt	05-04-01	ca. 1886 (HH); 1896 (WG)
HAER CA-313	Powder Works Bridge (Paradise Park Bridge)	Paradise Park, Santa Cruz County	Smith (4)	05-44-03	1872
HABS CA-1551	[Glen Canyon] Covered Bridge	Glen Canyon, Santa Cruz County	Howe	05-44-01x	1892

HABS/HAER Number	Name	Location	Truss Type	World Guide No.	Date
Colorado					
HAER CO-49	Hortense Bridge	Nathrop, Chaffee County	Queenpost uncovered	06-09-u03x	1880
Delaware					
HABS DE-162	Ashland Covered Bridge	Ashland, New Castle County	Town lattice	08-02-02	mid-1800s
HABS DE-1†	Smith's Covered Bridge	Granogue vicinity, New Castle County	Burr	08-02-01x	1839
Georgia					
HAER GA-138	Red Oak Creek Bridge (Imlac or Big Red Oak Creek Bridge)	Woodbury vicinity, Meriwether County	Town lattice	10-99-02	ca. 1840
HAER GA-140	Watson Mill Bridge (Broad River Bridge) [Carlton Bridge]	Comer vicinity, Madison County	Town lattice	10-97-01	1885
HABS GA-185	[Papermill Road or Sope Creek] Covered Bridge	Atlanta vicinity, Cobb County	Town lattice	10-33-01x	1886
Illinois					
HABS IL-243†	Eames Covered Bridge [Allman Bridge]	Oquawka vicinity, Henderson County	Burr	13-36-01#2	1865
HABS IL-25-19†	Wooden Covered Bridge [Homer Park Bridge]	Homer vicinity, Champaign County	Howe	13-10-02x	1865
HABS IL-242†	Jack's Mill Covered Bridge	Oquawka vicinity, Henderson County	Town lattice	13-36-02#2x	1845
HABS IL-1002	[Rock Island Railroad] Bridge Spanning Mississippi River	Rock Island, Rock Island County	Howe uncovered	13-81-u01x	1853 (WG)
Indiana					
HABS IN-24-20†	Whitewater Canal Aqueduct (Metamora Aqueduct)	Metamora, Franklin County	Burr	14-24-11	1846
HAER IN-108†	Duck Creek Aqueduct (Whitewater Canal or Metamora Aqueduct)	Metamora, Franklin County	Burr	14-24-11	1846
HAER IN-28†	Deer's Mill Covered Bridge [Bluff Mills Bridge]	Alamo vicinity, Montgomery County	Burr	14-54-03	1878
HAER IN-29†	Adams Mill Bridge	Cutler, Carroll County	Howe	14-08-01	1871
HAER IN-30†	Vermont Covered Bridge	Kokomo, Howard County	Smith (3)	14-34-01	1875; moved 1958
HAER IN-33†	Busching Covered Bridge	Versailles, Ripley County	Howe	14-69-04	1885
HAER IN-40	Leatherwood Station Covered Bridge	Montezuma, Parke County	Burr	14-61-25	1899; moved 1981
HAER IN-44†	Mansfield Covered Bridge	Mansfield, Parke County	Burr	14-61-20	1867

HABS/HAER Number	Name	Location	Truss Type	World Guide No.	Date
HAER IN-45†	Medora Bridge [Dark Bridge]	Medora, Jackson County	Burr	14-36-04	1875
HAER IN-48†	Jackson Covered Bridge [Rockport Wright's Mill Bridge]	Bloomingdale vicinity, Parke County	Burr	14-61-28	1861
HAER IN-49†	Narrows Bridge [Lusk Mill Bridge]	Turkey Run State Park, Parke County	Burr	14-61-36	1882
HAER IN-50†	Cumberland Covered Bridge [Matthews Bridge]	Matthews, Grant County	Howe	14-27-01	1879
HAER IN-57†	Ceylon Covered Bridge	Geneva, Adams County	Howe	14-01-02	ca. 1860
HAER IN-103†*	Pine Bluff Bridge	Bainbridge vicinity, Putnam County	Howe	14-67-03	1886
HAER IN-104*	Cataract Falls Bridge	Cataract, Owen County	Smith (3)	14-60-01	1876
HAER IN-105†	West Union Bridge	West Union, Parke County	Burr	14-61-27	1876
HAER IN-106†	Forsythe Bridge [Forsythe Mill Bridge]	Moscow vicinity, Rush County	Burr	14-70-04	1888
HABS IN-24-1†	Kennedy Bridge [East Hill, East 2nd Street, or Cemetery Bridge]	Rushville vicinity, Rush County	Burr	14-70-10x	1881
HAER IN-27†	Brownsville Covered Bridge (Wagon Bridge)	Brownsville, Union County	Long	14-81-01x	1840; moved 1974
HAER IN-31†	Dunlapsville Covered Bridge	Dunlapsville, Union County	Burr	14-81-02x	1870
HAER IN-39	Gosport Covered Bridge	Gosport, Owen County	Smith	14-60-03x	1870
HAER IN-46†	Bells Ford Bridge	Seymour, Jackson County	Post	14-36-03x	1869; collapsed and salvaged 2006
Iowa					
HAER IA-64	Holliwell Bridge	Winterset vicinity, Madison County	Town lattice	15-61-05	1880
HAER IA-92	Cutler Bridge (Donahoe Bridge)	Winterset vicinity, Madison County	Town lattice	15-61-02	1871; moved 1971
HAER IA-93	Hogback Bridge	Winterset vicinity, Madison County	Town lattice	15-61-04	1884
HAER IA-94†	Imes Bridge (Wilkins Mill Bridge) [King or Munger Bridge]	St. Charles, Madison County	Town lattice	15-61-06	1870; moved 1977
HAER IA-95†	Roseman Bridge (Oak Grove Bridge)	Winterset vicinity, Madison County	Town lattice	15-61-07	1883
HABS IA-30-2†	[Owens] Covered Bridge	Carlisle vicinity, Warren County	Howe	15-77-01	1866 (WG); 1882 (HHH); 1888 (R. S. Allen); moved 1968
HAER IA-76†	Red Bridge [Yellow River or Oelberg Bridge]	Postville, Allamakee County	Pratt uncovered	15-03-u02	1920

HABS/HAER Number	Name	Location	Truss Type	World Guide No.	Date
Kansas					
HABS KS-13	[Springdale] Covered Bridge	Springdale vicinity, Leavenworth County	Howe	16-52-01x	1859
Kentucky					
HAER KY-49	Bennett's Mill Bridge	Lynn vicinity, Greenup County	Wheeler	17-45-01x	1875; rebuilt 2004
HABS KY-20-11†	[Butler] Covered Bridge	Butler, Pendleton County	Burr	17-96-02x	1870
HABS KY-20-20†	[Cynthiana] Covered Bridge	Cynthiana, Harrison County	Burr	17-49-05x	1807 (HH); 1837 (WG)
Maine					
HAER ME-3	New Portland Suspension Bridge (Wire Bridge)	New Portland, Somerset County	Suspension	19-13-S1	ca. 1866
HAER ME-4	Lovejoy Bridge [South Andover Bridge]	Andover, Oxford County	Paddleford	19-09-01	1867
HAER ME-69†	Sunday River Bridge (Artist's Bridge)	Newry vicinity, Oxford County	Paddleford	19-09-04	1872
HABS ME-61†	[Babb's] Covered Bridge	South Windham vicinity, Cumberland County	Queenpost	19-03-01x	1840 (HH); 1864 (WG)
HAER ME-51	Meeting House Bridge (Sinnott Road Railroad Bridge) (spanning Boston & Maine Railroad)	Arundel, York County	Howe, boxed pony	19-16-P02x	1908 (HH); ca. 1905 (WG)
Maryland					
HABS MD-12†	[Jericho] Covered Bridge	Jerusalem vicinity, Baltimore County	Burr	20-03-02	1865
HAER MD-187	Jericho Covered Bridge	Jerusalem vicinity, Baltimore County	Burr	20-03-02	1865
HAER MD-174†*	Gilpin's Falls Covered Bridge	North East, Cecil County	Burr	20-07-01	1860
Massachusetts					
HAER MA-83	Hastings Bridge (spanning Boston & Maine Railroad)	Sterling, Worcester County	Howe, boxed pony	21-14-P01	1892
HABS MA-101†	[Railroad Combination] Covered Bridge	Montague City, Franklin County	Howe with arch (through & deck)	21-06-31#3x	1870
HABS MA-225†	Nehemiah Jewett's Bridge [Pepperell #1 Bridge]	Pepperell, Middlesex County	Town lattice	21-09-01x	1847
HABS MA-440	[Bannigor Heights or Red] Covered Bridge	Millville, Worcester County	Howe	21-14-49x	ca. 1888
HABS MA-497	[Collins Station] Covered Bridge	Ludlow-Wilbraham, Hampden County	Howe	21-07-17x	1851
HAER MA-94	Boston & Maine Railroad, Clark Street Bridge	Belmont, Middlesex County	Howe, boxed pony	21-09-P02x	1908
HAER MA-116	Boston & Maine Railroad, Essex Street Bridge	Swampscott, Essex County	Howe, boxed pony	21-05-P02x	1901

HABS/HAER Number	Name	Location	Truss Type	World Guide No.	Date
Michigan					
HAER MI-331	White's Bridge	Smyrna, Ionia County	Brown	22-34-01x	1869
Minnesota					
HAER MN-123†	Zumbrota Bridge	Zumbrota, Goodhue County	Modified lattice	23-25-01	1869; moved 1997
Mississippi					
HABS MS-90	Old Covered Bridge	Steens vicinity, Lowndes County	Town lattice	24-44-02x	Unknown
Missouri					
HABS MO-270†	Noah's Ark Covered Bridge	Hoover vicinity, Platte County	Modified Howe	25-83-01x	1878; moved 1965
HABS MO-1156	Sandy Creek Bridge [LeMay Ferry Road Bridge]	Goldman vicinity, Jefferson County	Howe	25-50-01#2	1887
HABS MO-1307	Bollinger Covered Bridge & Mill [Bollinger Mill Bridge]	Burfordville, Cape Girardeau County	Howe	25-16-01	1868
HABS MO-1325	[Allenville] Covered Bridge	Allenville, Cape Girardeau County	Multiple kingpost	25-16-02x	1870
New Hampshire					
HAER NH-8†*	Cornish-Windsor Covered Bridge (Cornish Bridge)	Cornish, Sullivan County	Town lattice	29-10-09#2	1866
HAER NH-33†*	Bath-Haverhill Bridge (Haverhill-Bath Bridge) [Woodsville Bridge]	Woodsville, Grafton County	Town lattice	29-05-04	1829
HAER NH-34	Bath Bridge	Bath, Grafton County	Multiple kingpost	29-05-03	1832
HAER NH-35	Wright's Bridge [Wright Railroad Bridge]	Claremont vicinity, Sullivan County	Double Town lattice with arch	29-10-04#2	1906
HAER NH-36†*	Sulphite Railroad Bridge	Franklin, Merrimack County	Pratt deck	29-07-09	1896
HAER NH-38†*	Contoocook Railroad Bridge (Hopkinton Railroad Bridge)	Hopkinton, Merrimack County	Town lattice	29-07-07#2	1889
HAER NH-39	Clark's Bridge [Pinsley Railroad Bridge]	Lincoln, Grafton County	Howe	29-05-14	1904; moved 1965
HAER NH-40	Kenyon Bridge (Blacksmith Shop Bridge)	Cornish, Sullivan County	Multiple kingpost	29-10-01	1882
HAER NH-41	Honeymoon Bridge (Jackson Bridge)	Jackson, Carroll County	Paddleford with arch	29-02-01	1876
HAER NH-42	Hancock-Greenfield Bridge (County Bridge)	Greenfield, Hillsborough County	Teco	29-06-02#2	1937
HAER NH-43	Livermore Bridge [Blood Brook or Old Russell Hill Road Bridge]	Wilton, Hillsborough County	Town, boxed pony	29-06-P1	ca. 1937

HABS/HAER Number	Name	Location	Truss Type	World Guide No.	Date
HAER NH-44	Rollins Farm Bridge (Boston and Maine Railroad, Western Route, Portland Division, Bridge No. 69.19)	Rollinsford, Strafford County	Howe, boxed pony	29-09-P1	1904 (WG); rebuilt 1929 (HH)
HAER NH-45	Mechanic Street (Israel River Bridge)	Lancaster, Coos County	Paddleford	29-04-06	1862
HAER NH-48†	Boston & Maine Railroad, Berlin Branch Bridge #148.81 (Moose Brook Bridge) [Boston & Maine Railroad #262 Bridge]	Gorham, Coos County	Howe, boxed pony	29-04-P1x/ 29-04-p1#	1918; rebuilt 2012-2016
HAER NH-49	Boston & Maine Railroad, Berlin Branch #143.06 (Snyder Brook Bridge)	Randolph, Coos County	Howe, boxed pony	29-04-P2	1918
HAER NH-50†	Whittier Bridge (Bearcamp Bridge)	West Ossipee, Carroll County	Paddleford	29-02-08	1871
HABS NH-21†	Contoocook Covered Bridge	Hopkinton, Merrimack County	Long	29-07-63x	1853
HABS NH-29†	[Fairlee-Orford] Covered Bridge	Orford, Grafton County	Town lattice	29-05-94x	ca. 1850 (HH); 1856 (WG)
HABS NH-30†	[Henniker Road] Covered Bridge	Hopkinton vicinity, Merrimack County	Town lattice with arch	29-07-62x	1863
New Jersey					
HABS NJ-442†	[Green Sergeants or Sergeantsville] Covered Bridge	Sergeantsville vicinity, Hunterdon County	Queenpost	30-10-01	1872
HABS NJ-654†	Old Covered Bridge & Flood Gates	South Pemberton, Burlington County	Stringer		Unknown
New York					
HABS NY-4-204†	Perrine's Bridge	Rifton, Ulster County	Burr	32-56-01	1850 (HH); 1844 (WG)
HABS NY-263	Hyde Hall, Covered Bridge	East Springfield, Otsego County	Burr	32-39-01	ca. 1825
HAER NY-330	Hyde Hall Bridge	East Springfield, Otsego County	Burr	32-39-01	ca. 1825
HAER NY-170†	Jay Covered Bridge	Jay, Essex County	Howe	32-16-01	1857
HAER NY-329	Beaverkill Bridge (Conklin Bridge)	Roscoe vicinity, Sullivan County	Town lattice	32-53-02	1865
HAER NY-332†	Powerscourt Bridge (Percy Bridge)	Huntingdon County, Quebec Province, Canada	McCallum	61-27-01	1861
HABS NY-359†	Blenheim Covered Bridge	North Blenheim, Schoharie County	Long with arch, double barrel	32-48-01x	1855
HAER NY-331	Blenheim Bridge	North Blenheim, Schoharie County	Long with arch, double barrel	32-48-01x	1855
North Carolina					

HABS/HAER Number	Name	Location	Truss Type	World Guide No.	Date
HAER NC-46†	Bunker Hill Bridge	Claremont vicinity, Catawba County	Haupt	33-18-01	1895
Ohio					
HABS OH-22-12†	[Spain Creek] Covered Bridge	North Lewisburg vicinity, Union County	Partridge	35-80-02	ca. 1859 (HH); ca. 1870 (WG)
HABS OH-2229	Roberts Bridge	Eaton vicinity, Preble County	Burr	35-68-05	1829; moved 1990
HAER OH-45†	John Bright No. 2 Covered Bridge	Carroll vicinity, Fairfield County	Bowstring, iron suspension truss	35-23-10	1881; moved 1988
HAER OH-87†	Germantown Covered Bridge	Germantown, Montgomery County	Bowstring, iron suspension truss	35-57-01	1865; moved 1911
HAER OH-122†*	Eldean Bridge (Allen's Mill Bridge)	Troy vicinity, Miami County	Long	35-55-01	1860
HAER OH-123	Crum Bridge (Knowlton Bridge) (Long Bridge) (Old Camp Bridge)	Rinard Mills vicinity, Monroe County	Multiple kingpost with tied arch	35-56-18	1867
HAER OH-125†	Pottersburg Bridge (Upper Darby Bridge) (Beltz Mill Bridge)	North Lewisburg vicinity, Union County	Partridge	35-80-01	1872; moved 2006
HAER OH-126†*	Harshman Bridge (Four Mile Bridge)	Fairhaven vicinity, Preble County	Childs	35-68-03	1894
HAER OH-127	Salt Creek Bridge (Johnson Mill Bridge)	Norwich vicinity, Muskingum County	Smith (2)	35-60-31	1876
HAER OH-130*	Rinard Bridge	Wingett Run vicinity, Washington County	Smith (3)	35-84-28_2	1876
HAER OH-138	Strength of Burr Arch-Trusses	Cleveland, Cuyahoga County	Burr		
HABS OH-45	Old Covered Bridge (Clay Pike Bridge)	Zanesville vicinity, Muskingum County	Multiple kingpost	35-60-49	1878
HABS OH-22-13†	[London Road or Reed] Covered Bridge	North Lewisburg vicinity, Union County	Partridge	35-80-05x	1884
HABS OH-44	Old Covered Bridge [Pleasant Valley Bridge]	Hopewell vicinity, Muskingum County	Smith (3)	35-60-30x	1875
HABS OH-270†	[West] Covered Bridge	Newton Falls, Trumbull County	Howe, double barrel	35-78-03x	1856 (WG)
HABS OH-623†	Covered Bridge	Collinsville vicinity, Butler County	Smith (4)	35-09-11x	1869
HABS OH-624†	New London Pike Covered Bridge (Hogan's Bridge)	Hamilton vicinity, Butler County	Burr	35-09-01x	Unknown
HABS OH-2224	[Clarksville] Covered Bridge	Clarksville, Clinton County	Burr	35-14-01x	ca. 1870
Oregon					
HAER OR-26	Grave Creek Bridge [Sunny Valley Bridge]	Sunny Valley, Josephine County	Howe	37-17-01	1920
HAER OR-119	Pengra Bridge (Fall Creek Bridge)	Jasper vicinity, Lane County	Howe	37-20-15#2	1938

HABS/HAER Number	Name	Location	Truss Type	World Guide No.	Date
HAER OR-120	Short Bridge [Cascadia Bridge]	Cascadia vicinity, Linn County	Howe	37-22-09#2	1945
HAER OR-123	Gallon House Bridge	Silverton, Marion County	Howe	37-24-01	1916
HAER OR-124†	Larwood Bridge	Lacomb vicinity, Linn County	Howe	37-22-06#2	1941 (HH); 1939 (WG)
HAER OR-125	Office Bridge (Westfir Covered Bridge)	Westfir, Lane County	Howe	37-20-39	1944
HAER OR-126†	Neal Lane Bridge	Myrtle Creek, Douglas County	Kingpost	37-10-07	1939 (HH); 1929 (WG)
HAER OR-136	Goodpasture Bridge (McKenzie River Bridge)	Vida, Lane County	Howe	37-20-10	1938
HAER OR-145	Fisher School Covered Bridge (Five Rivers Bridge)	Fisher vicinity, Lincoln County	Howe	37-21-11	1919
HAER OR-8	Jordan Covered Bridge (Thomas Y Bridge)	Scio vicinity, Linn County	Howe	37-22-01X	1937
HAER OR-15	Horse Creek Covered Bridge	McKenzie Bridge vicinity, Lane County	Howe	37-20-12X	1930
Pennsylvania					
HABS PA-19†	[Thomas Mill, Spruce Mill, or Megargee Mansion] Covered Bridge	Philadelphia, Philadelphia County	Howe	38-51-01	1855
HABS PA-415†	Bells Mill Bridge [Sewickley Bridge]	West Newton vicinity, Westmoreland County	Burr	38-65-01	1850
HABS PA-535†	Waterford Covered Bridge [Wattsburg Road Bridge]	Waterford, Erie County	Town lattice	38-25-04	1880s (HH); ca. 1875 (WG)
HABS PA-1020	Griesemer Mill Covered Bridge	Yellow House vicinity, Berks County	Burr	38-06-03	1832 (HH); 1868 (WG)
HABS PA-1108	Bartram's Covered Bridge [William Sager's Gristmill Bridge] [Lewis Garrett's Bridge]	Newton Square vicinity, Chester County	Burr	38-15-17	1860
HAER PA-67	Gross Covered Bridge (Klinepeter's Bridge) (Beaver Springs Bridge) [Overflow Bridge]	Beaver Springs vicinity, Snyder County	Burr	38-55-03	ca. 1878 (HH); 1871 (WG)
HAER PA-197	Cabin Run Covered Bridge	Pipersville, Bucks County	Town lattice	38-09-10	1874
HAER PA-198	Loux Covered Bridge [Loux Mill Ford Bridge]	Pipersville, Bucks County	Town lattice	38-09-11	1874
HAER PA-350	Felten's Mill Covered Bridge	Breezewood vicinity, Bedford County	Burr	38-05-03	1892
HAER PA-352	Jackson's Mill Covered Bridge [Barnhart's Bridge]	Breezewood vicinity, Bedford County	Burr	38-05-25	1889
HAER PA-361	Raystown Covered Bridge (Diehl's Bridge) (Turner's Bridge) [Williams Bridge]	Manns Choice vicinity, Bedford County	Burr	38-05-19	1892
HAER PA-458†	McConnell's Mill Bridge	Ellwood City vicinity, Lawrence County	Howe	38-37-01	1875

HABS/HAER Number	Name	Location	Truss Type	World Guide No.	Date
HAER PA-491†	Pleasantville Covered Bridge (Manatawny Bridge)	Manatawny vicinity, Berks County	Burr arch-stiffened pony	38-06-01	1852; 1856
HAER PA-586†*	Pine Grove Bridge [Little Britain or Pine Grove Forge Bridge]	Oxford vicinity, Chester County	Burr	38-15-22#3	1884
HAER PA-587	Dreibelbis Station Bridge	Lenhartsville vicinity, Berks County	Burr	38-06-07	1869
HAER PA-588	Uhlerstown Bridge [Lock 18 Canal Bridge]	Uhlerstown, Bucks County	Town lattice	38-09-08	1856 (HH); 1830 (WG)
HAER PA-622*	Kidd's Mill Bridge	Greenville vicinity, Mercer County	Smith (2)	38-43-01	1868
HAER PA-623	Mean's Ford Bridge (Burnt Mill Bridge) (Ralph Stover State Park Bridge)	Point Pleasant, Bucks County	Howe boxed pony	38-09-P1	ca. 1860s
HAER PA-624	Academia Bridge (Pomeroy Bridge)	Academia, Juniata County	Burr	38-34-01	1902
HAER PA-638	King's Bridge	New Lexington, Somerset County	Burr	38-56-06	1906
HAER PA-645*	Structural Study of Smith Trusses		Smith		
HABS PA-351	Snyder's Fording Covered Bridge	Hunterstown vicinity, Adams County	Burr	38-01-04x	1868
HABS PA-618†	[Grimes] Covered Bridge	Ruff Creek vicinity, Greene County	Kingpost	38-30-22x	1888
HABS PA-1173†	Johnson's Mill Bridge [Henry Musselman's Bridge]	Chickies, Lancaster County	Burr	38-36-35x	1866 (HH); 1854 (WG)
HABS PA-5184	Detters Mill Covered Bridge [Pickett's or Emig's Mill Bridge]	Detters Mill, York County	Burr	38-67-01x	ca. 1815 (HH); 1848 (WG)
HAER PA-68	Kuhn's Fording Bridge [Mummert's Grove Bridge]	East Berlin vicinity, Adams County	Burr	38-01-12x	1862 (WG)
HAER PA-119	Philadephia & Reading Railroad, Walnut Street Bridge	Reading, Berks County	Kingpost uncovered	38-06-u01x	1869 (WG)
South Carolina					
HABS SC-391†	Chapman's Bridge	Gowensville vicinity, Pickens County	Multiple kingpost	40-37-02x	1912 (HH); 1924 (WG); moved 1969
HABS SC-396†	Lower Gassaway Bridge [Rice Bridge] [Twelve Mile Creek]	Norris vicinity, Pickens County	Multiple kingpost	40-39-02x	ca. 1900 (HH); 1905 (WG)
Tennessee					
HABS TN-224	Elizabethton Covered Bridge	Elizabethton, Carter County	Howe	42-10-01	1884
HAER TN-41	Doe River Bridge (Elizabethton Bridge)	Elizabethton, Carter County	Howe	42-10-01	1884

HABS/HAER Number	Name	Location	Truss Type	World Guide No.	Date
HAER TN-48	Nashville Toll Bridge (Abutments)	Nashville, Davidson County	Modified Burr	42-19-02x	1823
HAER TN-31	Marlow Road Bridge	Clinton, Anderson County	Kingpost pony uncovered	42-01-u01x	1918
Virginia					
HAER VA-1†	Humpback Covered Bridge	Covington vicinity, Alleghany County	Multiple kingpost	46-03-01	1857
HAER VA-126	Link Farm Covered Bridge (Sinking Creek Bridge)	Newport vicinity, Giles County	Polygonal arch	46-35-01	1916
HABS VA-11-13†	(Trent's) Covered Bridge [Hornquarter Bridge]	Cumberland vicinity, Cumberland County	Town lattice	46-25-01x	1844
HABS VA-567	Covered Bridge	Lexington vicinity, Rockbridge County	Burr	46-78-02x	1877
HAER VA-20	Marysville Covered Bridge [Gladys Bridge]	Gladys vicinity, Campbell County	Kingpost	46-16-01x	1878
Vermont					
HAER VT-28†*	Brown Bridge [Hollow Bridge]	Shrewsbury, Rutland County	Town lattice	45-11-09	1880
HAER VT-29	Flint Bridge	Tunbridge vicinity, Orange County	Queenpost	45-09-11	1874
HAER VT-30†*	Taftsville Bridge	Taftsville, Windsor County	Multiple kingpost	45-14-12	1836
HAER VT-31	Pulp Mill Bridge (Paper Mill Bridge)	Weybridge, Addison County	Burr	45-01-04#2	1854
HAER VT-32†	Shoreham Railroad Bridge [Rutland Railroad Bridge]	Shoreham, Addison County	Howe	45-01-05	1897
HAER VT-33†*	Morgan Bridge (Upper Bridge)	Belvidere, Lamoille County	Queenpost	45-08-07	ca. 1886
HAER VT-34	Village Bridge (Big Eddy Bridge) [Great Eddy Bridge]	Waitsfield, Washington County	Burr	45-12-14	1833
HAER VT-36	Swallow's Bridge (Best's Bridge)	West Windsor, Windsor County	Tied Arch	45-14-10	1890
HAER VT-37†	Pine Brook Bridge (Wilder Bridge)	Waitsfield, Washington County	Kingpost	45-12-12	1872
HAER VT-40†	Hall Bridge (Osgood Bridge)	Rockingham, Windham County	Town	45-13-07#2	1982
HAER VT-1-A†	E. & T. Fairbanks & Company, Two-Story Covered Bridge	St. Johnsbury, Caledonia County	Town lattice with arch	45-03-68x	ca. 1876
Washington					
HAER WA-133	Harpole Bridge (Manning-Rye Bridge) [Colfax Road Bridge]	Colfax vicinity, Whitman County	Howe boxed through	47-38-01	ca. 1922
HAER WA-28	Grays River Covered Bridge	Grays River vicinity, Wahkiakum County	Howe	47-35-01x	1905

HABS/HAER Number	Name	Location	Truss Type	World Guide No.	Date
West Virginia					
HAER WV-8†	Barrackville Covered Bridge	Barrackville, Marion County	Burr	48-25-02	1853
HAER WV-31	Staats Mill Covered Bridge	Ripley vicinity, Jackson County	Long	48-18-04	1887; moved 1983
HAER WV-32	Milton Covered Bridge (Sink's Mill Bridge) (Mud River Bridge)	Milton, Cabell County	Howe with arch	48-06-01	1876; moved 2001
HAER WV-53	White's Creek Covered Bridge Abutments	Cyrus vicinity, Wayne County	Howe	48-50-01x	1877
Wisconsin					
HABS WI-28-12†	[Cedarburg] Covered Bridge	Cedarburg vicinity, Ozaukee County	Town lattice	49-46-01	1876
HAER WI-117†	Cedarburg Covered Bridge	Cedarburg, Ozaukee County	Town lattice	49-46-01	1876
HABS WI-13	Seventh Street Bridge	Hudson, St. Croix County	Howe pony uncovered	49-56-u01x	1910
Wyoming					
HAER WY-60	New Fork River Bridge	Boulder, Sublette County	Kingpost pony uncovered	50-18-u01	1917

NOTES:

This list includes all historic wood truss bridges in the HABS/HAER Collection, covered and uncovered.

HABS/HAER documentation for each bridge in this list can be accessed through the Web site of the Prints and Photographs Division of the Library of Congress, **http://loc.gov/pictures/collection/hh/**.

Bridge names in parentheses are alternatives noted by HABS/HAER.
Bridge names in square brackets are alternatives noted in the World Guide to Covered Bridges.

† Documentation includes drawings.
* Documentation includes engineering analysis.
[1] An "x" following a World Guide number denotes a bridge that is no longer extant.
(HH) Date of construction is from HABS/HAER report.
(WG) Date of construction is from World Guide.

Index

Note: Bolded page number indicates illustration